From Cowboy Trails to Soldier Tales

The Autobiography of Cowboy Chaplain Dann

Other Dann Slator memories:

Unwanted

From Cowboy Trails to Soldier Tales

The Autobiography of Cowboy Chaplain Dann

Dann Slator

Monsterwax Media

Tallahassee, Florida

From Cowboy Trails to Soldier Tales

The Autobiography of Cowboy Chaplain Dann

By Dann Slator

Third Edition

ISBN: 978-1533005212

MONSTERWAX MEDIA

3202 Enterprise Drive

Tallahassee, FL 32312

(850) 591-3080

monsterwax@aol.com

In Memory of my loving wife, Esther. She was born in York, Nebraska on June 6, 1924.
We were married 68 years.

TABLE OF CONTENTS

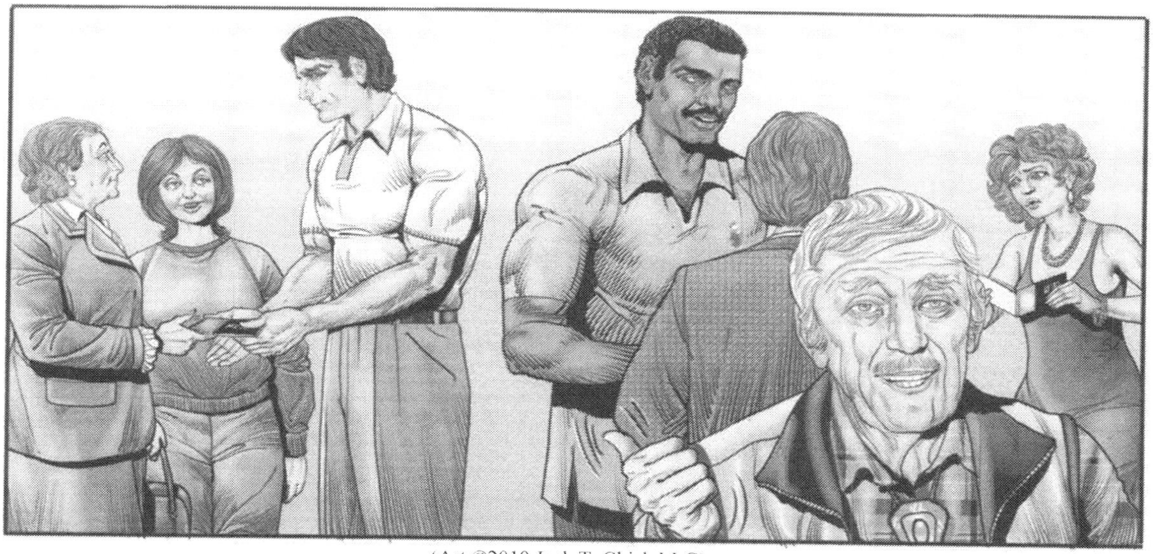

(Art ©2010 Jack T. Chick LLC)

Acknowledgments

I would like to thank Jack Chick and Chick Publications for letting me use Fred Carter's beautiful artwork from the *Crusader* comic book "Unwanted" to help illustrate this book. I would also like to thank Sara Owen for getting me started by making the tapes needed to tell this story. My appreciation also goes to Kurt Kuersteiner for editing, organizing, and publishing my story. Last but not least, I would also like to thank the contributors to our Kickstarter campaign for helping fund this project, especially Alan Bryant, Brian Blankenburg, Keven Rybolt, Ed LeClaire, Philip Reed, Kevin W. Christy, and Scot Horne.

Chaplain Dann's appearance in the "Reverend Wonderful" Chick tract. (Art ©2010 Jack T. Chick LLC)

Additional Dedications (by Chaplain Dann)

This book is also dedicated to the poor and downtrodden folks who believe they have no chance to make it and who feel that no one really cares for them. If Jesus can love and help me, then he can certainly do the same for you! My story is likewise dedicated to all of the military veterans who wanted so badly to be able to go overseas to fight for America but were stuck stateside.

Foreword (by Sara Owen)

Our friendship began in God's mind a long time ago. Chaplain Dann Slator and I met in 1991, when I was 15 years old. I was introduced to Chick Publications at the age of 13, and loved to read their Gospel comic tracts and *Battle Cry* newspaper. I saw an article written by Chaplain Dann which included his address. I wrote to him and was thrilled to receive a prompt reply. We became good friends right from the start. He had no idea how young I was. I started sending him a copy of my *Christ's Friends United Ministries* newsletter. God began *Christ's Friends United Ministries* in my heart when I was 13, and then on paper when I was 14. It all began with a little itty-bitty Chick tract titled "Somebody Goofed." As a young girl, I didn't have much money, but gathered what I had, joined the *Fishers of Men* club through Chick Publications, and sent $12 for my first 100 Chick tracts titled "This Was Your Life."

In 1995, a true "loaves and fishes" miracle happened in my life! The Lord Jesus Christ burdened Chaplain Dann's heart to help *Christ's Friends United Ministries* when he read in a newsletter that I was only 19. He sent me a box of Chick Tracts and I was amazed and bowled over at God's provision and goodness. The flow of Chick Tracts from Chaplain Dann has continued for all these years, and I have been truly blessed by Chaplain Dann's faithfulness and generosity. Chaplain Dann has faithfully sent Chick Tracts across the world for over 25 years. Many people have come to know the Lord through his ministry. Chaplain Dann and Brother Jack Chick, the founder of Chick Publications, are good friends and have blessed each other through the Lord for years. Chick Publications has a prison fund to help other prison Chaplains, and Brother Jack Chick has given the tracts to Chaplain Dann, who served an 18 year stint as a volunteer chaplain for prisons in Chino, CA. When Dann left the prison ministry, he started his own ministry and Chick Publications provided all the unstapled or miss-packaged materials for that effort. Meanwhile, Chaplain Dann has worked at a landscaping business to provide postage money, gas money and other funds for his ministry. He makes weekly trips to Chick Publications to pick up more tracts to share with folks like me. God is so good!

Chaplain Dann has felt for many years that God wanted him to tell the story of his life. He has drawn and written many tracts and has made notes for a book. Several people have thought of writing his book, but nothing ever came of it, so Chaplain Dann and I decided to work on it together. We both felt like it was the Lord's will. Chaplain Dann gathered materials and made tapes to send to me. Due to my growing family, I wasn't able to sit at my desk and start transcribing Dann's story until January 24th, 2006… and then daily interruptions prevented me from finishing it. Yet despite these stops and delays, Chaplain Dann and his ministry have persevered—and now, over a decade later, his story is finally being told.

I began this adventure backed with a lot of prayer. It is our prayer that you will be blessed and encouraged by this true story. May God richly bless you.

– *Sara Owen*

Editor's Preface (Kurt Kuersteiner)

I first saw Chaplain Dann in a Chick comic tract. He appeared in two different stories as a Christian who passed out Gospel tracts. The titles were *The Letter* and *Reverend Wonderful*. What I didn't realize was that Dann was a real person, and the tract character was the spitting image of him. His personality and manner of speaking were also accurately portrayed. Even his battered pick-up truck, with the license plate, "1 HOPE 4U" is depicted. The real life Dann has passed out over a million Chick tracts, earning him the nickname of "The Human Tract Dispenser." So it is little wonder that in 2006, while I was filming *God's Cartoonist* (a documentary on Jack Chick's comic tract empire), that Chick himself recommended I speak to Chaplain Dann.

I'm certainly glad I did so. I discovered "Cowboy" Chaplain Dann had lived a very rich life, and had a lot in common with Chick himself. Both were born in 1924. Both went overseas to fight in the Pacific during WW2. Both became Christians, and wound up back in California, and used comic tracts to witness to others. As a matter of fact, Chick himself was very instrumental in Dann becoming a Christian, and Dann was so impressed with the success of Chick's tracts, that he drew and self-published several tracts himself to reach Indians and prisoners who he often ministered to—Chick eventually did the same and adapted *One Way* for Native Americans with *The True Path*.

Chick and Dann continue to be close, calling and checking on each other every week. Dann told Chick a story that became the basis of the comic book, *Sabotage* (about how modern Bible colleges were undermining their own Gospel), and Chick ended up giving the lead character Slator's last name. Years later, Chick devoted an entire comic to Dann's true-life story, entitled *Unwanted*. But there are far more amazing things that happened to Dann than could ever fit into a 32 page comic book. He lived through numerous near death experiences, grew up in the Great Depression and the Dust Bowl, worked during the last generation of a real life cowboys, went to fight WW2 in the Pacific, and fought with his fellow Marines even more than with the Japanese! The fact is, Dann was born and raised a fighter. His parents fought constantly, Dann regularly fought with his brother, and he wound up fighting with other boys (and eventually men) all his life until he became a Christian in his later years.

Considering the poor conditions in which he was raised, it is difficult to believe how funny Dann's story often is. Dann had a real "devil may care" attitude in his younger years and it was routinely getting him in trouble, often with amusing results. His country-fried background didn't mix well in the military, and many of his experiences in the Marines are reminiscent of *Gomer Pyle, USMC*, only Dann never avoided a fist fight and the people in his story were not fictional (and in many cases, died tragically). His simple cowboy background and true love of animals (especially horses) helped him make some unusual friends—and enemies.

In the end, Dann's journey led him to wage another battle, one he continues to fight using his hands (but not his fists) to win. The million plus tracts he has handed out, as well as the ones he personally drew, are not only a testament to how much God loves humanity, but proof of how much Dann wants his fellow man to know they are never really alone.

As editor, I changed as little of Dann's grammar as possible, preferring to let him tell his story in his own homespun language. I felt it added to the authenticity and flavor of the life and times that he describes. Dann's recollections provide a rare insight into a nostalgic and historic time that many of us have heard about, but could never really imagine. Now we can do so from the perspective of a lone cowboy who traveled most of the Old West—and much of the Far East—during some very tumultuous times. I suspect you will find his experiences as enjoyable as I did.

Here then, is Dann's true story…

– *Kurt Kuersteiner*

Born in the Roaring Twenties

Blue skies before the storm. (Art ©2010 Jack T. Chick LLC)

Every life and tale has a beginning, and mine began when I was born on March 10, 1924—during the roaring twenties. I had an older brother (John Roy). He and I were left almost completely on our own except for a German Shepherd dog named Helmer Von Brudenbrock. I was abandoned in my mother's and father's hearts before I was even born. They didn't want me.

My grandpa and grandma were both born in 1844 in England. They came to America in 1863 and moved around for sometime before settling in Trinidad, Colorado. My grandpa was a building contractor and built the first three-story building in Trinidad, Colorado. He bought land on East Main Street to begin building houses. He built a lot of houses including the three-story hotel on Commercial Street.

While still in England, my grandpa was a captain on a British sailing ship. My grandparents had seven children and one of them was John William Slator, who was to become my father.

Dad started a grocery store before he was called to service in the Army at the beginning of WWI. After the war he continued his grocery store. The coal mines around the city of Trinidad were really bustling, but there were not many women around marrying age. My dad saw an advertisement in a local newspaper for a mail-order bride. He sent for the list and picked out from a picture a stunning brunette, Ruby Blanche. They were soon married with their first child on the way.

Ruby Blanche, circa 1920

They named my brother, John Roy, after Dad and Mom's brother. My mom didn't want any more children, but she became pregnant just five months after having John Roy. When the doctor warned her that she could lose the baby if she continued riding horses, she rode them every chance she got hoping that it would end the pregnancy. But it didn't work. I was born on March 10th, 1924. I weighed over 10 pounds. The last thing she wanted as another boy, so for a while, she dressed me as a girl and my nickname was Bunn (which was short for "Bunny", and it kinda stuck).

When I was two months old, my dad went on a fishing trip to Creede, Colorado. My mother saw an opportunity to go out on the town. She put six bottles of milk into my crib and left John Roy to run loose in the house for two days!

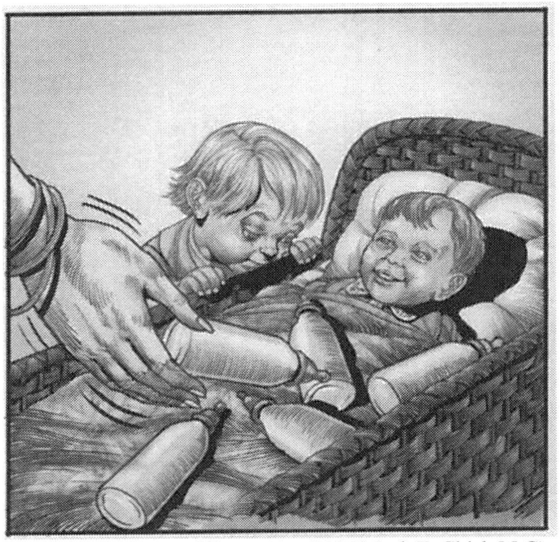

Leaving John Roy and Dann. (Art ©2010 Jack T. Chick LLC)

My grandma came to our house and heard us crying. She broke into the house and found us alone. We were in a mess—dirty, hungry, and heartbroken. My grandma kept me for three months because I was in such bad shape. She scolded my mom and told her to take better care of John Roy and me.

Scolding a bad parent. (Art ©2010 Jack T. Chick LLC)

Mom wanted to go back to Pennsylvania to visit her parents, so Dad planned the trip. He had just bought a new Model T Ford. I was four and John Roy five. It was a rough, long trip. All of the roads from Trinidad, Colorado to Altoona, Pennsylvania were graveled or dirt in 1928.

When we finally arrived in Altoona, we stayed with Mom's two brothers, Roy and Ike. My uncle's house was built outside of town near the railroad tracks. The tracks came straight towards the house and then made a left-hand turn carrying the trains away from the house. Altoona was a large railroad center and had a big round house in which to repair trains.

Dann at 4 years of age.

Ike and Roy fought and argued a lot. Once when Ike used Roy's shoeshine rag to clean the stove, Roy got so mad he picked up Ike's white cat and started to shine his shoes with it. That started a big fight.

Meeting Helmer

During our stay with my uncles, Mom was off visiting most of the time and Dad found a couple of bars in town. John Roy and I liked staying with Roy and Ike because they spent time with us and had dogs. We loved dogs.

Around three weeks later, Dad decided we needed to go back to Colorado. My mom didn't want to leave. After a lot of fighting and yelling, Mom finally did leave with us.

On the way home from South Dakota, we saw a sign that read "Registered German Shepherd Pups for Sale." Dad wanted to stop and look at the puppies. We turned off the main road and came to an old ranch house.

The rancher took us to the barn where the pups were. The mother dog looked like a wolf. The puppies were eight weeks old. John Roy and I fell in love with the silver grey male puppy. The rancher wanted to keep that puppy, so he priced him at $50—which was a lot of money back during the Great Depression. John Roy and I wouldn't give up wanting him and Mom also liked him. The rancher was surprised when Dad handed him the money. Dad had found a place to gamble in Altoona and had won a large sum of money. We went back in the ranch house to get our puppy's papers. His registered name was Helmer Von Brudenbrock. He would be our constant companion for the next eight years.

The Slator boys with Helmer. (Art ©2010 Jack T. Chick LLC)

John Roy and I took turns on the way home holding Helmer. By the time we got back to Trinidad, Helmer was really tamed down. When a reporter from the local newspaper found out that Dad paid $50 for Helmer, he wrote an article making fun of Dad.

When Helmer was grown, Dad put ads in cattle magazines that read, "Only Registered German Shepherd Male Dog at Stud: $50 Fee or Choice of Pups." Ranchers and others called or wrote to breed dogs as far away as Wyoming, New Mexico, and Texas. When people came they couldn't believe how beautiful and big Helmer was.

Dad's sister Eva lived in the downstairs of our house with her husband, three daughters and one son. Evelyn Mary, Aunt Eva's youngest girl (a red head), was my age, and we spent a lot of time together. One spring, a carnival came to town and Tom Mix was the main attraction. He was a world-famous cowboy. We both liked him, so we went to the fairgrounds to see if we could sneak in. We got in under the tent in the circus part of the carnival. Once we were in, we were able to go anywhere in the carnival. We saw a parade and I got to talk to Tom Mix. When we got home, Aunt Eva was very angry at us.

A week later, Evelyn Mary got sick. I went to visit her every day. She kept getting sicker and sicker. Aunt Eva called Dr. Espey to come check on Evelyn Mary. He examined her while I was in the room. Dr. Espey asked Aunt Eva, "Has this boy been around Evelyn Mary much?" Aunt Eva said, "Yes, he's been around her every day since they snuck off to Tom Mix's carnival." His expression darkened and he replied, "Oh, God help him. Evelyn Mary has spinal meningitis." She died three days later. Dr. Espey believed she contracted the disease at the carnival. Strangely, no one else in Trinidad contracted the disease. God had mercy on me.

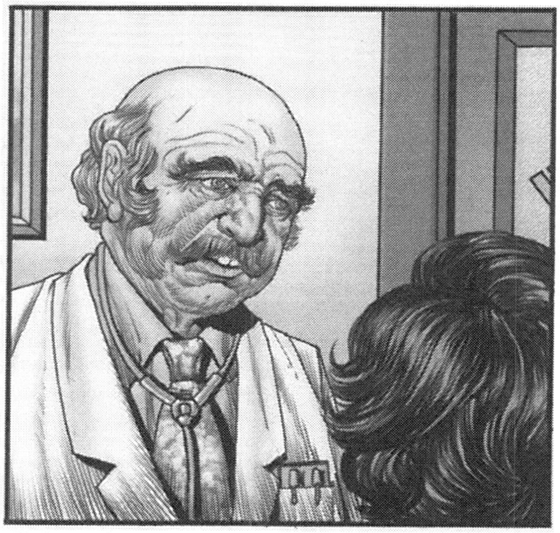

Bad news from Dr. Espey. (Art ©2010 Jack T. Chick LLC)

Two young brothers worked as cowboys on a ranch near my Uncle Louie's. A two-year-old steer had strayed and the brothers set out to find him. They finally found him stuck in some heavy brush and could not get him out. They went back to the ranch and got a wagon and tried to get him out once more with no success. They decided to shoot and butcher the steer. The owner of the ranch heard their shot and came to find out who was on his land. He found the brothers butchering the steer and thought they had shot his steer. He shot and killed both brothers. John Roy and I went often to Trinidad's three mortuaries. The week the cowboys were killed, we went to see their bodies. The mortician asked, "Did you know the brothers?" John Roy answered, "Oh, no; we just came to see the bullet holes."

My mother left my dad and took John Roy and me with her. Once in a while Dad would bring groceries over. They always ended up fighting when he came. Once, Mom hit him over the head with a shaving mug and knocked him out and cut his scalp.

Ruby decks dad. (Art ©2010 Jack T. Chick LLC)

We yelled at Mom because she had hit Dad, so she locked us out of the house in the snow. Later, Dad became conscious and came out of the house and left in his truck.

Chasing Wolves

A few weeks after their big fight, Dad heard of a big barbecue the state was having on July 4th to celebrate the opening of a pass on the Continental Divide, which had an altitude of 11,000 feet. The whole family went – even Helmer. When we left Walsenberg, it was a hot 98 degrees, but at the high altitude cook out, it was just 30 degrees with a light snow! We had a lot of fun. They had barbecued bison calves and served them with beans, potatoes, and pies. Everything was really delicious. We ate until we couldn't eat anymore and they sent food home with us.

The young Slator boys (John Roy left, Dann right).

On the way back to the house, Mom was driving and had her car window open. A pack of wolves ran across the road in front of us. Helmer was sitting between John Roy and me in the back seat. When he saw the wolves he jumped over the front seat and out the window. As Helmer was sailing out the window, his claws cut two deep cuts in Mom's arms. Mom stopped the car and we tried calling Helmer. Darkness was falling fast. Dad rubbed snow on Mom's cut to try to stop the bleeding. It worked, but Helmer was gone! We cried most of the way home because we just knew the wolves would kill Helmer. John Roy and I were heartbroken!

A month later, a state panel truck pulled up in front of our store. The man identified himself as a state trapper and told Dad, "I think I have your dog!" He opened up the back of his truck and Helmer jumped out! The man had been trapping wolves in the area because they were killing sheep. One day when he checked his traps he had caught Helmer. He raised his gun to shoot Helmer and noticed he had a collar on. He put his rifle down and started talking to Helmer and gave him a drink of water and some food. Helmer was still in the trap. Helmer finally let the man touch him and take his foot out of the trap. Helmer had not been in the trap long and hadn't broken any bones. His paw was swollen and bleeding. Helmer kept licking his paw and the man saw our name on Helmer's collar.

John Roy and I were thrilled to get Helmer back! Our dad gave the State Trapper groceries and some money for a reward. Helmer was happy to be with us and licked our faces and whined joyfully! He laid down and slept pretty solid for two days, only waking up for a bite to eat and something to drink. We all loved Helmer. He ran with the wolves!

The expensive (but well worth it) Helmer Von Brudenbrock. He chased wolves!

Dad loved to fish and hunt. One time he went to Creede, Colorado and took John Roy and me and left Helmer. John Roy and I didn't like to leave Helmer. He had to be put on a 30-foot chain and could only go partway under our porch.

When we got to Creede, Dad showed us some buildings that he had helped his dad build. Then we headed into the mountains where the trout streams were. While Dad fished, John Roy and I explored. We saw deer, elk and wild turkeys. We heard a lot of noise and saw a mother bear sitting in a small stream completely damming it up. She would look in the stream and see a trout and slap it out of the water to one of her cubs.

We camped for a week. We helped Dad hook the tent to our car. Dad salted the big trout he caught and put them in a frozen snow bank to take back to Trinidad to give to friends and customers. We saw only two other people that week. One was a sheep herder and his two dogs and the other we saw was a mountain man. We found his cabin and was he ever surprised to see five-and six-year-old boys at his door! The mountain man introduced himself as Ned. He had two donkeys, a pet bobcat and a big dog named Trouble. We were high above the timberline.

Ned went back with us to our campsite. When Dad returned from fishing upstream, Ned told him that it was really foolish for him to let us roam around in the hills by ourselves. He said there were mountain lions and cinnamon tip bears around. Dad gave Ned some trout and some whiskey.

Stilt Walking

I had never seen people walking on stilts until I went to the circus that time with Evelyn Mary. I was determined to make a pair out of some old bed slats I found in the garage. The bed slats were six feet long, thin and very strong. I made the footrest about three feet up the stilt and put straps on the hub of the stilt to hold my feet in like a stirrup and the handles were at my waist. After several falls, I managed to walk without falling. I was the only person in town with stilts. When I got used to the stilts I could run on them and cross the river using them.

My idea of homemade stilts caught on, and others in our neighborhood began making them. We were so good using them that we played a game called Kick the Can. This game was a lot like soccer. I even went to town on my stilts. The courthouse steps were a challenge I soon managed, and I could swiftly climb up and down them. I started making taller stilts and finally had a pair so tall I had to get on top of the house to get on them. I could walk on the big train trestles with open spaces between the ties. John Roy was never interested in my stilt adventure.

My stilt walking ended abruptly one day when I was chasing John Roy. A new house was under construction where we lived. The carpenters had a ladder leaned against the second story of the house. John Roy climbed up the ladder to the roof and I followed him on my stilts. When I was almost to the top, he pushed the ladder backward. I fell and broke my left arm below the elbow. The bone splintered and came out the skin. Dr. Espey came and set my arm with it lying on a pillow. John Roy said he was sorry. I had my arm in a cast for a long time and couldn't walk on my stilts.

The Danger Next Door

Once for a breeding fee, Dad obtained one of Helmer's puppies. Dad gave Major to our neighbors, the Gartsides, who lived behind us. They kept Major chained. He was almost as big as Helmer and was silver-grey also. He got loose a few times and he and Helmer would get into terrible fights every time. Several people in the neighborhood had to separate them because they would fight to kill each other. John Roy and I didn't like Major because he bit part of Helmer's left ear off. When the Gartsides were gone, we would tease Major and throw things at him. Major hated us and would bare his teeth at us like he would eat us alive. One day, we went to tease him and unknown to us, Mr. Gartside had lengthened Major's chain 15 more feet so he would have more freedom. Major came bounding out of his dog house and, to our surprise, grabbed John Roy by one leg and dragged him into his house. I ran over to our neighbor Mantelle's house and to the station across the street yelling, "Major got John in his doghouse and he is eating him alive!" Soon a lot of folks had gathered outside of Major's house because of the commotion I was making. The men got a hold of Major's chain and pulled him out of his doghouse. He still had hold of John Roy's leg. Several men had clubs and an axe in case Major attacked them. They got John Roy loose from Major's mouth. John Roy's pants leg on his overalls was torn off and he was bloody all over. Someone called Dr. Espey. They took John Roy to our house and Dr. Espey met us there. He poured acid in the deep bites and closed them with several stitches. John Roy didn't have any pain killers and three men had to hold him down. Jim Gartside told my dad he could shoot Major, but after my dad heard how it happened he wouldn't shoot him. John Roy healed up without any serious problems, but he had six very big scars for the rest of his life.

Climbing Simpson's Mountain

The steep cliffs of Simpson's Rest (near Trinidad, Colorado).

We loved Simpsons Rest. That's a giant sandstone bluff overlooking the Purgatoire River Valley and is located North of Trinidad. Pioneer George Simpson is buried high atop of it. It also has three caves that we explored on a regular basis. The best one was Lover's Retreat, but we also like Fatman's Squeeze, and The Drop. But Lover's Retreat had an unusual moss covered room at the bottom. We also found another exit to it. Most of all, we liked to go to Simpsons Rest to play.

We also like to play around the old mines that were boarded up and hunt for snakes. There were lots of things to do around them. We liked to hike and climb around there, and hunt for snakes. We also enjoyed throwing rocks down the mine shafts and listening how long they took to hit something, or calling out and trying to start rock slides. It was very dangerous for kids but we were too young or wild to care.

The deep, dark caves of Simpson's Rest. (Art ©2010 Jack T. Chick LLC)

Climbing the face of the cliff for fun. (Art ©2010 Jack T. Chick LLC)

We liked the view from on top of the bluff. You could see for miles around. But we got tired of going up the long, back way, so we decided to climb the face of it. It was at least 100 feet or more. Helmer was with us, but he had to run around the long way. When we reached the top, Helmer was waiting. He was so excited, he licked and pawed at me as I tried to climb over the top edge, and I almost fell down on John Roy below. It would have killed us both.

Roy and I were just five and six-years-old back then. We had taken a lunch and found the first spring and second spring that day, and we even signed the book in the box at the top of Fishers Peak (which has a 10,000 foot elevation). We made a lot of trips up there. During one trip, three bigger boys tried to take our lunches from us. We ran up a short cut but they kept chasing us so we stopped and started rolling and throwing rocks at them. I had a slingshot, and I started shooting marbles at them. They did run away from us but we knew they would be waiting at the end of the trail. So we decided to cross over this Narrow Ridge to the North Mesa.

We could never return to Fishers Peak, as we slid down big and steep rocks. We had to keep going. We finally made it to the North Mesa and home.

The Great Purgatoire

The Purgatoire River was rightly named. It had two desperate groups living on either side of it in those days. One side was the hobo's town, and it was really large. They had entire families living there, with kids and everything. Sometimes John Roy and I would steal things from my dad's grocery store and take the food down there to give to friends. But we had friends on the other side too, and they weren't too fond of the hobos. Those were the Gypsies. They also lived hand to mouth. You would think the two groups had a lot in common and would get along great, but there were fights that made them wary of each other. John Roy and I visited both sides a lot. The Gypsies had all sorts of colorful clothes and music and a very exciting culture. But once, while we were over there, we saw a hobo get in a fight with them and they killed him, and just dumped his body in the river like a dead rat. It never occurred to us that we were in any danger, but folks around there all told about how Gypsies stole children. We probably would have thought that was alright with us!

Once, after a flood, we saw a hobo roping lumber that was flowing down the swollen Purgatoire. He made the mistake of tying the rope to himself, and when he snagged a really big piece, it pulled him under and he disappeared. It drowned him. And he was the father of three kids, some of which we had played with. There's no telling what happened to those kids, but they already had it pretty bad, even before his death.

Our best place to swim was off the Purgatoire River where a dam was about three miles east of Trinidad. We rode the train down there and jumped off in a big pile of ashes that the trains dumped there. The dam was for irrigation purposes and had a big valve that let water out in ditches. A man caught us there a couple times and told us to get away from the dam, as it was dangerous. Instead of listening, we laughed at him and it made him angry. One day while we were swimming, he sneaked up on us and opened the big valve to prove his point. It created a strong whirlpool. John Roy was swimming further upstream and was unaffected, but my pal (a Mexican kid named Benny) and I got caught in the sudden current. We went under and were sucked through the open valve gate. I was knocked unconscious and scraped up by the metal gate, then spit out through the other side. But I was the lucky one. Benny was bigger and got caught on the gate underwater and drowned. A man that was irrigating saw me passed out in the irrigation ditch and pulled me from the water and saved my life. John Roy and I never went back there again.

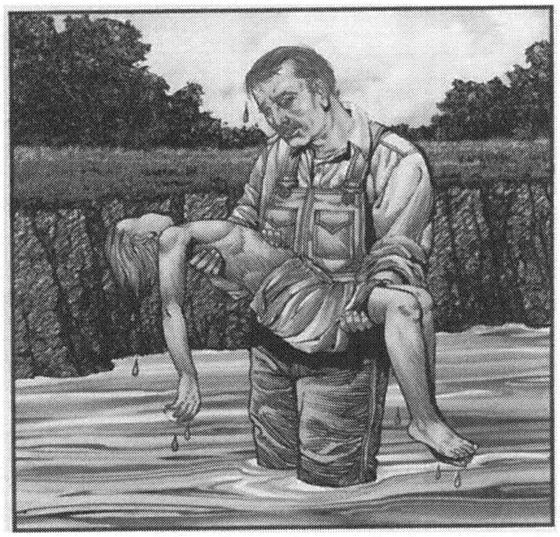
Dann was sucked through an underwater floodgate and saved by a stranger. (Art ©2010 Jack T. Chick LLC)

Fun with Guns and Speeding

My dad got us a BB gun pellet rifle for Christmas and we were told to share it. It was fine for a few days. That's until John Roy shot it three times and when I said it was my turn, he turned to me and said "It's going to be mine from now on." I asked him what he was talking about and then he pointed the barrel right at my head and said "I'm going to shoot your eye out." Of all the stupid things to say, I said, "Just don't miss." He pulled the trigger with the gun only eight or ten inches in front of my face. The pellet lodged in my left cheekbone and it hurt like the dickens! I grabbed the end of the gun barrel and yanked it out of his grip. He started to run away in the foot deep snow. I caught up to him and hit him on the head with a rifle and tore part of his ear off. It covered the snow with bright red blood. A man who saw the whole thing raced us to Dr. Espeys office as fast as he could. Doc sewed John Roy's ear back on, and he said I ripped a two-inch piece of it from his head. Then he removed the BB pellet from my cheekbone.

Mother loved to drive our new Essex town sedan. She always drove fast. One day when we were leaving town, the car spun out of control and hit a tree. The car flipped and landed upside down. A lot of people gathered around our car. They got Mother out of the overturned car. She asked the rescuers, "How are my boys?" They asked her, "Are you sure your boys were with you in the car?" "Yes!" she insisted. The rescuers feared we were under the car. Carefully, they pushed the car on its side. They didn't find us under it but they could hear one of us whining. The seat could go forward to make more room in the trunk. The back seat had been bounced enough to open and we had been knocked into the trunk.

Train Spotting

John Roy and I loved to get under the railroad trestle when the trains went over. This was a big thrill for us! John Roy had the bright idea that we could lie between the tracks and let the train go over us. To test his theory, he piled some gravel up between the tracks and put a rock on top of the pile. He then had me lie down beside the rock to see if I would be lower than the rock. I was lower than it was, so I got up and we waited for a train to come back. After the train had passed, the rock was still there. John Roy talked me into going first to let the train pass over me. It scared me so much the first time that I peed my pants, but I was braver after that. John Roy and I waited for the next train to come along and it passed over us. Our rock on top of the gravel pile was still there, too. We waited a long time for a fourth train to pass, but gave up and finally headed towards home. We were almost home when we heard another train coming. We ran back hoping to lay down on the tracks before the train went over our spot. Thank God for His mercy and grace that we didn't make it to our rock pile! When the train had completely passed our spot, the rock and most of the pile of gravel were gone! We would have been dead because the cowcatcher was lower on that train!

Dann and John Roy recklessly tempted fate on the railroad tracks. (Art ©2010 Jack T. Chick LLC)

The Killer Bull's Revenge

Just before my mom and dad separated, we lived in a house called Spencers house. It was as close as you could get to Fishers Peak by Setser's Dairy. We had guinea pigs and silver Martin rabbits and we also had a horse we both rode.

What we love to do when no one was around at the dairy was to tease their Jersey Bull. John Roy would get on one side of the corral and me on the other, and I'd tease him and then John Roy would and he would really get mad at us.

One day we went down to tease the bull and he was gone. It turned out that he had killed one of the worker's wives and they shot him dead and dragged him about a block away and dumped him in a deep ditch, belly up. We thought it would be fun to jump on his bloated belly from the top of the ditch. We would jump on him and bounce up on the other side. Then we decided to both jump on him together. Bad idea. With all the added weight, he burst open like a piñata, and we both fell inside. What a mess! We stunk to high heaven! We ran down to the creek and jumped in to wash our clothes and ourselves but it was an ordeal.

The Parting of My Parents

My dad and mom always fought and one day John Roy and I were playing in a field with Helmer and my mom drove our Essex loaded with everything she could get in it, and she got out and said she was going away for a while and Helmer would take care of us. John Roy never did see her again. She had gone back to Pennsylvania when dad came home from his fishing trip. He found a note on the table that said she was never coming back. Besides emptying the house, she cleaned out the bank account, too. Dad just sat there with us and got drunker and drunker. He had a gun on the table, contemplating suicidal thoughts, and he kept repeating, "Why didn't she take you two with her?"

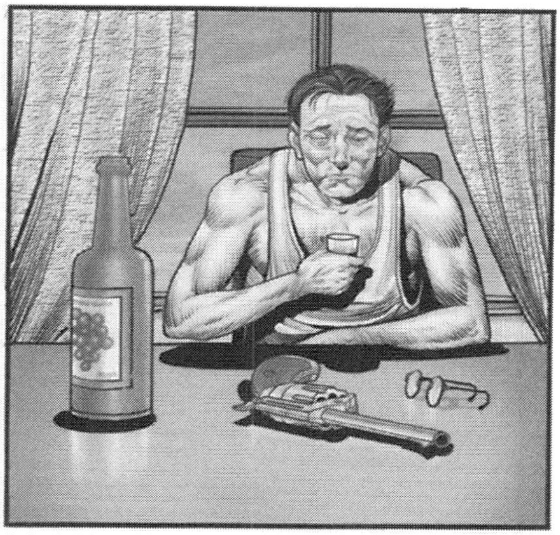

Ruby left her kids and husband with nothing but a bare house and empty bank account. (Art ©2010 Jack T. Chick LLC)

Our Dad soon decided to leave to California, so he left us with his mother (our grandmother) and that was the beginning of over 14 different people that took us in. Our dad didn't even send his own mother any money for us, ever. After grandma took us, our aunt Ava Gartside did for a while, then Jim Goodens and the Inmaus'. Then Ed and Abby Slaughter. Each one said the same thing to John Roy and me, that nobody wanted us, not even our own parents. It got so depressing, that at the Slaughter's house, I went into the basement and hung myself with a rope tied to a pipe. They heard the sound of the bucket I had used for a platform after I knocked it over, and they barely got to me in time. They were so disgusted with me and John Roy, that they sent us to the Abby's Family (dry farmers) way out in Tobe, Colorado.

Dann's suicide attempt. (Art ©2010 Jack T. Chick LLC)

The Bryants were the only ones good to us. There was Dennis, Willy, Gregory, Marybeth, grandpa Bryant, and grandma Bryant. They were all Christians and we went on a flat bed wagon pulled by two of our workhorses to church every Sunday in a two room schoolhouse. After church, we all went to someone's ranch or farm and had a potluck picnic.

The Dark Dust Days

I told John Roy we had to stop cussing and doing other bad things because I wanted to stay with this new family. But soon after we arrived, everything planted died in a drought and we got a big surprise in the distance as we could see coming from the east a large black cloud. It was a giant dust storm, the first of many.

The US government had paid all the farmers in Oklahoma 10 cents an acre to plow up the land, and no rain had come for over a year, so when the wind started blowing hard, it caused a major dust storm covering miles and as high as 1500 feet or more. The storms came often and blanketed much of Colorado. It happened most where we were and they called it The Dust Bowl.

The storms lasted 3 to 5 days. We stayed in the house and put wet gunnysacks over our heads and laid down on the floor to breath. The cattle and milk cows and six horses were all dying. So the US government sent men out to our place (and everybody else's) to pay $10 per cow and shot all of them. They said they would kill the horses too, but would pay nothing for them or the calves

The government sent men into The Dust Bowl areas to shoot all the cattle. (Art ©2010 Jack T. Chick LLC)

After all this, the Bryants decided to leave. Grandma and Grandpa both died of dust pneumonia.

They took John Roy and me back to Trinidad with the Goodens, Jim and Thora and nobody out of 14 different families ever got a dime from my dad or mom for taking care of us. The straw that broke the camel's back and forced us to leave Tobe was when billions of grasshoppers came and stayed a month or two. They ate everything is sight, even the bark off the trees. Between the dust storms and insect plagues, it really seemed like we were under some sort of Biblical curse!

First dust storms, then bugs. (Art ©2010 Jack T. Chick LLC)

Losing Helmer

Grandma then took us in again. Then our uncle Bernie and aunt Mildred (who owned the drugstore on Commercial Street by the rivers) decided to take us to California. Back then, Helmer was my best and only loyal friend. He joined us with each new family, but he was almost 10 and we could not take him with us to the west coast. So grandma took him. She said after we left, that he stopped eating and died of a broken heart.

Leaving Helmer behind. (Art ©2010 Jack T. Chick LLC)

On the way to California, we stopped at Carlsbad Caverns in New Mexico for a few days in tents. The day we all went in the caves, John Roy and I were really excited as we loved caves and those caves had bats, too. They had stores and shops way down hundreds of feet below the surface. We were awestruck. When they got ready to come back up out of the cave, I wanted to see the new room that was to open the next year, so I hid and stayed down there. What I didn't know was that after the tour left the area, they turned off the lights!

When everybody got back up out of the caverns, John Roy told them I was missing, so some Rangers went down and turned on the lights and found me. They said if I had gone another 50 feet in the dark, I would have fallen 200 feet down into another room. Uncle Bernie really got angry at first, but he laughed about it later.

Dann at age 12, Highland Park, CA.

When we got to Highland Park near Los Angeles, uncle Bernie took John Roy and me to his sister's (Rose's) house. We would end up staying with Aunt Rose for over three years. By this time, my dad was living with his brother and working nights. I was twelve then, and John Roy was thirteen. My cousins were Jack (10), Jess (8), Ruth (12), Dot (14),

Audrey (18) and Mildred (20). Aunt Rose also had four cats. She had to keep at my dad for help to take care of John Roy and me. I started to sell newspapers on a street corner in front of the 2nd See's Candy Shop in Highland Park to save money for a bicycle, and then got a paper route and rode that bicycle to school.

Aunt Rose took all of us to church every Sunday. I'll never forget one of my Sunday School teachers who was a doctor. He took his Sunday school kids to a lot of neat places. Aunt Rose would sign us up for any Vacation Bible School and anywhere else she could to get rid of us for a while. I guess we about drove her crazy sometimes.

One summer, she signed me up to go to Catalina Island for 10 days with a church group. The camp was at Emerald Bay near Avalon Bay. We had four hours in the afternoon to go to Avalon or just hang out near the ocean. I was a good swimmer and diver, so I would go up to Avalon and dive around the pier for coins. I braved it almost to the end of the pier where it was deeper. Sometimes I would find a silver dollar. Zane Grey Yatch's brought in Swordfish and Albacore tuna on the beach. He had a glass bottom boat. I got to stay another 10 days. These were fun days in my life.

Pre-Teen Boxing

When I got back to Aunt Rose's, she signed me up to stay for two weeks at Wallace Berry's son (Noel's) Ranch in Valyermo. This camp was located in the desert and was for boys from underprivileged homes. It was run by the Highland Park Police Force. It was a pre-curser to the Sherriff Boy's Ranch. It was something new for us. And the police force was really something else; they had everything there. We could go hiking or swimming. They had exercises. They also had baseball and basketball and boxing and horseback riding. I signed up for boxing and the horseback riding.

There was nothing religious whatsoever, not even praying or giving thanks for our food before we ate. But they kept us all busy all the time. Now, when I signed up for the boxing, I went down there with a couple of my friends. One of them I knew from the school. I went down and they had lots of blacks there and they had a couple of Mexicans, but mostly black guys. My friend said he wasn't going to fight any of those black guys and I said, "Well, they're just like us. They hurt just like we do." So, anyway, they had regular boxing bouts. They had a boxing ring, and trainers. They had referees: these were all police officers. My trainer signed me up for the biggest of the boys. I was about 5'9" and I weighed about 120 pounds, so I had mostly bigger kids to box.

Dann wanted to learn boxing at an early age.

We had a boxing competition between the different barracks that we were in. There were barracks and there were tents. After the first round of competition, it ended up that I just had to fight one guy to win the best boxer in my weight. My opponent was Chalky Wright and his brother was Wilbur Wright. They later both became professional fighters, but then they were just twelve years old. There were only three rounds for the main event. By the third round, I already had everything going for me. Everyone knew I had him beaten. No one saw it, but he butted me in the head with his head, and as I went backwards, he hit me, and I went down. He won the fight; I couldn't get up. After this was all over, a couple of my friends led me to their barracks that night and we looked for Chalky Wright and they said he was in the back bathroom – on the toilet. So, we all went back there. Some of the black guys in the barracks followed us and we went in there. He was sitting on the toilet with his pants around his ankles. I stood in front of him and said, "You know good and well how I won that bout. You know you butted me. No one seen it, but that's how you won was by butting me." He said, "Well, I don't know. You just have to accept it. I'm just the one that won." And I said, "Well, I guess so." He flushed the toilet and when he reached down to pull his pants up, I rabbit punched him hard as I could right behind the neck, behind his ear, and knocked him flat on the floor. He hit his head on the floor and we all started fighting. It got pretty heated up fighting until two of the barracks officers (who were police officers) came in there and broke us all up. They took us down to where the farmers had dug a big hole in the ground to store vegetables and stuff so they'd keep longer, before they had giant refrigerators. So they dug these holes and they put logs and planks across the tops. They covered it with dirt on top and rounded it all off nice. We were all thrown in there– all nine of us. But they hadn't used it for so long, that there was two or three feet of water along the bottom and we stayed stuck in it all day long. They listened to hear if there was any trouble in there. They eventually took us out one at a time to get our story. And when my turn came, I told them, "I actually beat him in that fight."

They must of believed me, because they announced a rematch for Saturday. My cousin who gave me boxing lessons and everything, Des, he drove all the way out there to watch it because it was a rematch for the championship of that camp. When it all ended up, I won the main event. The greatest part about the whole thing was just the experience – staying there that long.

Surfing Through School

In the fall of 1937, it was time for me to start school. There was a school about eight blocks from us in Highland Park. It was called Luther Burbank Junior High School. It was on Figueroa Street. I liked the school because I never saw so many kids in all my life and it was a good school. They had wood shop and they had all kinds of other things. I never did fool with the athletic part because I sold papers on the street corner after school. (I also had a paper route.) But I did sign up for wood shop. I made everything in wood shop that was required. I told my teacher, Mr. Toy, "I saw something in a National Geographic Magazine where these Hawaiians... they call them surfboards." I wanted to make one and he was excited that I try it. So we glued ten two-by-fours together and I started cutting and planning it until it was finished. Everybody came in there to see it and the teacher liked it.

Luther Burbank Jr. High School (torn down in 1975).

Then I wondered after I finished it how I could get it to the beach 22 miles away. I finally put pop-off wheels on it and made a hitch on my bicycle. The first chance I got to go to Seal Beach, I went. I tried all day to be able to stand on it and almost quit. I tried three more times, and finally got up on it, atop nice waves. But I got caught in a big wave and was knocked off my board and fell into heavy surf. I must have gotten knocked unconscious because all of a sudden, I saw that I floated out of the water above my body...my spirit, I guess is what you call it, left my body and I could see my body going in with the waves and being sucked out and back again and back in with the next wave. And all of a sudden, I looked down and I could see as far as from Alaska to Panama. I heard beautiful music and I could see my arms lifted up above me. Then all I could see was bare feet around me. A man was holding me upside down by my ankles, shaking me and bumping my head in the sand. Water was coming out of my mouth, nose and ears. God had spared me again! The man sat me down on the beach and hung around until he knew I was okay. After I gathered my wits, I went back in the ocean to search for my surfboard, but couldn't find it. I finally gave up and rode my bike home. I never told anybody about this at the church we went to because it was such a weird thing to see my body going in and out of the ocean, laying there in the surf. I didn't think anyone would believe me.

The Shrinking Collection Plate

The church we went to bought a lot next door to build an addition to the existing one. They had $40,000 saved up. Then the preacher stole it all and ran off with some woman from the church. John Roy and I had taken up the collection a few times before and we would pocket some money once in a while out of it. So after the preacher stole all the money, I asked Mr. Horowitz (my Sunday school teacher) if it was a sin for us to take money out of the collection now that we found out the preacher took it all. He said yes, it was—and he never let us take up the collection again.

Aunt Rose had a job at the general hospital in Los Angeles as a nurse's assistant. She had to take the streetcar to work. She also had a heart condition that she took medicine for – digitalis. Often she passed out and got stiff as a board, even in church. Mildred worked and got married to Desmond Selby who moved in with us. We had no heat in the house but the kitchen stove oven and a fireplace. Des was fun, and when he saw me come home kind of beat up, he started giving me boxing lessons. He also played soccer. However, he did drink a lot and loved to go to the races and bet on the horses.

Big Bear Lake (in San Bernardino Mountains, Ca.)

Aunt Rose signed me up for a church camp up at Big Bear Lake, a hundred miles from our house in the mountains. Des took me up there. I thought I wasn't going to like it there, but it was very beautiful. It reminded me of Colorado. Everything was church-oriented – boys and girls. We had free time – two hours in the afternoon.

Camping Pranks

One day, a boy I didn't get along with much was there and I took his jacket that he laid down, climbed the tallest pine tree in the camp and put his jacket on the top branch. He saw it. Everyone watched and he climbed up to get it. He was heavier than me, and when he got to the top to his jacket, he reached for it and the branch snapped. He fell through the limbs, clear to the ground. He was knocked unconscious and broke some bones. Everyone blamed me. The ones in charge called Aunt Rose and told her to come and get me. So Des came and got me. This was the last camp I ever went to. John Roy got into trouble and was sent to a reform school for a year and I never did go to see him. We weren't that close anymore. When we got in fights, I could finally whip him. He just hung around with others. When he got out of the reform school, they made arrangements to send him to my Uncle Louie's cattle ranch in Colorado and I never saw him again for a couple of years. He stayed there and worked on the ranch for two years, and then he ran off and joined the 1st Calvary down at Fort Bliss down in Texas in the Army. I never really missed him that much 'cause we weren't that close anymore.

We had a large Canary Island Palm tree in front of our house. It had big, long fronds that curved up at the end in the tree. When they dried out, they fell to the ground. I took three of them and made a sled with boards across the top to sit on. When it was all finished, I sanded and waxed the runners. All around us were round, steep hills. When the grass dried up, I would take my sled up these hills and go down super fast, then faster if I laid down on it. I had a rope tied to the side runners so I could kind of guide it. I went as fast as sleds in the snow. I made a longer, wider sled that two could ride on. It was really a fun thing to do. The hills were really steep and long to go down. I went up there whenever I had the chance to go. I really loved it up there.

Biking in LA and Meeting a Giant

My barber, Mr. Zimberlaw, came from England and raced bicycles as a boy. I had two bikes now and I rode everywhere I went around L.A. and to the beaches. There was a bicycle shop near his shop. He looked at my bike and said he could make it go a lot faster. He got some bigger sprockets and kept my bike a few days. He also put on some different handlebars – lower down, so I could get more pull on the pedals. I had to run beside it and jump on it to be able to pedal it. A bigger sprocket on the back and a smaller one in front made it that way. I couldn't go up a hill, but on level ground I could go almost 35 mph. I went to the beach only once because I found out it was mostly uphill coming back from the beach and was very hard to pedal. People in cars really looked when I passed them at 35 mph!

I won a new bike by having more subscriptions turned in on my paper route than anybody else. I really loved it. It was a beautiful thing; it had lights and all that on it. I kept it for just going to school and such.

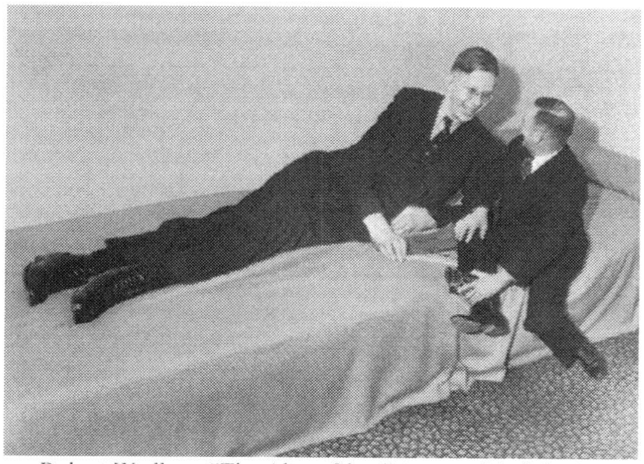

Robert Wadlow, "The Alton Giant" (next to his father).

One day, I saw in the paper that the tallest man in the world was coming to Carl's Shoe Store in Highland Park. The store had one of his shoes (size 37AA) in the window. It was full of dimes and who could guess the amount of dimes in it would get the shoe full of them. The day he came I went down on my stilts. They called him "the Alton Giant", but his real name was Robert Wadlow. He was 8'11" and I was 9' on my stilts. He really got a big kick out of my appearance on the stilts 'cause no one had ever done that before. He died at age 22 from complications of his size. He kept growing until the day he died.

At school, I made a big mistake of getting in a fight with another boy who had what you could call a "gang." I beat him up and the next day at the bike rack, he showed up with two of his pals. They all jumped on me and some other boys saw what was going on. Well, they got into it, too, helping me. We beat them up. That was the start of our so-called "gang." We didn't cause and real trouble, it was more of a social thing. We just liked to hang out together and pass the time.

The Newspaper Biz

My paper route boss asked me if I'd like to sell papers at the Rose Parade. I thought it would be a great chance to do something. He gave me almost fifty papers to sell. He said he would come by later and give me more if I needed them, but he never made it back because the crowd was too thick. I went to the parade; and I sold nearly all of my papers right away. It was real early in the morning; and most people bought them to sit on—although the paper contained the schedule of all the floats, and other stuff in the parade, including the bands. After I ran out of papers, I started standing every time I knew a float was coming. People were all sitting down until a new float approached and then they would stand up to get a better view as the float passed by. When they stood up, I would snatch their paper and sell it to somebody else. I'd grab it and run. I don't know how many people I did this to. Other folks would buy the same "recycled" papers. When it was all over, I did pretty good there at the Parade. My paper boss picked me up on a certain corner later. I made a whopping $8 that day.

I was ready now to start Franklin High School there in Highland Park. But I made a big mistake: at the same time, I took a morning paper route. So I had a morning route, and I sold papers on the corner, and I had an evening route. That was just a little more than I could ever handle. I should have known better, 'cause I'd never done too well in school since I never studied or nothing hardly. I was always cold and tired.

Benjamin Franklin High School, Highland Park, Ca.

But I did enjoy Franklin High School; I took up commercial art which I knew I had a talent for. I made all of the posters and all the things for different football games and everything else. I learned how to set up printing and all that stuff. But the greatest thing I enjoyed was a clay modeling and ceramics class taught by a real well-known artist named Mr. Andrew Bjurman. I started making everything. Mr. Bjurman took a liking to me as much as I did to him. He had me come over when I had the time to his big home in Alhambra to do his yard work and stuff. He was the kindest man and the best man I've ever known. We got along so good. I made all kinds of things. I even had stuff made that was put in a museum.

The Teacher's Pet Bull Dog

One day in the class there was a boy – I never liked him much – who got Mr. Bjurman all shook up. Mr. Bjurman would let me take over the class once in a while when he had to leave. When he left, I asked this boy something that got him all nervous and everything – I asked him to come and help me mix clay in the back room. There were two rooms. The far back room in the back of the building was where we had all of the clay and where we mixed it up and everything. He kind of sassed me. He said, "Why do I have to go mix clay?" And I said, "Because I'm asking you and I'm in charge."

So anyway, he was about the same size as I was and we got back in there to mix clay. I shut the door and I turned around and looked at him and said, "You didn't want to mix clay, huh?" and he said, "Well, no, why would I?" I said, "'Cause you and I is going to mix it up right here for what you done to Mr. Bjurman!" And, boy, we started fighting and I knocked him around pretty good. Then we went back to the classroom. He just sat there. A while later, Mr. Bjurman come back to the class when the class was about over and he looked around. Everybody left the classroom and I stayed behind to see how he was. He asked me, "What went on here while I was gone?" And I said, "I don't believe he'll ever sass you anymore."

In the class, I usually made dinosaurs and different animals and stuff. Mr. Bjurman made life-size statues of famous Indians, like Geronimo and such. I liked to do the work and I learned how to load the kiln and do all of that stuff and mix all of the glazes and everything. I really enjoyed it, but I failed in nearly all of my other classes. My report card was really something to see: "A" in metal shop, "A" in clay and ceramics shop, and the rest of the classes were pretty well down.

Getting To Know Girls

I started getting interested in girls at this time and I made another mistake. I always liked the prettier ones—like everybody else, I guess. I had quite a time going to some of the birthday parties and stuff. I really liked my cousin Ruth who was my same age. We had a lot of fun together like at the beach and stuff, and roller-skating and things. I liked to go over to Griffith Park with everybody and we all had fun there in this big park. No one ever rode bicycles with me, but I always rode to most of the places I went on my bicycle. I was super-thin on account of not eating proper but not only that, I was riding my bicycle all the time and going everywhere. I was busy. When I started the gym class at Franklin High School, they lined us all up and then they walked along and told different ones of us to take three steps forward. They came to me and told me to take three steps forward. So when the class was all over, they said all those who took three steps forward to go over to the other end of the gym. So we all went over there and I noticed they were all thin and some of them had kind of other things wrong with them. When we got over there, we met this Mr. Rigby, who was the teacher. We found out they called this the correction class. I got really upset 'cause I didn't think that I should be there. The first thing they ever done was sit us down, have us eat graham crackers and drink a glass of milk. I went there, and we had exercises; we had all these different things for about a month. I went there and said, "How long do I have to stay in this class?" They replied, "Probably the whole semester. You haven't gained much." I said, "I don't gain much because I have two paper routes and I'm always active." Anyway, he told me I'd have to stay the semester. So, when I left the gymnasium, I was pretty mad about it.

Embarrassing a Bully

Aunt Rose had made arrangements – John Roy had left Uncle Louie's ranch so now Louie said he would take me. He made arrangements in June when I got out to go back and work for Louie on his ranch in Colorado.

Anyway, I was starting to cross the street and one of the football players – a good-looking guy – and about six of the cheerleaders were sitting there. I crossed the street. He looked at me and said, "Did you get your cookies and your milk?" I said, "What did you say?" He said, "Are you deaf, too?" and the girls all laughed. I said, "No, I'm not deaf, I just want to hear you say that again." He looked around and they all grinned. So he kept at it and said, "Did – you – get - your - cookies and your milk today?" I said, "Would you stand up and say that?" He was way bigger than me and he looked around at the cheerleaders and grinned. They all smiled. So he stood up and repeated, "I said, 'Did you get your cookies and your—'"

He didn't get to say milk 'cause I hit him right square in the mouth and I just knocked him flat on the ground. Then I pounded him and pounded him. Somebody came and pulled me off of him. Instead of going back to classes, I went down and got my bicycle and I went home.

Leaving to Louie's

When I got home, Aunt Rose was there and I said, "I don't want to wait 'til June to go to Uncle Louie's. I wanna go now." She said, "It's okay with me." So you wouldn't believe this, by Friday I was gone back to Colorado. You know, I never took nothing of my things with me. I had all kinds of little personal things – never took one of my bicycles or nothing. My Lionel train. Everything was there. Of course, I wouldn't have had any time later to do anything with them. But at least I could have had the option.

Returning to Trinidad, Co.

So I left on a bus to go back to Trinidad, CO and I was so glad to just leave. And I never worried about my paper corner, my customers, nothing – I just left. And, you know, when I got to Trinidad, Uncle Louie was there and my grandma lived in Trinidad, too. He took me out to the ranch about twenty miles out in Barela, CO right below all these big, high mesas and stuff. I walked around out there and I went down the creek and I looked in all the corrals and barns. I thought this is really going to be nice. I just enjoyed myself thinking about how beautiful it was going to be.

Well, the next morning when he woke me up real early, I went out there and he told me to go with Mackie, his cousin. They all three came from northern Italy in the early 1900s. And they all three took out a homestead: 660 acres each on the same parcel of land. So they ended up with about 2000 acres and they built the ranch there. They had cattle; the main thing they did was buy people's weaned calves and feed them through the winter and sell them the next summer. When I got up that morning and came out there, he told me to go with Mackie. I started that day working eight to ten hours a day. Each one (there was Charlie, Louie and Mackie) had almost a different way of doing things. So I always told everybody that I knew how to do about everything three different ways. They even milked a cow different. When I would look around and see one of them coming, I would start milking the way he'd told me. I couldn't believe all the work there was on a ranch. But I soon found out there was no rest. And after I learned to milk the cows, then that was my job to milk the cows. I learned to separate the milk and all that, and clean the separator. That was all extra from the work you done out in the field, and horseback riding with the cattle and everything. I couldn't believe that I ever got into such a deal. In a way, I kind of liked it.

I got there just about in time for the haying period. He had an alfalfa field, and he had a *Timothy-grass* hay field (a perennial long stem grass), and they grew winter wheat over there in another ten-acre patch. I had to learn how to mow the hay, how to rake the hay, how to pick up the hay with buck rakes, how to stack the hay with a stacker, how to do all these things – how to irrigate, how to take care of all the fences and all the stuff around there. There was just absolutely no day there wasn't something you could do. But I did like the workhorses. We had six big workhorses: Bill, Jerry, Dobson, Daisy, Jack, and Bob. Jack and Bob were the result of two Percheron mares out in a pasture and a man's thoroughbred stallion got loose out there and bred them. Jack and Bob were half thoroughbred and half Percheron. They were big, lanky horses. Bill and Jerry were the ones I had most of the time. They were pure Percherons. And, you know, you think you're never going to get through with something when you start mowing a great, big field. But, before you know it, you keep going around and around and it's done. But I kept thinking all the time – and no one ever wrote to me – I wondered how things was back in California.

Mackie on a Buck Rake. (1940)

Uncle Mackie

Mackie was always so good to me and every time I made a mistake, Mackie would patiently show me exactly how to do it. Then he would ask me to do it and I would do it. If I didn't do it right, he'd say, "No, you gotta do it this way," and he never did raise his voice, never called me any names, and was always real nice to me. But my Uncle Louie, for some reason, he wasn't a very happy man and he was always angry. Whenever I made a mistake, he would blow up and say, "No wonder no one ever wanted you and John Roy. Your own mother didn't want you. Your own dad didn't want you." He started all that stuff with me. He never showed any kind of appreciation when I did something right. The only time I ever heard from him was when I did something wrong. And I was expecting to go up on the mesa where they take the cattle for the summer, but he decided to let Johnny Strasia or someone else take the cattle up and stay on the mesa at the cow camp.

Meeting Josephine

Well, during this time, I found out that there was a gal about three miles up the canyon. They were all Italians in the canyon: Diderros, Strasias, Corteses, Bassals, Duttos, Cousimanos. They all were Italians settled in that canyon. Well, I found out that there was a young girl up the canyon named Josephine. So one day I went up the canyon. I went to their house and Josephine was there and I talked to her for a while. She was a pretty little Italian girl and she was just a year older than me. So I says, "Can I come up and see you sometimes?" She says, "Well, yeah, any time." And so I set a date and I went back up to see Josephine. This really, really took a lot of stress off of me to have someone as sweet as her to go and see. She was always so nice. I got to be wearing the road out regular at night going up there and back – even in the snow.

Josephine Dutto, Dann's first sweetheart.

At our ranch, at Louie's, they had an outhouse way out from the house about fifty yards and they had the water pump outside – no water for inside. They had no heat in the house except the cook stove and a potbellied stove in the living room. They didn't have any electricity. They had kerosene lights and lamps. You know, when I went up to Duttos, he had a butane refrigerator, stove, a heater, inside water/plumbing, a water heater ... all of this stuff. I told Louie, "How come you don't have those conveniences?" I felt really sorry for Aunt Sarah because she was cold half the time and she was treated worse than anybody. He said, "Well, Dutto made all that money boot-legging so he could afford it." But that's the last we heard of it; we never got nothing else and Aunt Sarah did not have any of these conveniences.

Louie and Sarah had a daughter named Mary Elizabeth. She was going to school and living with Grandma in Trinidad. When she finished school, she came to stay at the ranch. That kind of brightened things up a little.

Meeting Trucker Joe

One day, a man delivered a big load of corn to our granary. He shoveled the corn off. Mary went up there to watch him. He unloaded the corn. His name was Joe. He left about a month or two later, Mary Elizabeth found out that she was pregnant. At just that time that Joe had unloaded the corn up there, he got Mary Elizabeth pregnant. Instead of letting her just have the baby and have it adopted or whatever, they made Joe marry Mary. He was really a wild, wild person. He was a truck driver; he hauled coal, corn, wood and all sorts of stuff. When Joe came to live with us after the baby was born at the ranch, they worked Joe hard.

Joe kept saying he could make more money with a truck than what they were paying him. So, Louie brought him a new truck – just a chassis. Joe and I would take this truck out of sight up on the back hills and go hill climb with it and go flying over the roads 50 or 60 mph, up hills and down hills. Well, that all ended when they got a big load of lumber to build a bed for the truck. I helped Joe and Mackie build a big bed on that truck. It was about a five-to-six-ton truck. There was a mine up above the hills there near the top of the mesa: Maraski's Mine, a coal mine. Well, Joe would get orders for coal and he would go up there and haul the coal to different ranchers and places, to us even. The other truck drivers—he was getting a lot of their customers. No one knew this but me, but Joe was a real fighter. He could fight; he very seldom ever lost a fight. And I think the reason was that he had a clubfoot. He told Louie and everybody else that he got his foot hurt in an accident and a car run over his foot. But, anyway, I think he learned to fight because when he was younger, kids made fun of him and everything. He could really fight; he was about 6'1" and weighed about 180-190 pounds and he was strong.

I went with Joe up to get a load of coal. On the way back, two of truck drivers were waiting for him. There was a cattle guard at the bottom where you come onto our ranch and these trucks had parked in the way. One was on one side of the cattle guard and one was on the other side to block Joe's way across the cattle guard. Joe just told me, "They better move. I'm not stopping." Boy, they jumped in those trucks when they saw he wasn't going to stop. He went flying across the cattle guard and the coal all jumped in the bed and away we went.

The next time we went up to get coal they had the trucks; they had the cattle guard blocked off without the trucks there. So, Joe stopped the truck and he got out and these two guys walked up to him. They were pretty husky, or looked that way anyway. Before they could even say one word, Joe popped one of them – knocked him flat on the ground. Then he started in with the other one. The other got up and I started to get involved. Joe yelled back at me, "Just stay back! I can handle it!" He knocked the heck out of both of those guys. He told them to clean that stuff out of the way. He was going to take his truck through there and they better not fool with him anymore. Anyway, we left. It was really something that Louie ever made him marry Mary Elizabeth. Then later on, when Joe wanted to go to California, Louie didn't want to hear it, so he stayed there and continued to work even more. (Eventually, Louie let Joe leave with $10,000.00 to go buy a house in California for his daughter, but Joe stopped in Vegas and lost every dime gambling!)

The Dam Builder

Louie was always in on different things that the government offered, and back then, the government would pay farmers and ranchers to build small dams in their creeks to keep them from flooding further down in the lowlands. These dams they called spreader dams; he got so much: 10 cents a yard for the amount of dirt he put in there. When I started building these dams, I had to take this beam plow out with the horses. I'd plow the ground behind where we were going to build a dam, then I'd take these scrapers they called *fresnos* and I drag them along to collect the dirt. They would hold a ½ yard of it. So I'd start building the thing. I'd go out there real early. After I milked the cows, I'd harness the horses – two teams – and take them out there and I'd work all the time for about eight to ten hours out there building these dams. I got one completed and then I started the next one. When I was building the third one, a guy came out and measured it and said I built it too high. My uncle got mad 'cause I'd wasted time making it bigger than necessary. He said that they wouldn't pay for the top four feet of it. So, they measured and deducted that. My uncle was so angry with me about that. Because we had real heavy, heavy rains, I had to go out in the pastures and fields and gather up rocks in a lumber wagon to make riprap—mounds of rocks to cover the face of the dam so the water wouldn't wear it out.

"Riprap" rocks helped the dams to stop from washing out.

Whenever these heavy rains came, the water was supposed to build up and go out a ditch – like an irrigation ditch – and it would be spread out over different areas. It had outlets; it would be spread out over the prairie to make the gamma grass and stuff grow.

It rained super hard for a couple of days or more and then it rained again. We went out there to check the spreader dam and if I hadn't put that four foot on top of it, it would have been gone over 'cause it just about three foot from the top—it had settled. It was not even that much—ready to go over the top of the dam. So, anyway, that was the end of my building these spreader dams. The next project I got into was really fun because Louie had went down and bought 500 head of calves from a man about twenty or thirty miles away. Mr. Newcomb sold him the calves. We went down to drive them up and that was so much fun, driving the calves all the way up to the ranch. When we got to the ranch, they were divided between the heifers and the steers. The heifers went in the south pasture and the steers went in the north pasture. I was to take care of the heifers in the south pasture, to go out there and feed them the cottonseed cake. We had the wheat straw from the threshing of the wheat and had a feed rack built to feed them the wheat straw. We had one of these ponds I'd built filled up with water. I had to break the ice once in a while for them. Really, now, I'd turned into what I'd wanted to be: a cowboy, instead of a rancher or farmer. During this time, I practiced a lot on the side to do all the things cowboys do, so I wouldn't be so dumb.

The Unsolved Murders

Well, by this time, it was about two o'clock in the morning. There had been some murders up on that mesa that no one solved. A couple of game wardens was killed and stuff – different things. Johnny Strasia was kind of scared to stay by himself. It was raining and I knocked on his window and he shined a flashlight out. It scared him to death and he shined a flashlight in my face and he had a gun in his hand. He came and opened the door. Well, the next day we done a few things he had to do. He had an extra horse up there; I had to ride bareback, though. We rode out to where the beacon light was. I told Johnny, "Down there, you can hardly crawl, down there where those three rocks was," I said, "That's where I came up!" They never did believe me that I climbed that rimrock all the way up there at night and the last part of it in the rain. They thought no one could climb it without falling off it, especially in rain. Anyway, we went back to the camp. Johnny was the best cook that ever lived. He liked to cook. We ate and then I had to get back down to the ranch. I went a different way. Johnny showed me a better way to get down off of the mesa. I went down and I told Louie about that and he was like the rest of them. He couldn't believe that I had climbed up the face of that rimrock by the beacon light.

Dann the mountain climber, showing off new boots.

We were just about through haying at that time. I was on a Sulky Rake with Bob and Jack. Something happened that spooked the horses. They ran off with the rake and they ran over the brim. When they went over this brim, they threw me off of the rake. I wasn't hurt that bad. They ran around—it was a good thing they didn't go down into the fence or anything, and they ran around and they finally stopped on their own in the middle of the field. But Louie was so mad at me. Everything was always my fault. I was really shook up 'cause I got thrown off that thing when it was almost a full run. This is the way he treated me. He always, always, always had to swear at me. And I couldn't ever do anything to please him.

A horse drawn Sulky Rake—with not much to hold on to.

Another Joe Rumble and Mackie's Big Plan

I had to help deliver the calves from Mr. Newcomb's Butcher Block Ranch down about 20 or 30 miles south of us there on the ranch. We had to go deliver these calves up to Louie; drive them all the way up there. So Joe had to help do that, and he refused to wear a cowboy hat, and he was almost bald-headed. We got about halfway driving the cattle, and this guy rode up that liked to fight, too, and he rode up and told Joe, "You'd better get your hat, you're going to get your head sunburned!" and Joe said, "Well, you'd better get your mouth sewed shut before you get in trouble." And the guy just stepped off his horse and said, "What'd you say?" And Joe got off his horse, and I'm telling you, that was some fight, but that guy had no chance with Joe; Joe just played with him and he finally just knocked him flat.

But anyway, wasn't long after this that the baby was born. They named him Richard – Richie – and they still stayed on the ranch, and Joe and I went together a lot, and we talked a lot, and I always said I'd like to get a motorcycle, and one day Joe told me, "You figure out a way to kill Louie accidentally, and I'll buy you a new motorcycle."

And when Louie would get mad at me and cuss me out and call me "ivory-headed S.O.B." and all these names, I felt like doing something to him, but I never, ever acted on it. Mackie was just the reverse. He never raised his voice to me, and he always wanted to help me, and we became really close, especially after Joe left. One day, Mackie got me aside in the bunkhouse and he said, "Bunn, I wanna ask you something," and I says, "What's that?" And he says, "I'm plannin' on sellin' my part of the ranch out, and I'm gonna leave, and I'm gonna go back to the old country of Northern Italy near France," and he says, "I won't do *none* of this unless you go with me." And I said, "Mackie, you don't have to do nothin' for me – I'll go anywhere with you; anyplace. I'd gladly go anywhere with you."

So we'd sit and talk about the different things we was gonna do. I think he really was gonna go look for a wife – never had been married; I'm positive he was a virgin. Never had been married, he was 56 years old. But he said, "When we come back—we're gonna come back to Colorado, and when we do, we'll buy about a two-or-three-hundred acre ranch enough to just kinda keep us busy, and I'll get you the best horses in the country, and get two milk cows," and he'd go into all this detail with me about what we would do.

So one day, April the 21st, we were all sittin' in the kitchen and talking about Ireland being bombed, and they said it was the Germans, but Mackie said, "I betcha the English bombed Ireland to get 'em in the war," and my Aunt Sarah got so mad, she says, "You don't know nothin'. You can't read, you can't write, hardly. What are you sayin'?" And he looked at me and he said, "Let's go out to our room," and I said, "Okay," and when he started to get up, he just fell forward and hit his head on the floor– he died, right there, he had a heart attack. And I cried, and it was about two foot of snow outside, and still snowin', and Aunt Sarah got there and pounded on his chest, and he never liked her ever. And she said, "Speak to me, speak to me," and I said, "Aunt Sarah, you wouldn't want to hear what he had to say; don't say that."

VAN HOUTEN'S COCOA

The Irish Press

PRICE THREE-HALFPENCE

AIRMEN WRECK IRISH CREAMERY

GERMAN BOMBS KILL THREE IN CO. WEXFORD

Government Protest To Berlin: Demand For Reparation

Showing the wrecked creamery at Campile

A debate over the bombing of Ireland led to Mackie's death.

We were all stunned. I said, "Let's put him up on the couch," and uncle Louie said, "No, we're not going to move him; he hurt his head pretty bad, and the coroner, when he comes, he'll think maybe we—" I said, "Why would he ever think that? I'll do it myself," so he didn't help me put him on the couch. Then I went down to the Barelas, since they had a phone two or three miles down the road, and I raced down in the snow. I cried all the way as my tears froze on my face, and I got down there and the phone was out. So I walked back, and the next day they came and got Mackie.

Mackie's Final Farwell

I remember once that Mackie showed me a brand-new grey suit he had, and it looked real fine. I said, "Why don't you ever wear that?" and he said, "Oh, I will." But I never saw him wear it alive. Then they had the funeral in Trinidad. All the cattlemen were there and everything; it was an awful day. And I heard my Uncle Louie say to some cattlemen there that Mackie had worked for them a long time, and I went over and I said, "He didn't work for you, he owned a third of the ranch, you know, until now," and anyway, I was really disturbed. And I looked in the casket, and there was Louie's old suit on him. And I told Louie and Sarah, I said, "How could you ever do that; that was the only suit he ever bought. How come you couldn't bury him in that?" And she says, "Well, that's crazy to bury him a new suit when it fits Louie," and I couldn't believe that, and so it went on.

He had a little ring from his mother. He wanted me to be sure that if he ever died that that was on his little finger. And I looked and his ring wasn't there, and I says, "Where's his ring?" and she said, "Well, Mary Elizabeth has it." I told them what Mackie had told me. And then he gave me a brand-new lever-action Winchester rifle and I put it in my room, and Louie come out there, and he says, "I couldn't find Mackie's rifle. Is it in here?" And I said, "Yeah, he gave it to me," and Louie just laughed out loud, and says, "Yeah, how are we ever gonna know that he gave it to you? He isn't here to say," and I said, "Well, we'll never know because you won't be where we are, so we'll never know in the hereafter either."

Mackie was the best person I ever knew, and we had plans that when he was already planning to sell his interest in the ranch and the only way he would do it, he said, is if I would go with him, leave with him and we would go back to where he'd come from on the border of France and Italy, and he'd take me with him, and then when we'd come back, we would buy, like, maybe just 100 acres up near Colorado Springs or somewhere, and he would buy the best horses there was for me and have a few milk cows – we talked about all these things. And we had made plans for November. He died April the 21st. When they shipped the cattle he was gonna sell out. And he had $67,000 dollars saved which Louie got, and plus they got the third of the ranch that Mackie owned. He never got really nothin' out of life except hard work, for he built all the barns and all the corrals and feed racks and everything. I helped him with a lot of it, but he done all that. He never even ate decently. And I can't believe, to this day, how they could have ever treated him like they did.

Leaving Louie

A couple of days later, Louie got real mad at me for just something small, and he called me all kinds of names, and also that I oughta be so thankful that they kept me, and the only reason they did is because I was related to his wife, and that my own mother and dad didn't want me.

About a week later, a cattleman came from Texas, and he saw how hard I worked, and he asked me if I was related to the people at all there, and I said, "No, I'm just workin' here." He says, "Well, if you ever want a job, come down to the Matador Ranch in Channing, Texas, and we'll give you a job."

After a week or so, Louie blew up again, and I said I was leaving. He laughed out loud and asked me, "Who would ever want you?" And I said, "Don't matter if anybody wants me or not, I'm going somewhere, I'm leaving this place." So I started planning on leaving.

Uncle Louie Cortese and the horse, Dude. (1941)

A few days after that, we were branding and dehorning and everything, and the Strasias were up there helpin' – Johnny and Charlie, and Mitchell – and I was handling the chute, and they had left a young bull that probably weighed about six, seven hundred pounds or so. They left him for the last to brand, to make the chute bigger, and he was really mad, this bull, and I was over there. They had the gate open when they let the bull out, and the bull ran, instead of going out the gate he knocked me down and he got a knee on each side of my chest, and he put his head down on my chest and he kept pushing, and they all just laughed and kept laughing. Finally, I got a hold of his head and pushed his head off and I got out from under him, and they were all just roaring, laughing. And I went to my bunkhouse, and I just got so mad. I had a single-shot .22 rifle, and when I had went to town, I didn't have enough money for a pump rifle. I'm thankful I didn't have that, 'cause I thought, well, I can't shoot 'em all with just a single shot; they'd all run. But that's how mad I was.

A few days later, they brought the subject up, and they were laughing again, and I took off my shirt, and I showed them my whole chest was black and blue, just purple. And they didn't think it was so funny then.

Louie had given me a horse before that, and his name was Dude, he was a beautiful blood bay, and I really liked him, and I was planning on taking him with me. I had already wrote a letter to the Matadors Ranch in Channing, Texas that I was coming down there, and one of the Strasias had worked there before (George Strasia), so I told Louie and Sarah, I says, "I don't know whether you believe me or not, but I'm leaving the first of the month, and I'd like to have what money I got coming," and finally, toward the end of the month, I told Aunt Sarah I wouldn't be there for supper 'cause I was leaving. She tried to talk me out of it by saying how much they'd done for me, but I wouldn't listen. I went out to the bunkhouse and I tried to figure out what I could carry on the horse, 'cause I decided to ride down. So I had nearly all my stuff on the horse and everything, and Louie walked around and saw me, and he said, "What do you think you're doing?" And I says, "I told you I was leavin'." He said, "Not on that horse, you're not." And I said, "What do you mean? I thought he was mine," He says, "Well, as long as you stay on the ranch here, he's yours. But the minute you leave the ranch, I'm gonna report him stolen." So I just hugged Dude, and I says, "Well, I guess I'll have to leave you behind," and I took off my saddle and all the stuff, and he kinda looked around at me like, now what are you gonna do now? I took my saddle and put it over my shoulder, put all the stuff I could carry, and I headed down the road on foot. That's when it started to snow.

Heading to Matador Ranch

So it was about 12, maybe 15 miles over the hills – I didn't go down the road, I should've, maybe someone would have picked me up – but I walked over the hills with all that rigging stuff to the Trinchera where the trains stopped. And when I got there to the train stop, I went to the train depot and the stationmaster told me, "There's not going to be any trains here going to Channing, Texas for a couple days." And I thought, "Oh, boy," and he said, "But there's a freight train coming by in a few hours that's got a caboose, and you can ride in the caboose for just seven dollars to Channing." And I thought, "Well, man, that'd be different." I said, "I'll do it," so I paid him. And the train came and I got so excited, and I got in the caboose, they had a little stove in there, and you could look out the windows or you could go out the back and look at all the scenery as you went down. Anyway, I enjoyed the trip down there.

When I got to Channing at 2:00 in the morning, boy it was really cold, and there was a little hotel across from the railroad tracks. I went inside and a man come out to the counter. I asked, "Is there a room here or anything?" He said, "No, there aren't any vacancies," and I asked, "Do you mind if I just sit in here? I'm gonna work for the Matador Ranch, but it's freezing outside and my ride isn't here yet." He said, "No, I don't want you. You can't do that." So I went out and I crossed over there to the railroad station and I tried the door and it was locked. So I messed around a bit and then I saw a red-hot stove in there inside the room there, and I managed to get a screen off, and I got the window open and I went in and set my stuff through the window, my saddle and stuff, and I crawled in. I set my saddle blanket out and laid down on the floor and went to sleep.

Well the next thing I knew, someone kicked me in my ribs and I turned and I yelled and looked up and it was a marshal. He had the station master with him, and a big dog, and he put a double-barrel shotgun over the bridge of my nose, and he said, "Boy, don't you know that you'll get 20 years for breaking in to a railroad station?" And I said, "Well, I was cold, and I didn't really break in, I just took—" "Yeah, that's all you did, but you broke in," he repeated. And I said, "Well, I'm coming down to work for the Matador Ranch, and I'm supposed to meet John Stevens here." I was lucky they finally let me get up and get my stuff together, and John Stevens picked me up, took me down to the headquarters where I was gonna have my new job, and I couldn't believe it. It was the most beautiful place I ever saw, and the ranch had the most gorgeous horses right there, I could see 'em all and everything, and as we walked, he showed me all my chores I was gonna do. He told me how to take care of his stallions and how to halter brake colts and go feed the registered cattle and go feed the mares and all these different things.

Fellow cowboys at the Matador Ranch.

I finally got through with all the information, and I went to the bunkhouse and it was time for supper. And I could not believe it at all – there at the table was steak, potatoes, gravy and all kinds of other things, and pasta on the table, and the men all come in there to eat at the table, and there was about 15 of us or so, and Mr. King, who became a real good friend of mine later, was the cook. Well I ate there about three days, but the men talked so filthy and used such vulgar language, that I wanted no part of it. I saw a little table in the kitchen, and I noticed Mr. King. He sat there and ate at the little table. So I asked him, "Could I eat with you in the kitchen?" He said, "Well, sure! I'd like that." So I never ate again at the table with the men on a special day, even, and they said, "Aren't you gonna come in there and eat with us?" I'd say, "No."

Mr. King, after everybody left, he would point to the oven. He'd have a pie in there or something for me, and I really loved it. The whole place was just something else.

More on the Matador

The ranch was 35 miles wide and 50 miles long, and it was divided by the Canadian River that runs through the middle of it, and they had a standing herd of 65,000 cows, and then they had about 200 bulls they kept separate. And everything was just so, and these stallions I had to ride were magnificent. One of them was a beautiful stocking legged Golden Palomino. He was double registered. He was registered in the Palomino Horse Association, and he was registered in the Quarter Horse Association. And I got to ride all of these guys.

The Matador Ranch had 65,000 cattle, and some cowboys had to haul bedrolls with them to patrol all 879,000 acres.

The ranch also was one of the few ranches left that had a chuck wagon. And at certain times, I would have to go help the cowboys at the chuck wagon. The wagon boss, Dale Simons, was really a nice guy. The guy who owned the ranch, Mr. Mackenzie from Scotland, would sometimes come down there once in a while. And Dale or the manager would take Mr. Mackenzie on a ride in the pickup around and show him what was going on and what the cattle all looked like and everything. One time they took a ride over where they could look across the river to were the bulls were (they kept them separate until they were putting them with the cows later). And they couldn't believe their eyes – right in the middle of all those bulls, about 200 or whatever – I was riding horseback. I loved bulls, just lookin' at 'em, and ridin' through there.

Later that night, John Stevens, the manager, came up there to the bunkhouse, and he told me, "If one of those bulls would have made a pass at you, they would've all tore you to pieces, and the horse, too. Don't ever do that again."

The manager was always going off to stock shows and stock sales, and he went to Denver to the International Stock Show. He bought the international champion blood bay young stallion at the stock show, and had him shipped in a box car by himself to Murdo where they have a spur (a switching section in the tracks) and they have a stockyard thing, and he got a notice that the stallion would arrive a certain day, and he told me he wanted me to go and receive him. So I rode down there, and here was a lone boxcar on a side track, and I opened it up. They had broke about 20 bales of straw in there for him, and I looked in there and no horse. I thought, "Oh, no; somebody must have got there before me." But all of a sudden, I saw a head raise up out of the straw, and he nickered, and I called out, and got in there, and there was an unloading chute there, and I talked to him a while, and we went and I unloaded him and I took him back to the ranch. The manager told me, "Don't do anything but food, groom and take care of him. Don't be messing with him, don't be trying to ride him, 'cause he's just a stallion." And so after a while, I kept talking to *Jocko A* (They called him that.) One day I thought, well, I'm gonna start handling him.

I just couldn't resist messing around with the new young stallion. He was so beautiful, a blood bay, and so full of life. I rubbed him all over with an old sheepskin vest of mine, continually talking to him. After about a week of this, I took him out to feed the registered cattle on a lead rope. He really liked it. The next couple of days I put my saddle on him and rode him all around in a big corral. Johnny Stevens was gone for a while. I taught Jocko to neck rein, and about the third day I opened the gate and rode him an hour or so outside in the pasture. He responded well to all the things I worked on him in the corral. A couple days later, I rode him clear down to Emmitt Smith's camp. He said he'd never seen such a dandy horse. I came back halfway up the riverbed. It's all sand. I wanted to run him. Boy, could he go, and he loved it. I really spent more time on him than my other 10 horses.

John Stevens came back, and first thing he asked was, "Did anything different happen while I was gone? Or exciting?" I knew others would probably tell him anyway, so I said, "Come up to the barn when you can in 30 minutes or so, and I'll show you something new." That gave me time to saddle up Jocko and put him through his paces.

When he came up, his wife was with him. They both were very pleased with what I'd done with Jocko. John Stevens smiled and said, "I just knew you couldn't stay off that horse."

At this time, in the early '40s, the U.S. Remount from Reno, Oklahoma would lease certain stallions to ranchers that passed their qualifications. The matadors put a request in for a thoroughbred stallion to put with their smaller range mares. They sent a seven-year-old stud by the name of Reno. He had won races on the racetrack. He stood 17 hands and weighed 1200 pounds. They quit riding him because he was what they call a "cold jawed" (he had nerve damage in his mouth from riders who pulled too hard on the bit), so you couldn't stop him now if he wanted to keep on running. I had already used hackamore bits (which squeeze their jaw) on other horses, so I decided I would try them on Reno, because I wanted to ride him for quite a while. He hadn't been ridden since he came to the Matador. I took him around in the big corral. He reacted okay with the bits. So I took him outside and just rode him off. When I got to the river where it was all sand, I let him run. He loved it. Now the test came: in a full run, I gently pulled on the bits, and he stopped. Never had any trouble with him at all. He was a beautiful and fast horse. He was also one of my favorites.

Dann on Reno

Racing Reno by the River

The cowboys would gather at Emmitt Smith's cow camp on Sundays to drink and have horse racing in the Canadian river bed. They had asked me several times to come down and race with them. I decided to go down and check it out. To my surprise, two young prostitutes from Amarillo were there, too. I rode Reno the remount stud. After visiting a while, they decided to go down to the river and have the race. It didn't bother them that I had brought Reno, since he was a lot bigger than their cow ponies. The seven of us each put a dollar in a bucket, and the winner would take all. It was worth it! We headed to the riverbed, which was dry that time of year.

When we got to the riverbed, they agreed to race to the only Cottonwood tree by the riverbank about a mile away. Their horses were rested, but they had not bought their best horses out of their string of six or so horses. I had run Reno before I got there, so I didn't know what to expect. One, two, three, and we were off! Reno took a slow start, but I caught up with the rest and we passed all of them. I was really suspicious of them, 'cause two of them had ramrodded me before. That is when one sneaks up behind you while others are on each side of you on horses with ropes stretched across between them, and they knock the rider off his horse. I was only shook up, and I had a rope burn across my back, but when I passed all of them I just kept going, leaving all seven of them far behind. To my surprise, next time I went to see Emmitt, he had my seven dollars that we left in the bucket, 'cause I just kept going when I won the race; I didn't go back to where they were.

Dann "bulldogging" a bull. (Art ©2010 Jack T. Chick LLC)

When I got back to the ranch, they were unloading a long-horned steer that the ranch had bought just to have around the place for looks. Really a beautiful long-horn, already had about two-foot-long horns on him. When no one was around, I'd practice *bulldogging* him (grabbing him by the horns and wrestling him to the ground). I'd run alongside of him against the corral, and I'd nail him, and I'd bulldog him. And I just kept doing this all the time, and he was getting bigger all the time, too, and so one day after doing this so many times, John Stevens came up to the corral, and when we walked in the corral, the long-horned steer looked around and he laid down. And the manager said, "Is there something wrong with him?" I said, "No, I don't think so. He's alright." So he looked all around at the stallions in the barn and the feed thing, and we came back to the corral, the steer was standing in the middle of the corral. As soon as we opened the gate and went in the corral, the steer laid down again. He says, "You sure he's alright?" I said, "Sure. I know he's just layin' down." So anyway, I found out later that every time I went in the corral, I'd bulldog him so much that the steer got to thinkin' that when I'm around he's supposed to be layin' down. And no matter if I'd leave and come right back in the corral, when he got up he'd lay down again. So that was the end of my bulldogging.

The ranch was almost completely divided by the Canadian River, and there could be heavy rains a long, long ways off, and it'd be nice and sunny and the whole river would be just a solid flood. It'd move real fast and real, real deep and wide. And so when things happen like that, Mr. Stevens, the manager, if he wanted to go on the other side of the ranch he'd have to go about 50 or 75 miles out of his way to go around by Amarillo and come back down the other side, and it always took a lot of time and effort.

Getting A Message Across the River

He needed to get a message to the wagon boss on the other side of the river, and he asked me to go first thing in the morning to take the message across the river to the wagon boss 'cause he had to have that message that day, and he didn't want to drive all that distance. It was a full moon, so I left about 2 AM in the morning onto my favorite little Palomino stallion, named Manotobian. When I got to the river, it was really swollen and at least 100 yards wide and deep. I decided to try and cross. Manotobian swam most of the way. I got off him and held on to the saddle horn so he could swim better. With me off—I'd swam horses before—we ended almost a mile downstream by the time we crossed. It took me about an hour to find the chuck wagon, and Dale Simmons, the wagon boss, they were surprised to see me. I gave them the message and left.

When I got back to the river, I couldn't believe I'd ever made it across as I pondered if I should try to cross again. Manotobian made up my mind for me and just plunged into the swollen river. We made it; I got back to the ranch headquarters, Manotobian had dried off, I rubbed him down good and went to the bunkhouse and hit my bedroll. John Stevens came in and saw sleeping. He shook me and yelled, "I told you it was important to get that message to the wagon boss!" I said I already done it. He said, "What horse did you take?" I said, "Manotobian." He said, "The horse could have drowned. Don't you know that?" (Sometimes you're damned if you do, and you're damned if you don't!)

I was still interested in boxing, so I set up a workout area in the feed room. I put rolled oats in a big bag and hung it from the rafters as the punching bag. I skipped rope when I had time, lifted bags of feed and other kinds of workouts. One day, two cowboys came up to headquarters. I was mixing feed when they came in and they made fun of me because I had my shirt off and had a medal around my neck that my grandma had given me for protection, a Catholic medal. The one that made a lot of remarks opened his mouth real big, laughing. So I took the feed scoop and filled it full of feed, at the same time I threw it in his mouth, I hit the other one. We really got into it. Virgil heard all the commotion and broke it up. I removed the medal after that and continued training.

At 17, I was 6 foot tall and weighed 148 pounds. I read in the Amarillo news that they were having a golden glove tournament. I asked John Stevens if by any chance I could go and try out. He said, "No. Period. I can't believe you would even think of it."

The manager John Stevens would send me to other cow camps and to the chuck wagon to help out once in a while. This time, he sent me to help at a cow camp to round up the two-year-old steers that we were going to ship. The man at the camp was a horse abuser. I'd seen him beat and jerk and kick horses for doing nothing wrong. He had married a young prostitute, and it was common knowledge some of the cowboys were seeing her when he was not around. John Stevens came down to give us tips on what to do and help us get the roundup started. I was saddling my horse when he asked where Earl was. I said, "He's lying down in the corral last time I saw him." John Stevens walked off, and then suddenly turned around to me and said, "What do you mean he's lyin' down in the corral?" I said, "A horse kicked him a while ago, knocking him flat." He yelled at me and said, "Come with me. I can't believe you didn't help him." I said, "You know yourself he beats and treats your horses something awful, so I just figured he got what he deserved."

When we got to him, he was up and dusting himself off, and no more was said except when we were out rounding up the steers, Earl rode up to me and said, "If you ever get in any kind of life-threatening situation, don't count on me to ever help you; I don't care what happens." I said, "Good. We *do* understand each other then."

This roundup was the largest shipment of two-year-old steers ever shipped to anyone's knowledge, and a lot of people came from the cities around to watch the loading of them at the stockyards. The stock cars were all lined up, and not just one train, but two. I had taken Manitobian, the Palomino stud so we started loading and driving the steers into the holding pen and into the cars. John Stevens came over to me and grinned and said, "A lot of the folks looking on out here watching us say that that girl on the Palomino horse is as good or a better rider than any of the cowboys." They were referring to me! So I cut my own hair the next day.

Getting bucked off a stallion. (Art ©2010 Jack T. Chick LLC)

Manitobian was to be turned out with 20 or so mares in a week or so. I wanted to take a long last ride, so I decided to let him run as fast as he could. It was cold and the ground was frozen. In a full run, he bucked me off. I landed on my back. When I came to, I couldn't move and I had melted the frozen ground under me to mud. The young stud was standing nearby. I was surprised to see him. I tried to move and did finally manage to get up. I found out later I had knocked my tailbone in. I told no one about this.

Cowboys had separated the mares into groups with the four stallions. I had the job of taking the studs down to the different pastures where the mares were. I rode the studs and led a horse back to headquarters. When I got in sight of the mares, Manitobian got so excited, he was so anxious to go, that I got excited, too. I tied my horse and unsaddled Manitobian I put my hobbling rope on his nose and jumped up on his back with a handful of mane. He took off toward the mares. As he came up on them, I wasn't prepared for what was about to happen. The mares kicked at him and sprayed squirts of urine on him and me. He reared up and threw me off. I went to a windmill tank, took off my clothes and rinsed them off and got in the tank myself. It was worth it all to get the ride of my life.

Going Loco from Locoweed

As I rode all over the land, I saw wild horses that were eating *Locoweed* that comes up in the spring before anything else does—that's why cattle and horses eat it, because it's green. It produces a poison that drives horses crazy. Horses even eat the roots. Some that should weigh 1,000 pounds or so get down to 600 pounds or less. They are unaware of their surroundings. If they see their reflection in a tank of water, they will spook and won't even drink. I asked the manager if I could shoot them to put them out of their misery. He said on my own time. I took a rifle a couple days later. I found one who had got stuck in the wet sand by the river. A lot of horses and cattle die every year in the quicksand in the river. This horse was once a beautiful bay horse, and he couldn't be saved anyway as he was belly-deep already. I talked to him and said, "You'll be out of your misery soon." As he looked at me I shot him once in the head. He paused a while and collapsed in a heap, and sunk into the sand. I found a couple more. John Stevens had talked to a man that told him they never kill any horses or cattle that are Loco because they eat most of the Locoweed that comes up, so others don't eat it. So the manager told me not to kill any more of them.

I was writing to Josephine in Colorado 'cause I felt like I loved her, and she wrote back how she missed me. I can't believe I'd ever leave the Matadors, but the war had started and they already were drafting some cowboys. I'd be 18 soon, so I figured I'd have to go into the service soon, and I'd like to go see Josephine before I got drafted. So I told Johnny Stevens I might leave. He said, "It's up to you if that's what you think you want to do."

Matador Cowboys crossing the Canadian River.

I truly loved the ranch and I really liked Johnny Stevens and his wife also, and there was Earl who took care of the yards, and inside the main house where the office was. And Johnny Stevens and wife lived there. One day, Earl asked me if I'd like to change some chores with him. We talked it over and we decided to. One thing I had to do was keep stove oil in all the stoves and heaters in the office and on the ranch part. As I said before, Mrs. Stevens was a beautiful woman. She was left alone a lot, and would ask me to stay and talk to her. When I went in to check the heaters, she had little things she wanted me to do in the house, including building a fire in the big, beautiful fireplace in the living room. She asked me to stay and talk to her. I'd almost fainted when she came out by the fire with her nightgown on. By the fire, I could see right through it. She had found out about the trip to Amarillo that the cowboys tricked me into going with them, and she asked me if that bothered me. I said they were going to visit Mr. King's girls, so I went. Turned out she knew more about what they had planned than I did.

The House of Ill Repute

They did go to visit them along with six other prostitutes at this big house in Amarillo. The women, 18 or 21 years old, paraded around us, some in just their panties and others had bathrobes opened up. The cowboys all laughed when I ran out of the place and sat in the truck 'till they were finished and ready to go back to the ranch. While in the truck, one woman came out and asked me, was it because I didn't have the money – five dollars is what it cost – or was it because I'd never been with a woman. I said both. She said, "Come on in – I won't charge you anything. And I'll show you all you ever need to know." I said, "I really don't want to go back." She left. It was really tempting, as she had her breasts hanging inside the truck!

Mrs. Stevens asked me if I was really 18. I said, "Yes," I was only 17 yet. To change the subject, I asked if Earl ever built fires in the fireplace. She said, "Oh, yes, but not as good a fire as you do." Anyway, the next day I asked Earl to trade back with me. He agreed. I could see now that I was getting more interested in Mrs. Stevens than I should be, and I figured I'd better just leave.

I told Johnny Stevens I was going to leave the first of the month. Then I started making plans. Mrs. Stevens came out to the corral and said, "I can't believe you want to leave us. Why are you going?" I said, "I'll have to go into the service soon, so I'd like to go back to Colorado and see some of my friends back there before I leave." I can say for sure, I was attracted to her. Trying to make up my mind and thinking about it, all these beautiful horses and all, I thought it over and told Johnny Stevens I'd like to stay on after all. He said, "You have already been replaced. But stay a while if you want to. But as I said before, you have been replaced."

I knew now that I had to go, so I made arrangements. A couple days later, Johnny Stevens took me through the ranch there, and I had turned the stallions out in their paddocks. Some of them ran up to the fence when they saw me in the truck, and then knickered and stuff, and I really was kind of sad to leave all that behind, but I knew I had to go, that was the best thing.

So I got off the train in Trinchera and walked down to Charlie Strasia's place, and he was glad to see me and he had a lot of things to do, so I stayed – I just automatically stayed there with him; he was the best cook. He loved to eat, so he cooked and bought all kinds of things, and he was in the process of trying to get married. I stayed there a while with him, and he told me that he was going to leave for a couple weeks, and he wrote down some things for me to do around there just to kind of keep the place up while he was gone a-courting Gabe, his future wife in Spanish Peaks. So I watched over his place while he was gone a few weeks.

Sundance

I built fences, and I messed around, and one day I caught one of the saddle horses and

I rode down to the ranch down below, Jimmy Fox's ranch, and as I rode down I saw this beautifully stocking-legged red sorrel running down a grassy slope. He was quite a sight. The sun was shinin' on him. And so when I got down there, I visited a while and I ask him if that sorrel horse was for sale, the stocking-legged red sorrel. And he said yes, so I ended up buying him. I had some bonds, and he wanted 75 dollars for him because he knew I liked him; he made it more than what most people pay for horses, and I signed the bond over to him and took him back to Charlie's with me. I even got up during the night and looked at him; I was so proud of him. My first horse, really, that I had bought, and I named him Sundance. And I started breaking him and handling him, and within a few days I was riding him all over the pastures and everywhere. He never, ever tried to buck or do anything wrong. He was just beautiful. I would go out at night and whistle—when I fed him I always whistled. So when I'd whistle, he would come runnin', and I'd hear him coming, but I couldn't see him 'till he got right up to me in the dark.

Charlie was a lot of fun to be around. He was having some wells drilled there, and this man that drilled the wells weighed almost 400 pounds, and his son was real skinny. Honneycut was his name. And Charlie had a really old house, and when Mr. Honneycut came in the house, he broke through the floor in a few places, so Charlie said, "I think it's time for me to build another house." And one day, someone took a picture of me standing in one leg of Mr. Honneycut's overalls and Charlie standing in the other leg, and we had it fastened up – it was really funny to see.

I enjoyed the responsibility of taking care of his place, and I'd done a lot of things in the yard and in the corral, cleaning things around and doing stuff, and when Charlie finally came back home, they had made arrangements to get married. Then he walked out into the Corral and he saw my horse Sundance. He said, "What's that horse doing here?" And I said, "Well, I went down to Jimmy Fox just for a little ride to visit, and I saw the horse and I liked him so much I bought him." And Charlie told me, "Are you ridin' him?" I says, "Oh, yeah, he's already broke to ride," And he says, "Well, I'll tell you what – right now, either the horse goes or you go or both of you go." So I said, "Well, if that's what you want." So without any hesitation, I went and I saddled him, took a few things that belonged to me and I rode on down to Jimmy Fox's. Jimmy Fox had told me that if I needed any work, he could use me, 'cause he was gonna start breaking some young broncos. So I went down there and Mrs. Fox was the greatest lady I ever met. Right away I called her "Mom Fox." She was Mr. Newcomb's daughter who owned the big Butcher Block Ranch.

Dann next to one of his favorite stallions, Jocko.

Rondo

When I started working for Mr. Fox, we were running the broncs and there was this beautiful coal-black horse, and they said that two or three different guys had tried to break him, and I just fell in love with him, too. I should have never done it, but I bought Rondo for 75 dollars, and I tried to break him, too, and I had the two horses, then.

Mrs. Fox was so nice, and she was a good cook and everything, and it was funny, 'coz one time, some people came to visit the Foxes, and we were all eating at the table (she had four children), and a lady kept looking at Mrs. Fox and me, and she says, "Pardon me for staring, but I never saw a boy that looked more like his mother than that boy right there," she was talking about me. No one said, "He don't even belong to us," or nothin', they just laughed. That was really an odd thing, I thought.

I stayed there at Jimmy Fox's helping him with all the things he had to do around there, fixing fences and going and checking on the cattle and all of this and that—and I found out that Rondo had been really abused; they tied tires on him and everything to try to break him from bucking and everything, but I still decided to take him anyway, so I took Rondo and Sundance, and I went down to Jimmy's father-in-law, the big Butcher Block Ranch. Originally, it had the chuck wagon and no fences at all when they first moved there, back when Mr. Newcomb first homesteaded it, and it was really a remarkable ranch.

At the ranch I met one of the best cowhands I ever met; he was crippled, but he never did ever believe he was crippled because he rode and he was one of the best calf ropers there ever was. His name was Hardy Roberts. And he kinda took me over, showin' me things and tellin' me things and helpin' me, and when we started breaking the broncs, he went with me all the time when I rode the broncs out into the open. And it was really funny one day; Mrs. Newcomb, her boys were real heavyset, and I was real thin, and she always said she was gonna put some weight on me. Well, when we finished breakfast, if there was any biscuits left, she would put a little butter and honey on 'em and put 'em in a wrapper-like, and I'd put 'em in my sheepskin coat, and away I'd go. And one day, as I was ridin' this bronc, he ran off with me, and he fell with me on a bunch of rocks and stuff, and it didn't hurt me none, but Hardy came ridin' up to me and he says, "Bunn, are you hurt?" And I said, "No, sir, but I busted all my biscuits." They got a big kick out of that one.

Mr. Newcomb asked me to go over to the open range on the other side of the river and take my time and see if I could count how many wild horses there was there. They all belonged to him, but he didn't have no idea how many they were, so I came back and he said, "Well, how many are there?" And I says, "How many do you think there is?" And he says, "Well, there's probably at least 60 or 70." I said, "There's way over 100." He was really surprised. So we decided that we'd get all the help we could and we'd round 'em up. Well, I didn't know this, but he had sold them for six dollars each to the Cutler Laboratory. So when we got 'em all there, we picked out ones that we might want to keep for saddle horses, cow ponies, and we picked out a few colts and stuff, and the rest all went to Cutler Laboratories in Texas, and no tellin' what – they make vaccine and stuff, but I sure hated to see all them beautiful Appaloosas in there, buckskins, beautiful grey horses, every color you could see, or think of, sent off to whatever fate.

Mr. & Mrs. Newcomb

Mr. Newcomb had three sons, and Dave Newton was across the river where the horses were, and Junior Newcomb stayed at the main ranch with his dad and his mother and his new wife and baby, and I stayed there with Dave. Well, Dave never did like me much, and I never – the two months I stayed there, I never was in their house. She always fixed my plate, that was it; whatever was on the plate, that was what I got, and she set it on the steps of the porch for me. And I kinda watched that I got it before the dog did. And I slept in a horse trailer – I never was in the house, and I went to the bathroom down behind some trees. But you know, I slept in that horse trailer, and – he had loaned the horse trailer to somebody, and the guy came real early, and I heard the commotion, kinda woke me up, and he'd already hooked up the horse trailer and was goin' down the road, and I was yellin' and hollerin', but he had to open a gate about a mile from the ranch, and when he stopped to open the gate I got out and I said, "Just a minute, I got my saddle and stuff in here." And he laughed about it, he was gonna take me all the way to the horse sale or something. So I managed to walk back to the ranch from there. We were breaking horses that day.

Another Dann sketch of him getting kicked by a horse.

The Chief of Police's Son

I only went to Trinidad once all the time I was there, and the one time I went, I went to see some of the guys I used to know there and went to school with, and I gave them directions so that they would come out to the ranch sometime. About a week or so later, Dave, his wife and kid, they went to town and said they wouldn't be back for a couple days. Well, I thought it would be a good time, so I run the horses in and we had five or six old saddles around there, and I managed to saddle 'em all up. There was two girls and Tony, and there was five of them all together, and they had enough saddles and stuff for all of us to go riding. So we rode down toward the beautiful canyon, it was all sandstone and Pinyon Pines and everything, and pools of water, and this one young guy, Palmer, he was riding Mr. Newcomb's horse, Dynamo, and he was going kind of through the cedars and stuff, and I looked over and all of a sudden I saw Dynamo, the horse, by himself, and Palmer had fallen off the horse and hit his head on a rock, and blood was coming out of his left ear, and boy, they shot over there, and they put him in the car, and I raced to town with 'em, and when we got there, they took him in the hospital. His dad was the chief of police in Trinidad, and he found out that he'd fallen off of a horse, and that I was the one responsible for the accident. He was still unconscious, in critical condition, and the police chief walked out there by me and he told me, "If my boy dies, you're next." I says, "What do you mean?" He says, "If my boy dies, you're gonna die, too, 'cause you're the cause of it."

He lived—and so did I—but he was permanently deaf in his left ear. I left the hospital and I went back to Dave's. Dave was staying in town and I always wanted to ride his big buckskin horse. It had a turkey track brand on his back leg. I always liked that big buckskin. He would never let me ride him, so I thought I'll ride him. So I caught Dave's big buckskin horse (we called him Turkey Track) and I went for a ride on him.

So happens, Dave Newcomb was coming home and he had already heard all that had happened out at the ranch while he was gone. And to make things worse, he saw me riding his big buckskin horse. I didn't think he saw me, so I turned, and kinda went down the hill fast so I could get there to the ranch before he did. Just as I got almost there, the big buckskin bucked me off and he ran on in, into the corral. I landed on my feet. Well, when Dave got out of the car, he told me angrily, "I just came from the hospital and I heard you had all of these people down here riding the horses and the one was seriously hurt. I just want you to know, I'm glad my horse bucked you off. That's it. I want you to leave and I want you to leave now!"

It was in the afternoon. There was this real steep canyon. In daytime, it was almost impossible to go single file down this canyon between the boulders and the Pinyon pines and real deep ridges – places were just four feet wide where you could just barely take a horse. He told me he wanted me to leave then. I caught Sundance and I braided Rondo's hackamore lead rope into Sundance's tail 'cause I knew the only way I could lead him was behind Sundance. As I got to the canyon's edge, it was getting dark, and I could barely see. I started down the narrow trail into the canyon. I went back down in the bottom, across, and came up the other side. I'm positive the horses were the ones responsible for me getting through there. As I got back to the other side of the ranch – where the main ranch was – Mr. Newcomb was really upset. He says, "I suppose you put that boy on the wildest horse we had." I said, "Well, sir, I don't know about that. I put him on Dynamo, your horse. I always used to say you could build a fire under Dynamo and nothing would happen." Well, he wasn't so mad at me then when he found out it was his horse that he had fallen off of.

Out for Eight Days

We had started rounding up the horses on this side of the river, near the main ranch. Just as we got them all rounded up and headed, something scared the horses and they got away from us and ran off. They were headed for a barbed wire fence. I tried to head them away from the fence. I did turn them, but my horse stepped into a hole and fell with me. I hit on my face and my head-knocked unconscious. They took me to the Trinidad Hospital. I remained unconscious for eight days or so. I woke up but could not talk, move, or realize what had happened to me. Mr. Newcomb, Hardy Roberts, Louie Cortese and the doctor were standing there. Mr. Newcomb asked if he could take me to his house and put me in his back bedroom, which was on the porch. Louie looked right at me and said, "Isn't he out of it now?" The doctor took his thumb and pressed it against my eye. I felt nothing and the doctor said, "See, he can't even respond to that." Newcomb said, "I just can't keep paying $35 a day for him to just lay here." They all left.

I tried to move my legs after many attempts, and I could finally do some movement. Then I tried to move my hands and arms. Soon, I was able to sit up. I opened the cabinet near my bed and saw my dirty, bloody clothes and boots. I got up and dressed and left the hospital. I walked down to the highway and just as I stood there, I thought I had only been in the hospital a couple of days. Soon, the mailman that goes to Trinchera came by. I flagged him down and asked if I could ride with him to Newcombs'. He said okay. I hadn't seen my face yet, but I could see my right eye over my nose. I could even feel the bandages on my head, plus I was awful, awful stiff. He took me clear to the Butcher Block Ranch as the mailbox was a mile from the ranch on the main road. I saw horses in the corral, so I went to see them. When I got there, Rondo was there, so was my saddle and tack. I caught Rondo and took off for a ride. I let him run. As I was coming over a small ridge, I saw Mr. Newcomb's car coming down to the ranch. Mr. Newcomb said to Hardy Roberts that was with him: "Isn't that Rondo, Bunn's horse? Who would be riding him?" Just then, something spooked Rondo and threw me off. My bandages flew off my head when I hit the ground. Mr. Newcomb drove over to where I was. They got out and I was standing up. Mr. Newcomb said, "Jiminy Crickets! What in the world are you doing riding that wild horse of yours in the shape you're in?" I had no idea that I had been unconscious for seven or eight days.

Dann's drawing of getting thrown from a horse (yet again).

Next morning, he told me I had to go, as he had already spent over $400 on me at the hospital. They had turned Rondo out with all of his horses, but Sundance was in the lower pasture. I went and got Sundance. Mr. Newcomb said they were too busy to run all those horses in just to get Rondo. As they all left, I rode along with them. We were going in the same direction. We went through the big pass to where Rondo was. I could see him afar off – just a black dot. I rode over to a little ridge and whistled loud as I could. The cowboys all laughed, saying, "You think he'll come to you?" and laughed harder. I looked and could see this black dot with a dust stream behind him. He would disappear in gullies and come up all of a sudden he'd be coming again and disappear. I whistled again and here he came. I took my hackamore off my saddle horn and held it up. Rondo ran right up to me and put his nose right into the noseband and I fastened it. Mr. Newcomb said, "How in the world did you ever get Rondo to do that?" I said, "One word, sir: love."

They all rode off and I went back up to Jim Fox's ranch to say good-bye. So happened, he needed me to help him round up his cattle to put them in another pasture. I really wanted to see Billy Fox and his three sisters, and most of all, Mom Fox who was always so nice to me, before I left for a rancher in New Mexico. He told me once, when I was on the mesa, that if I ever wanted a job just to come down to his ranch. His name was Tom Farmer. No one liked him and he was also a fighter. It was once said that he and another cowboy rancher got into a fist fight at the stockyard. They'd fight until they were tired, then rest a while and go at it again. After three rest periods, Tom finally won 'cause the other cowboy couldn't get up to continue the fight. After helping Jimmy Fox, I was ready to take off to New Mexico with Rondo and Sundance. I had to go over the mesa but it got so late that I decided to stay in a cow camp in the Scavarita pasture at the bottom of the mesa. I had stayed there one time before with Johnny Strasia. We spent two weeks at this cow camp. We had to build a new fence to divide the main pasture. This area had been a no-hunting area for over thirty years already. Wild turkey, deer, elk, bears, foxes and so forth, you name it—and up near the rimrock were eagles and mountain lions plus coyotes.

On the open range with Jr. Newcomb (Dann on right).

The Bear Attack

After kind of getting things in the cabin cleaned out and chasing all the rats out and such, I went and checked the fences around the five-acre cow camp. All was okay, except a couple of barbed wires were down. Next, I went up to get my two horses – Rondo and Sundance – to show them where the watering tank was. It was always full as a year-around spring kept it full. I put a rope halter on Sundance while Rondo was busy eating grass. I just took the end of the lead rope from the rope halter and tied it around his neck. As I got up to the tank, a large bear ran out into the open, right out of the choke cherry bushes. Both of the horses bolted with me in the middle running in between them: the one on one side and the other on the other side of a small birch tree. I hit it and busted it off at the ground level. I let loose of the horses' rope and fell. I got up and heard brush snapping and horses thrashing and squealing. When I got to where they were, I couldn't believe what was happening. Both were dead still, laying on the ground, and the halter had slipped down on Sundance's neck. Rondo's lead rope from the halter was pulled as tight as could be. I always had a knife on me, but I had given it to Johnny Strasia earlier that day and he hadn't returned it. I needed something to cut 'em loose fast and I started to panic. I ran up to the woodpile and got the axe. I ran back to where the horses were down. I cut the rope and took it off their necks. I put

Sundance's head in my lap and I sat there and cried. I glanced over at Rondo and cried even more. Rondo made a strange gurgling sound. I quickly crawled over to him. I put one hand over his left nostril and put my mouth over his right nostril and blew as hard as I could. Then I put my hand over his right nostril and kept doing this; all of a sudden, after quite a while, I felt breath coming back at me. I blew harder yet and in complete amazement, I saw his eyes blink. Then he let out a faint nicker. He was breathing on his own. I lay down by him and stoked and petted him all this time – talking to him. Soon, he was trying to stand up. He finally stood up and started snorting over and over when he saw Sundance lying so still. I led him back to the cabin and let him stay inside that night with me. (There were only two rooms.)

Next morning, I went down to where Sundance was. All that was left of him was scattered around – bones and some hide. I took his head and put it on top of a tall fence post with his head looking down to where he was raised on the prairie. I went back to the cabin and in the chow chest, I found some oatmeal and syrup. So I made myself breakfast. Rondo got the rest of the oatmeal. I messed around awhile and decided to go on to the Kerr camp on top of the mesa, thinking Johnny Strasia was there. I took a knife out of the chow chest, in case Johnny was gone, 'cause you always needed a knife to open the door. (That's why Johnny had borrowed mine earlier.)

When I got to the cow camp, a dark cloud hung overhead with lighting and hail as big as golf balls. Johnny was gone. There were seven steps to go into the two-room cabin. I gave Rondo a tug on the reins and he, without hesitation, came up the steps into the cabin with me. We stayed until the storm passed. Rondo was not concerned at all about the stove, and so forth. I did take the chairs and table out into the bedroom. Rondo was still kind of in shock. I noticed every once in a while, he'd shiver and shake and nicker at me. I kept stroking him and talking to him. I had this thing I did with horses where I'd put my head against the side of their head and try to imitate their nickering and other sounds. The vibration helped more than the sound to get it right. Soon it was time to get some rest. I put the table in the doorway with a chair on top of it to keep Rondo in the kitchen for the night.

Next morning, I looked into the kitchen and saw Rondo's head flat on the floor. I nickered and he raised up his head and nickered back. As I went into the room, he stood up. He had only made one mess of "road apples" on the floor. I took him outside down the steps. He then relieved himself. I wanted to leave the mess to prove he stayed all night with me, but I cleaned it all up.

During the night, I decided not to continue going to Tom Farmer's ranch for now. But instead, I'd go back to Jimmy Fox's place. First, I'd like to go see Josephine. So, I rode off, and down at the bottom of the mesa, Rondo kept glancing down to the riverbed bottom. I looked and there was a Yaqui Indian carrying a tree type cactus on his bareback. John Roy and I would see this happening from time to time. We'd then follow them to see where they'd meet later around Easter time. They are called Penitentes because they torture themselves and build big fires. They believe that when you sin, the only way to be forgiven is to hurt yourself some way. He had carried that cactus a long ways as they grow several miles from where he was. The Trinidad fairgrounds let them use it once or so, but stopped it after they realized what they were doing and so forth.

The Yaqui Indians sometimes served "penance" on themselves.

Jilted by Josephine

Mrs. Mary Strasia's place was on my way, so I decided to stop and visit there as she was always so good to me. We had a nice visit, then I continued on to see Josephine. It was dark by the time I got to Josephine's. I noticed there was a car in the yard, so I looked in the window and there was Josephine on the couch kissing somebody. I think it was a man I knew from Trinidad that was already married. Anyway, I decided to just forget it. I got on Rondo and rode all the way back to Jimmy Fox's through the night. He said I would always be welcome.

I found out Louie bought the Butcher Block calves and Jimmy Fox's 16 calves. So, I was going to stay and help him round up cattle. We had to cut out the calves from the cows. It was a big day. We branded, de-horned, castrated and vaccinated all the calves and earmarked them. Then we started on the long drive to Louie's – about twenty-five miles, at least. He came to the Butcher Block Ranch to be part of the drive. Louie found long yearlings, blind calves, alkalized calves and all, as he rode and looked through the herd. Mr. Newcomb saw me talking to Louie, and later on he said, "Did you tell him about these calves that he's found in the herd?" and I said, "Mr. Newcomb, you should know what a cattleman he is. He could spot them. I never said nothing to him, just barely talked to him."

And then as we got closer to Louie's place, I was just kind of wondering what I was going to do. So, Newcomb said I could stay there but he couldn't pay me, which he never did anyway. And Jimmy Fox – I just didn't want to stay there. Charlie Strasia wouldn't have me back at the time. So, I asked Louie if he'd like me to stay on. He said, "Yes, you know where you sleep." So, I turned Rondo out into the alfalfa field for one whole month. Boy, was he ever beautiful. He was just shiny black when he had eaten that alfalfa for a whole month and gained about 75 to 100 pounds.

By then, I was in the regular routine of doing all the work there on the ranch. The worst part of the whole thing was I got there during the threshing time, when they threshed the wheat, and get the straw, and you got to stack the straw into bundles, and all this and that. It's really a hard job, 'cause the guy that has the threshing machine charges so much an hour or day to run the machine so they're all in a big rush to get done. You finish taking the bundles off of one stack, then you get right down and get on another stack. They tell you to always have one going in the threshing machine, one in the air, and one on your fork at all times until you get to the bottom of the 18-foot stack.

The old style threshing machines required several workers.

Anyway, during all of this time, I thought I was registered for the draft. I actually wasn't. Louie Cortese's brother (Charlie's son-in-law) was the head of the draft board in Trinidad. So, Louie and Charlie had talked it all over, and they decided to put some cattle in my name and land in my name. That way they could keep me out of the service. So they did all this without me realizing what it meant. I just knew I had new heifers to feed in the South pasture. I had to fill all the feed racks out in the big pastures where the cattle were with straw from the threshing of the wheat. I was rather confused what all this meant and I wasn't the least bit contented. Louie was still the same almost as far as relationships and his stuff were concerned.

A Winter Baptism

One day, it had snowed and the ground was covered with ice, and I was carrying a 100-pound sack of cotton seed cake on my shoulder. I slipped and fell with the cotton seed sack on the back of my head and hit my head on the frozen ground. It knocked me out completely cold. When I opened my eyes, the cattle had chewed through the burlap bag and they were all standing around me. They had eaten most of the bag that was busted on the back of my head. I got up and had a horribly bruised forehead. Next day, it was all black and blue. It wasn't long before everything froze and I had to cut the ice on the stock ponds that I had built a couple of years before. So I was cutting the ice and didn't realize I was a little too far out on the ice to cut it. I broke through the ice and I went into the water. Before I got to the house, my clothes were frozen on me because I had gotten completely submerged in the pond.

The next day was just about as bad or worse. It was one of those days with sleet and wind blowing and the sky real dark. You couldn't see anything anywhere. I got down off my horse and I got down on my knees in the snow and I looked up toward the swirling dark, black sky. I said, "God, if you can hear me, please take me. I'm tired of all of this. I can't do this anymore. Just take me!" Then I paused a minute to think of something and all of a sudden, I said, "Oh! And God, if you don't mind, I'd like to go to hell for at least three days to really get warm once!" I really meant that, but God didn't take me at that moment.

I got on my horse and went about my business. That day when I came back in, Charlie Cortese had bought a new Hudson. He said I could go to town with him at least once a month if I wanted to. So, I went. The first time I got in his car, he had newspapers all over the back of the seats, the floor, and on the seat where I sit. I was clean; I had clean clothes on but he thought I would get his car dirty. And the strangest thing – there's quite a few little curves going down the canyon and on down into Trinidad. He would stop quite a ways from the curve and have me get out of the car and go look to see if anybody was coming. You know, it was so funny because we only met two cars in 25 miles anyway. But anyway, I got to go to town with him once in a while. He used to drain the oil out of his car just before he was ready to go to town. He'd put it on the stove and warm the oil up and put it back in the car. He was really something else.

He had a lady working for him, an old lady. Her name was Mrs. Milton. He paid her $12 a month. I stayed there just long enough that I didn't like it there. She was always bitching about something. One time, Charlie was to take a few eggs to the lady's sick brother in Trinidad and a few other little things from the ranch. She finally asked for a raise and he gave her $15 a month. When he started to take stuff to town the next time, she was going to send more with him. He said, "Now that you're getting $15 a month, I'm not taking anymore stuff to town."

One day I was out with Louie. He was looking my heifers over and checking everything over there in my section. He had the north pasture with the steers. I asked him, "Louie, you said to keep me out of the service, you'd put cattle, land and so forth in my name." I said, "Will that land and those cattle be mine when all of this is over?" He looked at me and just screamed at me almost, "Are you kidding? We're just doing this to keep you out of the service. You ought to be so glad we're doing it because otherwise you'd be in the Army or somewhere!" I found out later he even lied about his age in the first World War so that he wouldn't have to go.

Joining The Marines

I looked in the paper and I found out that a United States Marine Corps recruiting officer would be in Trinidad for a week or so. Then I found out that Louie Cusimano had joined the Marine Corps. So I went up to the Cusimanos' to see him and visit before he left. I always felt welcome. Mr. Cusimano and Mrs. Cusimano settled in that canyon on leased land where the railroad was once going to try to put a railroad line through Cisco canyon. So the railroad owned the land and they just paid a little to keep it up and lease it. Believe it or not, they had about 300 goats to milk, morning and night. They made cheese and stuff. There were four brothers – Victor, Louie, Johnny and Joe. They all worked in milking the goats and making the cheese. Mr. Cusimano was a hard-working soul, but Mrs. Cusimano was the best cook you ever saw on earth. They killed all the male kids [goats] and ate them when they were only about a month old or so. They had them most of the time to eat. Boy, they were good, too.

I talked to Louie and he told me he was leaving for the Marine Corps in the next few days. I told him that I thought I'd like to join the Marine Corps if they'd take me. A few days later, I asked Uncle Louie, "There's not much doing. I'm going to go up and see the Cusimanos again." Well, instead of seeing the Cusimanos, I walked over the hills and valleys to Trinidad. I looked for the recruiting office and found it. I saw the US paratroopers recruiting poster and I went inside for more info. I asked the funky where the Marine Corps sergeant was that was taking the recruits. He said, "He's off somewhere." So, I started talking to him; I thought that would really be interesting – the paratroopers. About that time, here came that Marine and I got to thinking I'd like to be with Louie Cusimano anyway. I talked to him and I almost lacked a couple pounds of being too light to join the Marine Corps. I was 6' and weighed 142. He signed me up and told me when I had to report to Trinidad to take the train on to San Diego.

Dann Slator and Louie Cusimano. (1942)

Well, when I got back, I found out Louie had been given a horse by Mr. Newcomb. Every time he bought his calves, he usually gave him a horse. So, Louie asked me if I'd go down and pick up that horse. They were going to leave it at Charlie Strasia's place. So I rode Rondo down to Charlie Strasia's to get the Butcher Block horse.

Louie's Kind Offer

I asked Charlie if I could leave Rondo there for a while. Charlie said, "Well, sure!" That's where Rondo stayed for almost four years until I got out of the Marine Corps – with Charlie Strasia out on the open plains.

When I got back to Uncle Louie's, Louie had gotten the paper from Trinidad and it had in there that I had joined the Marine Corps. He came out to my room. I had just gotten there and he came out to my room with a brand-new .38 super automatic and he laid it on my bed. He said, "I read about you joining the Marine Corps. If you want to die so bad, why don't you kill yourself here so we can bury you here where you belong?" I said, "No, thank you. I'll let the Japanese kill me or whatever." He left the room real mad. He didn't know I had to be in Trinidad the next day.

I got up real early and secured the few things I had to do. I headed across the hills again to Trinidad. I had to be there by noon. When I got to town, I stopped at my grandma's house for just a little while and visited with her. I went down there and the sergeant handed me all of my papers and said I had to go down to the depot, that the train was coming in an hour to pick me up and I'd better be there. The train left Trinidad for Denver to pick up more recruits on the way to California. Louie Cusimano and I were the only two guys who enlisted all the time that he was in Trinidad trying to get recruits.

I arrived at the base. It was cold and fogged in. I couldn't believe that I was where I was. Here were all of these men standing around in the fog, waiting to go God knows where for heaven knows what. Then I got my first insult: I had my cowboy hat and cowboy boots and the vest cowboys wear in those times, and I was talking to somebody and this sergeant walked up to me and said, "Hey, listen here, you sheep herder!" He said, "You better not be talking in ranks. You understand?"

I said, "Yes."

He said, "You better say, 'Yes, sir!'"

I said, "Yes, sir! I'm not a sheep herder, I'm a cowboy."

He said, "What's the difference?"

I kind of figured right then I'd made a mistake but it was too late now. I was already on my way. Boot camp is ten weeks of training – special training – from six in the morning 'til six at night. I was in platoon 1110. I made a mistake of telling them I was from Texas; I found out nobody liked anybody from Texas. Everybody made fun of me and picked at me and I got in quite a few fights and stuff.

One day, we had an inspection. I had a picture of Rondo on my locker door and a picture of Sundance – 8-by-10s that I had on my door. When they had the inspection, they came to my locker and my bunk. The sergeant and the two corporals – he looked and he says, "What the hell is this?"

I says, "Those are my horses, Rondo and Sundance."

He says, "Well, Rondo and Sundance aren't allowed in here."

An angry Marine inspection. (Art ©2010 Jack T. Chick LLC)

I said, "What do you mean?" He tore them off of the locker – just tore them off of the door. I said, "You'll be sorry for that someday."

He said, "What did you say?"

I said, "You'll be sorry. You had no business doing that to me. That's my whole life. I worked a whole year almost to buy those two horses. Anyway, they were my treasure."

He glared back at me and said that after lights out, he wanted to see me out between the barracks. One of corporals liked me and he told me, "Why don't you just go apologize to the Sergeant? He's really mad at you and if you go in there and apologize you can get out of seeing him tonight after lights out 'cause he plans on working you over, I think." But I refused and told him, "Why should I apologize? He's the one that should apologize to me. I can't believe he done that to me."

Getting to Know the Drill Sergeant

So at 10 o'clock, he came to the door and called my name and I went outside there with just my dungaree pants and a t-shirt on. He said, "I'm going to teach you not to be so smart, you got to learn right now, without any hesitation, to obey orders, to shut up, and to only speak when you're spoken to." He doubled up his fists and I stood there and looked at him and I said, "You're just going to beat me up then? I'm not allowed to fight back?" He dropped his hands and opened his mouth and looked at me. He said, "You think I'm just going to beat you? Sure, do your best. Do your best."

Being called out at night to fight with the Sergeant.
(Art ©2010 Jack T. Chick LLC)

I said, "Then I can fight back without getting in any trouble?" He said, "Sure, sure, do what you can!" So, he kind of waddled around a little bit, and then he attacked me. He never knew how much experience I had. I just ducked, then I popped him. Anyway, when it all ended up, I won. I really beat him up and the two corporals looked on, and one said, "I hope he don't get upset over all of this." Nothing happened, except a few days later, he asked me, "Where did you learn to fight like that?" I said, "Like what? What do you mean?" He just walked off from me.

Talking to Wind Talkers

In our platoon, there were two Navaho Indians – Kiosi and Pina. They were the best friends I had. We would sit and talk about horses, cowboys, Indians, and they were going to invite me to Monument Valley where they were from on the Navaho Indian Reservation and all of this. We had a great time talking. They took these two Indians before they even finished boot camp and sent them off. I found out later, they went to communications. They used them because the Japanese could never understand what they said. They have a tongue, not a language, a dialect that no one can hardly understand but the Navaho Indians. They call them "Wind Talkers." The Japanese never figured out how to decode what they said. Each Indian was given someone to guard him at all times with the radios and the communication, plus some of them carried cyanide capsules. If they were captured, they would take the cyanide capsule because they knew they would be tortured to death to try to get the code of how they decipher messages so the Japanese could understand it. I really missed them when they were gone.

Navaho Wind Talkers.

I had all kinds of problems after this, because the sergeant never showed me any mercy. He made me do nearly all of the dirty things and put me in all this and that. One day we went offshore on a ship, a small landing ship that would hold about 200 men. We all had to go over the side on these rope ladders, either that or we could just jump off the side or whatever. He called my name and I went up there. I took a real deep breath and I dove down into the ocean and swam underneath the ship to the other side. I came back up the other side and it had a rope ladder hanging on it. Everybody was looking and they said I had dived off the ship and had never come up yet. Everybody was really wondering and they looked around and I was standing there. I told them I had just swam under the ship. They didn't know I was such a good swimmer. He told me, "You stupid jerk! You were supposed to go ashore! Go ahead, do it right this time!" Then I did jump off and swim to the shore like I was supposed to. We had these offshore maneuvers for about a week.

When I got back, we were all through with the boot camp. They had trucks parked there for destinations unknown. When they called your name you went by and shook hands with the two corporals and our sergeant. When they called my name and told me—they had the trucks numbered 1-2-3-4-5 and they were loading them up with men from all the other platoons—my number was 5. I went and shook hands with both corporals and I just ran and jumped in the truck. Then one of the corporals came over and said, "You know, we have put thousands of men already through this boot camp and you're the first one ever to refuse to shake hands with the sergeant." I said, "I just don't feel like shaking hands with him. I don't consider him any part of a friend of mine or anything. I just won't do it, no matter what." So they finally left off.

Finding Fritz

When I found out for sure where we were going, we was going to go to the rifle range first. It was really out there in the boondocks. The machine gun range, also. There I met Fritz Truan. I had a horse drawn on the back of my dungaree jacket and put Matador Ranch, Texas on there. I put some cattle brands on there and I heard a man say, "Are you a cowboy? I said, "Well, I was a cowboy." He introduced himself, and I had already heard of him. He was a world-champion cowboy in 1939 and 1940. We sat and talked mostly and I was so glad to know somebody like him. No one else around there was ever related to the ranch or anything. We had a lot of fun. I'd look for him and he'd look for me and we'd go together.

We were walking back from the rifle range and there was a boxing ring there behind the mess hall. There was this guy – a big Marine then was 180 pounds and over six foot tall, wasn't hardly any bigger than that—this guy was a cook. He yelled over at us walking by; he says, "I can't get anybody to box with me. Everybody's all chicken!" I looked up there and I said, "Well, I'll box you." So, we got up in the ring and put the gloves on. I could tell right away that he had some experience because I couldn't pull these foxy moves that I usually had, and all this and that. He kind of counter-punched me; anyways, he kind of beat me up and I finally held up my arms and I said, "That's enough for me!" I pulled my gloves off and climbed out of the ring. Fritz said, "Wait a minute! Give me those gloves! I'll box you!" The guy says, "Okay." He got in the ring and I never saw a guy move—you could tell Fritz never had any professional training at all, but he was rugged, boy, and he could hit hard. He just waded into that guy and finally plowed and knocked him down. Then he walked over, took the gloves off, and threw them in the ring. The other guy eventually got up.

Fritz Truan. He quit rodeo at the height of his career to join the Marines in 1942. He was killed Feb. 28, 1945 at Iwo Jima.

As Fritz walked away, I said, "Why don't you take up boxing? Man, you're really something else!" He was 26 years old and he'd had a rough life with the rodeo and everything. He said, "I don't like to fight, but when I saw what he done to you, I decided I was going to go in there and work him over." We became good friends and planned on meeting up after the war, but Fritz didn't make it. (He was promoted to Sergeant and he was leading his men on an uphill charge during the Battle of Iwo Jima when he was shot and killed by enemy machine gun fire.)

I was really surprised when I got back to my tent area. They had a list there of those who could go on liberty. This would be my first liberty from the rifle range. I knew the best beach on the whole coast, Corona Del Mar, wasn't far from there. I just wanted to get down and go swimming in the ocean. I loved the ocean. When I got my liberty, I went right down to that beach. I went swimming and really had a lot of fun eating hot dogs at a hot dog stand. I met this girl and we went swimming together. We talked a while. She pointed up to a house overlooking the beach and she said that's where she lived. "Why don't you come up after a while?" and I said, "I don't know—" She said, "Why don't we go now?" She took me up the pathway – the steps up to her house. She had told me her dad was a Navy commander. I said, "I don't know what your dad's going to think when he sees a Marine." She said, "I don't think he'll mind." He was nice to me for a little bit.

We were in the room there talking and she told me she had shaven her legs that day and she said, "Feel how smooth." I said, "I can see that." She said, "Well, feel how smooth!" and just as I was feeling her legs her dad walked by the room where we were sitting. I planned on coming back the next liberty I had to see her. I got her address and she got my address. When I was ready to leave, he said, "I'll walk down to the highway with you, Dann." And she said, "I'll go, too." He said, "No, I just want to get better acquainted with him. I'll just go." We started down the road; we had gotten just out of sight of the house and he turned to me and said, "This is as far as I'm going." I said, "Okay, sir." He said, "But I want to say something to you." I said, "What's that?" He said, "I don't ever want to see you at my house again. I don't ever want to see you with my daughter."

"'Cause I'm a Marine, huh?" He said, "No, I saw you had your hand on her leg." I said, "Would you believe, sir, she asked me to feel her leg? Otherwise, I would never have done it." He said, "Whatever. I don't want you around anymore." I said, "That suits me. There's plenty other places I can go." And I just walked off.

Night Visits to the Zoo

"Speed" the giant 150-year-old Galapagos tortoise, died in 2015. He weighed over 500 pounds and had been in the San Diego Zoo since 1933.

A couple of days later, I had a notice on the bulletin board of Marines that were going to be transferred to San Diego at the Balboa Park for a special weapons and training school. I was on the list. I was glad to get out of there and get graduated from the rifle range. We went down to San Diego and what a beautiful place we were in. It was like the Spanish apartments or hotel or whatever you want to call it. It was Balboa Park. I knew, in the '30s – '37 or so – I had gotten to go to San Diego Zoo and I knew the zoo was in Balboa Park. So about the third night, I was in a second story barracks. It had curfew at 10 and reveille at 5 in the morning. It was guarded at the doors so no one could come in after 10:00. Anyway, there was a big tree by my window. I was in the second story. I opened the window—I was in the top bunk—I opened my window and I seen that tree. I could reach out for one limb and I climbed out the window and I got a hold of that limb and I went down the tree to the ground. I sneaked around and I came to a fence. I had asked several different people where the zoo was. One actually knew; he pointed to exactly where it was. I climbed one fence and I waited because I saw the second fence was guarded by the Navy. So it must have been Navy personnel there. I waited for my opportunity and I climbed the second fence. Later on, I worked my way – still going kind of north – and I came to a tall fence right by the highway. I climbed over that fence and got down. I went by the highway and I saw the zoo. I crossed this highway and I went over to a fence; I could see some of the animals in the zoo. By climbing over that fence, I was in the zoo. I wandered all through the place until early morning – 2 or 3 o'clock it seemed like, 2 o'clock anyway.

When I left, I went back over the same route that I had taken to get in, all the way back to base. I climbed the same tree to get back into the barracks, but I couldn't reach my window from the tree. I had quite a bit of maneuvering to do to get in that window, but after several attempts, I finally managed (thank goodness), and I got in my bed, and snatched a little rest.

Well, we went to all of these special schools. We had to learn how to disassemble machine guns blindfolded and had special training and other things like exercises and formations and such. That night I was pretty tired. I kept thinking about how beautiful that zoo was at night. I never saw one person in the zoo. I saw one vehicle going down a little road, but that was it. So I decided to go over to the zoo again the next night. I continued doing this for the whole time I was there. I went over there and I met Osa Johnson's gorilla: his mate had died. Martin and Osa Johnson had brought this gorilla in the '20s to the zoo. I would go over the zoo and I'd laugh and I'd sit and talk to him. He would hold his hand out to me and I would just hold his fingers as I talked to him. I'd try to mimic and make the same sounds he would; I was getting pretty good at it. One night, after about a week or so, he didn't have his arm quite all the way extended and I had my hand there to hold and he grabbed me by the wrist. He tried to pull me through the bars and I lost part of my jacket. It took everything but I finally got loose from him. I said, "I'm not coming to see you anymore after that," and I left. It was about 15 days after I started going in there. I had gone every night almost. I didn't stay as long sometimes.

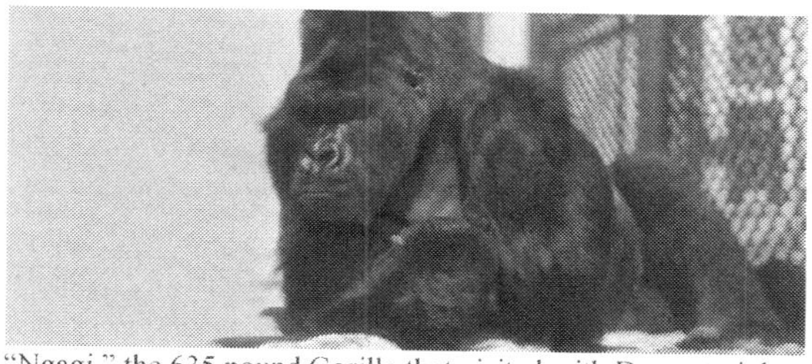

"Ngagi," the 635 pound Gorilla that visited with Dann at night.

I saw the zebras and they looked so much like horses, especially in the moonlight. I wondered if they were tame enough to go up to. They had about a twelve-foot fence around them. I climbed the fence and I went in with the zebras. There were about a dozen, and there were some young ones—colts, too—in there. They all snorted and kind of whistled. I tried to imitate their sounds. I got right in the middle and I started talking to them. This one kind of walked toward me. Well, I found out later what he was doing. I started to take a couple of steps forward and they all ran at me and knocked me down and ran over the top of me. Then they ran over and made those funny sounds again. When the dust all settled, I got up and I went to the fence. I got over the fence. I went back over the fence and got to the base and back to my sack. The next morning, in the showers, this guy said, "What happened to you?" I asked, "What do you mean?" I had horseshoe marks on my back. I had some hair taken off the side of my head that was a horseshoe shape. I had horseshoe shapes on one leg. I said, "I must have got that when I fell the other day." But I figured the zebras had stepped on me when I was in there.

Sleeping with an Elephant Seal

So then, a couple of nights later, I always wanted to see the sea elephant and I'd go by where he was. There was a really big, flat rock and I climbed inside there and sat atop that flat rock. I kept looking all around to see where he was; it wasn't that light. As I was looking for him, I got kind of sleepy, so I laid down on the rock and dozed off. All of a sudden, I got real wet and I hurt. This sea elephant had come out of his thing and practically laid on me. They weigh about 1200 pounds. He got me soaking wet because he splashed water on me when he came out. When I yelled, he jumped back in the water. I did get to see him. I tried to get up and I felt like a car hit me or something. I finally got up and I was just soaking wet. I went back over the fences.

San Diego's giant Elephant Seal.

Well, about the last day, I heard that we were going to be leaving in a couple of days. The last time that I went in there, I went over there to see the gorilla and kind of talk to him and visit all around the different places. I never ever did get to see the black panther. I sat there by the side of his cage and kept staring and staring in his pen. It was kind of dark. I couldn't see no movement or nothing. All of a sudden, I heard a wild-like little yawn. He was sitting there all the time. When he opened his mouth. I could see his teeth. He was sitting there all the time I was but I never saw him. That was my last trip in there. I had to get everything in order. I made it there about 26 days and we were there 30 days. I only missed about four days of going into the zoo every night.

We had formation and the platoon sergeant told us – he was an old master sergeant, really – he told us, "The San Diego Zoo is going to give us a treat. We can march through the whole zoo and see the whole zoo." Everybody just cheered. We got through chow and we all lined up and marched over there, down the road and into the zoo. We met some of the zoo officials and wandered all around the zoo. We finally, at last, came to Martin and Osa Johnson's gorilla. He was sitting in a big old tire – absolutely like he was sleeping and not paying attention to anything. The guide kept trying to get his attention. He would move a little, but he wouldn't turn around or anything. The guide said, "Oh, well; I guess he just don't feel like getting around today." I said to the guide who was standing close to me, "Sir, would you ask the sergeant if I would be allowed to talk to the gorilla?" He looked real surprised at me and said, "What?" I said, "I used to talk to gorillas in the zoos." He said, "Oh, yeah?" He went over and asked the sergeant who said, "Suit yourself." I walked over there. The gorilla had his back to me. He weighed about 600 pounds. I started in my voice I always use for horses and I said, "What's the matter? Don't you want to see us today? Don't you want to come and see us?" He heard my voice and he kind of like jumped like he was shocked. He got out of the tire and he came right over to the fence. He saw me, and I said, "How are you doing today?" and I made a couple noises like he made. He got so excited: held on to the bars, looked me right in the face, and he made these noises and kind of jumped up and down. They said, "Well, we got to go." It's strange. No one ever said anything, why or how that I got that gorilla to come up to the fence. We went on out of the zoo and a couple of days later we were getting our stuff ready. We were going to be transferred to a new air base near there called Miramar. It never even had a fence around it yet. It was kind of out there in the boondocks. I was going to be assigned there to go to air traffic school to be a traffic controller in the Marine Air Corps. It was beautiful out there. We had different kinds of work details all the time. I was put, as a regular job, into ordnance to take care of all the firearms that came in and to check everything in ordnance. I really thought it was fun.

In my time off, I would just wander off and I found a horse ranch. The horses would come up to the fence and I'd talk to them and pet them and stuff. I knew that I would love it there. I had no idea of all the things that took place there. We had to go to Marine aircraft identification school. We had to do other things – more things than you can imagine to take care of and what we had to learn.

Camp Elliot

I heard my uncle's neighbor, Louie Cusimano, was stationed just at Camp Elliot, which was a base training for infantry, and heavy tanks and stuff. So first liberty I got, I went into Camp Elliot, and I checked all around and I finally found out he was at Green's Farm. So I went over there and I found Green's Farm and I went through all the areas asking, and finally someone told me that they think he was in this last tent. So I went in there and I looked in the tent and he was inside, and we were just so glad to see each other and to celebrate there.

The first 12 barracks at Camp Elliot were ready in Oct. 1940.

I found out he had some liberty yet, so I figured I could go on liberty at the same time. He had a family friend, Mr. Decara who lived in El Cajon, so Louie and I hitchhiked over to El Cajon, and we finally found out—he lived on the only little hill in town, right at the top of the hill he had this incredible Spanish architect tile roofed, an amazing home. It had a swimming pool in the basement and a small bowling alley, and tennis courts, and he owned an olive grove and some other trees, and he was just so good to us. He had the table set at all times, a big table in the dining room. And he had two daughters. And one of them was engaged, but the other one wasn't. And Louie and I went there about three times, and then I went over to see Louie, and he had a notice that they were going to ship out in a few days. So I found out when they were going to ship out and I went back over there, and I saw Louie on a bus. He waved at me, and I just about cried; I wanted to go with him. In fact, that's why I joined the Marine Corps, so maybe I could be with him. Anyway, that was the last time I ever laid eyes on him. He survived the war and lived to be over 90, and we kept up with letters and on the phone. But he died just as we were planning to visit each other in person.

And so I stopped going to San Diego. When I had liberty I'd go see Mr. Decara over in El Cahon, and it was so nice over there I went there most of the time. As I hitchhiked, we had another friend of mine that went hitchhiking with me, but when we got to our destinations we separated. We played poker with license plates, and we would bet a car would go by that had two pair on the license number, or the next one would go by, and we could draw one card from the next car after we decided what we wanted. It was a lot of fun to do just to pass the time while we were hitchhiking. But when I got back to the base, they put me in charge of ordnance there, testing new weapons and such, and there was still no fence around the place; I could wander off in my spare time into the hills or down to that horse ranch.

One weekend, I (and some other Marines decided, too,) to visit Tijuana. Well, we got in trouble in Tijuana; we got in a fight with some sailors, and the Tijuana police put us in a jail down there, and we were about 25 or so servicemen in this room, and I asked the guys, I said, "Where does that door go, does anyone know?" and they said, "It goes to the alley." So I got way back at the end of the room, and I run the whole distance, and I broad-jumped and hit the door with both feet. Instead of the door flying open, the whole door frame that held the door flew out in the street and we all ran off. I went as fast as I could and got across the border. I never did go back; I'm sure they would have recognized me. It was amazing that they all managed to escape.

Anyway, we got all loaded up and ready to move to a new base in Santa Ana called El Toro. It was donated to the Marine Corps for an airfield; the Irvine Ranch donated it. What a joy to see the different squadrons there: fighters, dive bombers, torpedo-bombers, trainers... and I was put in a torpedo-bomber squadron. I worked in the tower, also, some days. I saw a lot of crashes and explosions.

El Toro Airbase was opened in 1942. They also trained F4U-4 Corsairs, which finally made it into combat in early 1945.

I was on the airstrip when the first F4U-4 Corsairs were delivered (24 of them). The pilots were kind of afraid of them because they were so heavy, and they crashed a lot of them. So a lot of the accidents I saw because I was standing on the airstrip. I stood in front of all the planes as they came in to land from 8 o'clock in the morning 'till 5, and I stayed on the airstrip. I had to watch the patterns as they came over the Capistrano Mountains, and if they didn't make the right pattern, I would wave 'em off and they would have to go around again. Plus, I had a flag in each hand, and I'd hold my arms out like their wings were as they'd come in for a landing. I would tip my arms like their wings so they could try to make a perfect landing. I had the only job that was ever given in front of landing aircraft; no one else done that but me, and I stayed there all day long till closing.

A Visit from Lindbergh

So one day, out of a clear blue, they secured the field. I was on the airstrip. And I found out that Colonel Charles Lindbergh was going to fly a Corsair there and demonstrate how this plane should really be handled, and so they wouldn't be so scared of the Corsairs. He went way up out of sight and dove down, he went upside down, did barrel rolls, and I was on the strip where he done touch-and-go strip landing tests and all this, and I stood before him out there. Anyway, they'd go over 100 miles an hour to land, most of the planes, and when he finally landed and taxied over to the hangars, I went over there, and I went right up to him and he looked at me and he says, "That's that crazy person that was out on the airstrip! How in the world...what were you doing out there?" and I told him that was my job, to stand out in front of the planes like that. And he says, "No way should they ever have anyone do that," he said, "that's the most dangerous thing you could ever think of." So that was the end of my job at the airstrip. They had a lot of crashes because I wasn't there, because planes would come in with the nose too low, or they'd come in half sideways and they'd go off the runway and everything. I missed my job, but they wouldn't allow that to happen anymore.

Lindbergh himself cancelled Dann's airstrip job. (Art ©2010 Jack T. Chick LLC)

The Tower Telephones

I went to a special trading school to be a traffic controller in a tower built on top of a large aircraft hanger (so that we could see all the airstrip and control outgoing and incoming planes). To get up there was a long wooden ladder fixed to the side. All went well until they packed all ten of us together in a small room and started removing us, one by one, to interrogate us in private about the improper phone use in the Control Tower.

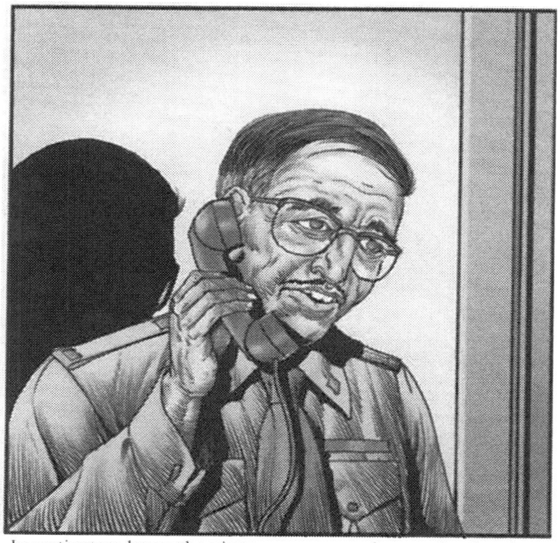

Investigators knew the air tower personnel were abusing the phones. (Art ©2010 Jack T. Chick LLC)

I was the last one they called in to the private room and they proceeded to question me by asking if I had ever used the phones for anything other than official military use on the base. They looked really surprised when I said, "sure." Then they asked, "In what way?" I told them I called Mr. Irvine's daughter at the ranch, and Mr. Irvine himself (since I worked for him on my day off). I also told them I made a few calls to other women I saw every once in a while. They looked at each other rather confused, unsure what to say. Then one of them told me I could leave. It turned out the investigators already knew everyone was guilty, because they checked the phone records. The other guys became furious because they were all rationed bread and water for five days, while I wasn't punished at all. They accused me of ratting on them, but I explained the only one I told on was myself. I just told the investigators the truth about my calls and they never even asked me about anyone else. That cooled them off, because they all knew they lied and they weren't asked about anyone else either.

The Morse Code Test

The squadron I was in at that time, 141, was going to be shipped out soon, and they were getting all ready and prepared to go. This was a torpedo bomber squadron, and each plane had three men: a pilot, and a gunner and a radioman. And their use in the war was to carry an 18-foot torpedo and go toward enemy ships, and just before they'd get within range they'd lay the torpedo in the water and it goes about three foot or so under the surface of the water toward the target.

They needed 50 radio gunners for these Torpedo Bombers. So they had to know Morse Code (in case the radio man was injured and the gunner needed to replace him). I was one also taking the test. It had 60 codes for us to decipher, all dots and dashes. Everyone taking the test was already a machine gunner.

When the test was over, the officer in charge came out and asked who Slator was. I said "Here, sir!" He told me the Major wanted to see me on the double. I went into his office where all the testing was. The Major looked at me and sighed. He said "We've been giving this test for years and you're the only person who missed all 60 of the codes list. I just wanted to see who could miss *every single one.*"

When I went back to where all the other men were, someone yelled out to me to ask what the Major wanted. I said, "He told me I had a score of 100%."

The ones with the highest scores were all put in the Torpedo Squadron, and all of them got killed, 'cause they lost every single plane.

A Last Minute Change

But none of us knew that then. I was just excited my squadron was soon going overseas. So we had a big party, a beer party to do everything or whatever we could do, and just five days before being shipped out, I was called into the office. They said they were going to transfer me – they wanted me to manage the skeet range that they set up, and they said that I would be transferred into another squadron at that time. So the 141st left without me. I wanted to go with them, but I also was wondering why things like this happened to me when I wanted to go so bad.

So three days a week I had the skeet range. I got so good by self-practicing that I could actually – there's 12 from a low house, and 13 from the high house, and I had this all set up that the high house would be 65 miles an hour, they'd come out, and the other house would be 70 or whatever; I could adjust it either way. And I got to the point where I knew where they crossed by certain speeds. And I would shoot my shotguns there right where I knew where they crossed, and a lot of times I got a possible 25 out of 25. But I got 15 out of 25 that time, although I maxed it out ten other times.

I had this extra time, so I decided that there was a chance for me to go to chemical warfare school. So I went to that during the daytime, and I enjoyed it a lot; it was into different kinds of gases and different kinds of grenades and all this stuff that we could use if we had to in the war. Anyway, in my new chemical warfare, the sergeant in charge there was really a master sergeant; he had 20-some years in the Marine Corps, and I confided in him that I was supposed to go overseas twice now and didn't. And he told me, "You know, the best way to go overseas is to get in trouble." So I kept getting in a lot of trouble down there, but nothing seemed to be that bad to do anything about it.

Just Hanging Around

When I was about 8-years-old, I always went to the old Adobe museum in Trinidad to admire the section where all the famous outlaws were being hung. One of my favorites was Black Jack, and a lot of the others. I know now that this had an effect on me later when I tried to hang myself in the Slaughters' cellar.

As an adult in El Toro, I noticed they started building a two-story overflow barracks. To me, the structure was so high, it looked like those pictures in the Trinidad museum. My best friend was an aerial photographer. He printed my cowboy pictures. I thought it would be fun to rig myself up like I was really getting hanged and have him snap some pictures of me. I made it look good, and even tied the thirteen wraps around the rope for the hangman's noose. When I swung out in the open for him to take the photograph, someone saw me from the main office building and yelled out to everyone else. They all poured out to see what was happening and my friend took off. I was stuck and could not release myself. Two marines had to undo all the ropes to get me down!

A few days later, they came and took me to the Naval Hospital for observation in Corona, California. I sat at a table with six officers asking me a lot of questions. One asked if I had ever been knocked unconscious. As I took a moment to answer, the Marine officer barked, "Did you hear the question?" I answered, "Yes sir, I'm just counting all the times!"

The El Toro Baseball Wall

The captain's wife was an Olympic skater, Sonja Heni. She made the cover of Time Magazine on July 17, 1939.

The baseball diamond was in the farthest corner of the base at El Toro Air Base. It was the last game against the nearby Navy Base for the title. About in the 8th Inning, the baseball went over the 9' fence with six rows of barbed wire on top. Captain Dan Toppings was the recreation officer; his wife was the champion Olympic figure skater, Sonja Heni.

With about 1,500 spectators in suspense, Captain Topping asked what the heck we should do. I told him, "Sir, I can get the balls on the other side of the fence." Without hesitating, I started up and over the security fence, got on the other side and started throwing the balls back over. I tossed about seven or so (as some balls were from other games). Then I came back over the fence and the crowd applauded. Our commanding officer knew me and said, "Slator, what a beautiful display in front of all those people!" Not one of them could do it without being cut up, but I could, because I had all that practice climbing fences meant to keep us in or out!

Confronting John Roy

On weekend liberties, I used to go see my brother John Roy up in Beverly Hills and I went up there one day to see him, and I found out he was abusing my aunt in more ways than one, sexually and physically. So I confronted him about it; I said, "What do you think you're doing? You shouldn't be doing these things; Uncle Bernie's so good to you and everything." And anyway, he left the room and I was sitting in a chair, and he come up behind me and he called my name, he said, "Bunn!" and I turned my head to look around and he had a 38 revolver pointed at my head; I could see the bullets in the chamber. And he said, "You don't get scared at all, do you?" and I says, "Well, I don't know, what do you think you're going to do?" and he pulled the trigger, and there was a loud click of an empty cylinder, and I snatched the weapon from him and threw it on the floor and I beat him up pretty bad, and I left. And he got in his car, he bought a brand-new '41 Ford convertible, and he followed down there where I went and I got on a streetcar, and he'd come alongside the streetcar, and when it stopped I got out and got in the car with him, and we went back to the house.

Well, when he left the house, he didn't bother to open the garage door, and he backed the car out and knocked the garage door out into the street, and the police were there, and they were checking to see what the heck was going on. They decided it was an accident, and we drug the garage door back, and was trying to put it back on. Later that night, John Roy went out with his car again even more drunk, and I didn't know at that time, but he was also smoking marijuana, too. The cops were chasing him in his '41 new convertible, and he ran a red light on Manchester Blvd., and went under the second trailer of an oil tanker with the convertible. They had his car on display for drunk drivers. It was four foot wider, and it was flattened to only 3.5 foot high, what was otherwise a brand new car. John Roy was hurt pretty bad, but not enough. He couldn't work, but that didn't stop him from his drugs or alcohol.

Facing the Music for John Roy

Dann stands in for his brother before an angry officer.
(Art ©2010 Jack T. Chick LLC)

I had another Marine Corps uniform there at the house, and he didn't know what to do, and I said, "Well, come and stay with me at the base." So we went and we got on the Marine Corps base alright, no problem. He stayed there for over a month 'til he got better. I lent him my dog tags and they doctored him and took care of him and everything. One day he was out of uniform and the colonel saw him, and he forgot to salute the colonel. He was dishonorably discharged just before Pearl Harbor from the Cavalry, 1st Cavalry down there in Fort Bliss, and he knew the basic military regulations, but he didn't salute the colonel for some stupid reason, plus he was out of uniform, so the colonel wrote him up. When the time came to face the music, John Roy said, "I don't know what to do; should I just take off?" and I said, "No, I'll go there in your place." So I went up to face the colonel during his office hours and stood there at attention. The colonel stared at me (John Roy and I looked kind of alike, but not really that much) but the colonel looked puzzled and he says, "You're Slator?" and I said, "Yes, sir." He says, "You don't look like the one—there's something I don't understand—" I said, "Would I come up here if it wasn't me? Why would I show up if it wasn't me?" and he said, "Well, I don't know—" so he gave me 20 days EPD, which is Extra Police Duty, doing work at night in different places.

Getting Married on a Lark

After John Roy finally stayed there over a month, he left and I started going up to see my uncle in San Dimas, and one of the Marines there had married a prostitute, he told everybody he saved 5 bucks every time he went to town, and so—in the back of my mind, I didn't like messing around that much, I thought I'd ask different ones to marry me when I was loaded and stuff, but none of them really wanted to, so I went up to see my uncle in San Dimas and— this was on a Tuesday. And I bought some bottles of gin from my uncle 'cause he couldn't sell much of the Seagram's Gin, so he let me have 'em real cheap; just a few dollars per. And I started drinking a little, and I went uptown to San Dimas, and there was a little restaurant there, and I went in there, and there was a real beautiful little curly-headed gal in the restaurant, and we started talking, and she says, "What are you doing in San Dimas?" I said, "I don't know; I'm looking for someone that will marry me." And she looked at me and she says, "Well, that shouldn't be so hard," I says, "Well, it is." And she said, "I'll marry you." And I said, "You'll marry me?" and she said, "Yeah." And I said, "Well, that's unusual—that'd be nice." And so when she got off work, we went over and we talked awhile, and on Friday night, in a Baptist church there in San Dimas, we were married. It turned out she was only 15! And I had just turned 19. Anyway, I got loaded and they drove us – her twin cousins (the Humphrey twins) drove us around in the car, and they both sang, and they let us off at my uncles house, and I was so loaded I just passed out–went up to bed. And the next day, I went over to her house and she was there busy doing something, so I crawled between the wall and the couch to take a nap. I felt so bad, I just laid on the floor behind the couch. Her two sisters was there talking to her. She had three sisters, and all three of them had married servicemen. (She also had a twin brother I didn't know named Billy.) My bride's name was Betty Oldham and they were talking there, and in the conversation, one of them said to Betty, "Well, for one thing, you're luckier than any of us 'cause you married a Marine. Most of them are bound to get killed." And she says, "Yeah, I guess so," When I heard that, I crawled out from behind the couch, and I stood up there and they about fainted, and I told them, "Things are rough enough for people; I'm not going to have people praying that I get killed so they can get $10,000. I'm out." I had no insurance anyway.

Dann visits an old friend. (Art ©2010 Jack T. Chick LLC)

So I left and I went back to the base, and when I got back to the base I found out they had me AWOL (Absent Without Official Leave) cause I just forgot how long I'd been gone. So I decided to go back over the fence and down to the highway to visit Colorado, back to see my horse before I turned myself in. So I hitchhiked all the way back to Colorado, way out in the country, and I went down to see Rondo. I rode him around a little bit, and I finally decided to go back to the base and turn myself in. Well, I messed around a little bit on the way back but eventually got there and turned myself in. They immediately took me down and put me in the brig. And I found out that they had me down for more days than I thought Absent Without Official Leave, and Failure to Report for Duty, and all this combined. They had a big case against me. So I got hard labor. I worked every day 10 hours. As time went by, they never done anything about having me have a trial or anything; I never heard a word, so I planned to escape, and I worked on a way to get out.

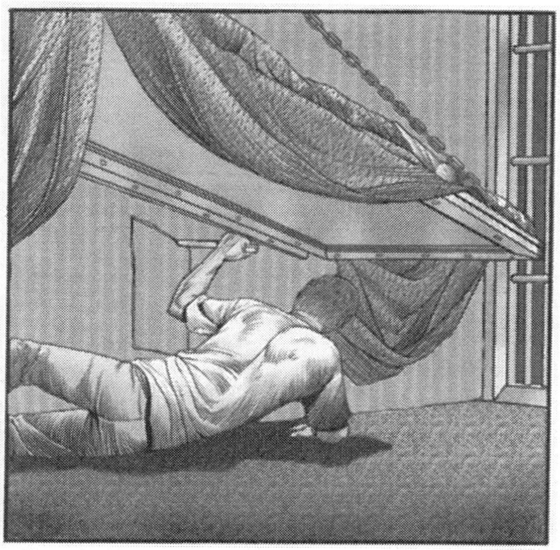

Dann decides to escape. (Art ©2010 Jack T. Chick LLC)

The brig had thick wood walls. I sneaked a small knife in there, and I slowly cut a hole real neatly in just one side of my room, and I put the sawdust and stuff down the toilet, and finally I started cutting on the other side, and when the time came, I pushed the two things in and I crawled through the hole about an hour before Reveille. I went out and headed down the airstrip and down to the main highway. I climbed over the fence and dashed along the canal, and I got clear away from there. Well, I didn't know it, but they had a big fire that night and they blamed me for the blaze, too.

So I was gone for about four days, and a Marine that knew me saw me in one of my favorite beer joints, and I knew they gave 20 Marines side arms and arrest papers if they saw me; they even offered a $50 reward if someone brought me in, and I told him, I says, "I see you're carrying (your gun)—what's that for?" and he answered, "Well, I'm supposed to arrest you; but I just wanted to warn you." So I decided, instead of messing around and getting in more trouble, I'd turn myself in.

Turning in The Prisoner

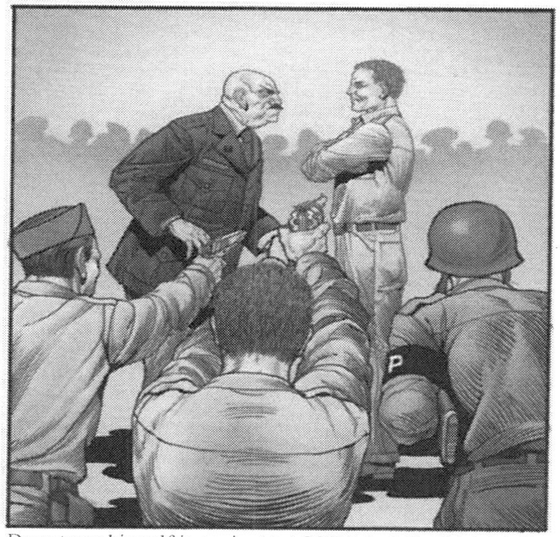

Dann turns himself in again. (Art ©2010 Jack T. Chick LLC)

So I went over the fence and I went right up to the brig, and they were having a big meeting. There was the chief of police of a few cities around there, Anaheim and Orange and Tustin, and there was a whole bunch of officers there, and the brig officer was there, and our colonel was there, and I stood beside my colonel almost with my arms folded. And they were talking about the best way to find and capture me, and I listened to all this, too, as I stood there. The colonel looked at me, and he says, "Who are you supposed to be?" and I said, "I'm a prisoner, sir," and he said, "*You're* a prisoner?" and I said, "Yes, sir," he said, "Where's your chaser?" and I said, "I don't have one, sir." (A chaser is one who takes you on work details and supervises you.) So he interrupted the meeting, and says, "I want to tell you – no wonder stuff like this happens around here. Here's a man standing here saying he's a prisoner, and he hasn't even got a chaser." Then he turned and asked, "What's your name?" And I said, "Slator." Boy, all hell cut loose then. They drug me in the brig. The captain (the brig warden) pulled out his 45 in front of about 30 men and guards and officers. He put the thing directly under my chin, and – they're sensitive; I know a lot about 45s. He had it cocked, and, you know, tucked under my chin, pushing up on it. And he said to me, "Say you're a no good S.O.B." and I said, "You're a no good S.O.B." and he just about pulled the trigger, but then an officer standing there said, "He said exactly what you told him to say."

90 Days Hard Labor

So anyway, it ended up that they gave me 90 more days hard labor and they didn't include the time that I'd served before, and I really worked like a dog. You never would believe the hours and stuff. They had me driving 1 ½ inch steel pipe that was six feet long, and I had to drive it into the ground three feet deep to hold rail road ties, to make a retaining wall for foundations. I did that all day under armed guards and a hot sun. After ten hours, they told me I could put the ten pound sledge hammer down, but I said I couldn't. They raised their shotguns at me and told me I better set the hammer down right away, but I told them I couldn't unwrap my hands. They were stuck! They came and peeled my hands off and they were bleeding real bad. They were covered with blood blisters and puss. Most the skin had split open. They wouldn't take me to sick bay because they didn't want the doctors to see my hands, but they took me off of detail long enough for them to heal. So they kept me in my cell without the hard labor, and I started to do all I could to slow down the healing. I rubbed them on the floor, and let the flies crawl on them, hoping to get them infected, but it didn't work. They got better and in a week or two, they put me back to work.

Back in the 1940s, "hard labor" meant ***HARD LABOR!***

The Warden called me out of my cell to inform me that I could write one letter a month. He gave me two pieces of paper and a stamped envelope. I went to my cell and tried to think who I could write to. The only one I really loved and longed to see was my horse, Rondo. So I wrote a long letter to Rondo telling him I finally knew how it felt when he was taken from his mother and it scared him when I started breaking him to ride and all. But I loved him enough to take him to my friend who I worked for once, Charlie Strasia, who just turned him out with his other horses for over three years.

Anyway, I addressed the letter to Rondo, in care of Charlie Strasia, Trinchera, Colorado. When I turned it in to the Warden, he called me back in to answer some questions. The one he wanted to know the most was if that letter was to a horse. I told him it was. He said that was the craziest thing he had ever heard of. I said, "No sir, if Rondo writes back, that will be crazier!"

A Visit from a Navy Chaplain

They still thought I had outside help to escape, so they got a Navy chaplain to come to my cell – I slept naked on the floor; no blankets, nothing – and they brought a blanket in, and two chairs in my little cell, and they said I had a visitor. And I couldn't figure out who that could be. So it happened to be a Navy chaplain (the Marine Corps didn't have 'em; it was Navy). I wondered why the heck he wanted to see me. They let him in there as I put a blanket around myself in a chair, and the Navy chaplain (I think he was a lieutenant commander), he looked at me and he says, "Slator, why don't you tell these people the truth; why don't you?" And I says, "I've been telling them the truth," and he says, "No, you haven't. There are a lot of things that you gotta tell yet; there are some things you're not telling," and I looked at him and I says, "Well, sir, I guess you're right," I says, "If I tell you a real truth, will you believe me?" He says, "Well, yes, yes," I said, "This is heavy stuff," I said, "You *will* believe me if I tell you?" and he said, "Yes, I will." And I says, "Well, sir, if you're not out of this cell in two minutes, you're gonna be a dead S.O.B!" but I used profanity, naturally. He screamed out the cell door for someone to let him out of there, and then he told the guards what I said, and they got so mad at me they done some things that no one would believe to me after he left.

After threatening a Navy Chaplain, Dann was relentlessly hazed by the guards. (Art ©2010 Jack T. Chick LLC)

A couple days later they knew I was in ordnance. They were all too lazy to clean their firearms and their Thompson sub-machine guns and all this stuff, so they brought a big table about eight foot long (my cell was 10 foot long) and they put all these on the table, and they brought in all the stuff for me to clean 'em all. So I started cleaning them and everything, and I picked up this one Thompson sub-machine gun, and it had a *full clip* in it. 24 rounds. So I took and I shined all the bullets, and I put 'em down the middle of the table, and about chow time they come in there, two or three of 'em to take the stuff out of there, when they started moving 'em they looked, and there was that row of bullets! And they looked at me and I says, "That was the most tempting thing in my whole life, all those bullets," and they really had a big deal.

This went on 'till my time was up. Now I never smoked in my life, and the warden, they never would offer me cigarettes or nothing. He told me I was the best prisoner as far as obeying and doing everything right that they ever had in there, that he was going to give me his own personal carton of cigarettes. And I said, "Well, sir, why don't you just give 'em to the men, I don't smoke." And he got all uptight. What a name: Warbriton was his name.

So anyway, this was something else in my life—I was ashamed and sorry I done it—but it happened. The last few days, I found out I had a couple of visitors. I didn't know who they could be, but it was my wife (Betty) and her cousin who had come down to see me. And she wanted to find out how I was and everything, but I'd already told my dad and my uncle to go ahead and get the wedding annulled (which they soon did), and I felt better knowing that I had never really touched her. Anyhow, she shows up with her older cousin (Pauline) and I end up flirting with her in front of my (then) wife! That was kinda mean, but I did it. I guess I was still sore about her marrying me in hopes I'd get killed.

Arrested for Sign Removal

I was put in a fighter squadron, and they gave me liberty; I couldn't believe it, I got liberty – and I got all set to go on liberty, and I went uptown and I was just walking along with another Marine, and there was a sign on a post about a month old advertising a rodeo, and I said, "Why don't they ever take their signs down?" and I saw it was a rodeo thing, and I kinda liked the picture anyway, so I took it off the post and the shore patrol come along, and they stopped and they started saying it was stealing. So they just took me in, but not the other Marine.

They took me down to the police station, and the back part of the police station was a mobile unit where the shore patrol had their headquarters, and it happened to be that this Captain Donnely who hated me so much, he just happened to be there, and he was in charge of the shore patrol that night. And when they brought me in there, they told him what I was doing, and in front of all the police officers and in front of all the shore patrol officers and the guards, he started swearing at me. Captain Donnely, and I stood there at attention, and while he was on this rage I just kinda smiled at him, and he yelled, "You wipe that grin off your face!" And I just kinda grinned back at him and he hit me, and he knocked me down. I was standing at attention.

I got up and I stood before him again, and he said, "Look, I just want to see you dare give me that grin of yours." So I stood there a minute, and I when I looked at him I let that little grin slip, and he hit me again. He did this to me four times! And the fifth time that he hit me, I went through the wall! It was a flimsy wall, but he hit me hard enough, regardless. I smashed through the plaster with my back and my head, and I fell between these old panels, or whatever they were, outside to the hall. They brought me back in through the door and Donnely told them to haul me back to the brig. But before they could, he called me names, and said, "You really think you're smart, you're gonna really get it now," and he doubled his fists and I said, "Sir?" He says, "What do you mean, 'sir?'" I asked, "Will I be allowed to fight back?" So he hit me one more time, and they locked me in a straitjacket, they tossed me on my belly inside this panel truck and they sat on me all the way out to the brig. I could barely breathe with them sitting on me.

Well, when we got to the brig, and in the brig they have a pecking order, what they call the big dog and the little dogs, and the big dog is the one that's got the most time, usually, and they're voted in by the prisoners, and they agreed that I was still the big dog because I hadn't been gone too long. Well, the one under me—Big Jake from Alabama—he decided it wasn't right, and he says, "I've already been named big dog." I said, "well, there's only one way to settle it," and he says, "What's that?" I said, "Tonight we'll settle who's big dog."

Deciding Who's Big Dog

So anyway, we got in there after chow, and everything was secured. No guards stayed in the tent part where the big brig was. And we pushed back a bunch of the bunks and I said, "Okay, if it's agreeable with you, whoever wins is big dog." And he was big and husky; kinda had a face like Frankenstein's monster. And everybody thought I was nuts to even think about it, but some of them kinda knew me, too. So he made a run at me, and I just got him by the arms and went over backwards and stuck my foot in the middle of his gut, and I threw him clear over amongst the bunks, and it didn't knock him out, but it shook him up so bad he decided he didn't want to continue. That's a little bit of the only jujitsu that I knew. But anyway, I was big dog.

Dann's airstrip help is missed. (Art ©2010 Jack T. Chick LLC)

So a couple days later, I was on a work detail by the main gate, and a couple officers that were present when Donnely hit me and all that stuff, they asked my guards for permission to speak to me, and one of the guards says, "Yeah, but you can't get in between the prisoners and myself, but I'll allow you to talk to 'em." So the officer asked me, "Is this all in regards to what happened the other night uptown in the shore patrol office?" And I said, "Yes, sir." They could hardly believe it. " So these officers, they were flight officers, and one of them knew me from bein' on the air strip, and he always commented how much help I've done and how many lives I've probably saved on the airstrip. (None of us could believe that they stopped having anybody do it.) Anyway, they both went up to Captain Stout, who was my commanding officer in the fighter squadron, and they told him what happened, and he went down to the brig and he had me released, and he had me come up there for office hours, and I went up there to see him, and the guard – I still had guards 'cause I hadn't been completely cut loose yet – and the guard says, "We shouldn't leave Slator here with you, sir; we're supposed to stay right here." So the Captain laid a .45 on his desk, and he says, "I wanna talk to him personally."

So they left the room and I stood at attention and he looked at me and he says, "At ease," and he says, "I'm lookin' at your record book, you're in our squadron, you're gonna be in our squadron; you're gonna ship out with us," he says, "I see you were a cowboy and a rancher," and I says, "Yes, sir." And he had an interest in the Wyoming Hereford Ranch. And we sit there and talked about bulls and cattle and horses and the Matador Ranch, and I took care of a bull they bought from his ranch, Prince Domino Mixer, Jr. II, and we had a big time talkin', and he says, "Well, you're gonna be out of there by the night; you're gonna be out in Donnely's. They've already fixed him – relieved him of his duties, and he's gonna be shipped out, but you won't be in the same area ever because of the friction between you two," so he said, "Just do me a favor: don't get into any more trouble before we get shipped out, which is soon," and I said, "I'll try, sir; I'll do my best."

Dann with Prince Domino Mixer Jr. II, a prize bull bought by the Matador Ranch.

So I left and they took me back down the brig, and they filled out some papers, and they let me loose. So I was sent back to the barracks, where verybody was still hanging around, plus some new guys , and a new Marine put his watch and wallet on his bed there, near mine, and I heard another Marine, who didn't see me, say, "Hey, you better watch out how you lay your stuff out around here, because that guy who just came in's a brig rat," and I walked around there and I said, "Yeah, I'm a brig rat, but it wasn't for stealin', it was for beatin' up guys like you!" And I shoved him against the bunk head, and he swung at me and I really let him have it. And naturally, they called the ones in charge of the barracks, and they showed up and took me up to Captain Stout, and he said, "You know, you haven't even been gone an hour and you promised me—" and I told him what happened, and he says, "Well, I don't blame you, but if any more instances like this happen, I'm not gonna have much more faith in you." So nothing else happened, and I was so happy because we started getting everything ready to leave, and we were going to go on a liberty ship clear to New Guinea, and I was so happy to finally go away overseas. I always felt so bad about others who wanted to go overseas, in fact one of the guys – a Master Sergeant Major – had 30 years in the Marine Corps. They wouldn't let him go back overseas, and he shot himself for that reason. He left $40,000 to a clerk in his office; that's the only person he liked, but he killed himself because he couldn't go back overseas.

Going to New Guinea

So one real foggy morning they loaded us all up to take us down to San Diego. The ship we were going on was the U.S. Liberty ship, *Extavia* was its name, and they got down there and they loaded us all up on the ship. We were going to go unescorted all the way (we didn't know then) to New Guinea, and everybody was assigned different places on the ship, and what was really interesting when we crossed the equator, they have a tradition and a ceremony they go through to make you "shellbacks". (They call you "pollywogs" until you graduate.) They take all the men that's never crossed the line overseas, and they initiate 'em. They use big paddles, and they have all kinds of things they do to 'em, and funny outfits they make them wear, and they have 'em do this and say that, and someone always dresses up as King Neptune. This has been a tradition for generations. I took pictures of some of the stuff that showed what they done and everything. And when you're all done, you get this card to show that you crossed the equator on the U.S.S. *Extavia*. Lots of interesting things happened on her.

Shellback ceremony as the *Extavia* crosses the equator.

One day, they announced that they were going to have boxing matches on top of the hatch. They rigged up a boxing ring and anybody who was interested in boxing could go to the fantail of the ship at a certain time and meet there. And so there was two coaches there, and there was about 40 sailors, and about 20 Marines, and they asked each sailor, they'd say, "How many of you are heavyweights?" and, "How much experience have you had?' and they'd raise their hand, and then one would have more experience than the other, and so forth. So they finally got down to me, and I fought the golden glove champion of Nevada. And he was about my size—shorter, a little huskier—but there were 10 bouts, and we were the last bout, and the Marines lost every bout up to that last bout. Everybody was lookin', and when I got in the ring, a lot of guys just went, "Oh, no," 'coz I looked so plain. The other guy was built nice, he moved around, he was doing his little dance, pulling on the ropes and stuff, and I got in the ring and just looked average. So I acted like I was half-Indian to add some drama, and I kinda chanted some chants and everybody thought I was up to something, but I just done it for show, and I kinda took little short steps in circles. It was three rounds, it was 100 degrees out in the sun with regular old field shoes on, and 12-ounce gloves, and we went for three rounds. The last of the three rounds, I got off balance when I swung, and I just happened to hit him. And I had everything behind that punch that could be, and he went out of the ring onto the floor, and he stood up and they called the fight off and they called it a draw. Boy, what a lucky punch that was!

Earning some Easy Cash

So, a lot of interesting things happened on the ship. I went back, and the sailors were all practicing – two or three of my Marine buddies – they were practicing tying knots, and this one sailor looked over at us and he says, "You guys, that's about all you know how to do is tie your shoes!" and then they all laughed. And I says," I got five bucks here that says none of you can tie a knot that I know how to tie." And they all looked like, "What's this; what's this?" and I says, "Like I say, five bucks – for each one that wants to try to tie the knot." So there was four takers, and so I turned around, they gave me a piece of rope, and I tied a hackamore knot. It's a double knot that goes under on the nose band to hold the lead rope of the hackamore, and I tied this and I threw it on the deck, but I'd already stated that they had 15 minutes to tie the knot. So anyway, they all looked at that in astonishment; they never saw nothin' like that, and they was wiggling around the ropes and trying this and looking at it, handing it to each other, and none of them could tie it. So I picked it up, and the guy said, "That's my rope," so I said, "Well, just a minute—" I untied it; I didn't want him to practice on it. So I won 20 bucks.

A couple of days later, this one sailor came up to me and he says, "Will you teach me how to tie that knot?" and I said, "Why would you want to know? That's a cowboy--" "Oh, a cowboy," he laughed, "No wonder you can tie knots!" So anyway, that was the end of the easy bets.

Finally, in the distance, we passed by some of the main islands that had already been secured by the Marines, and we was just at the French Haven Harbor in New Guinea, and we found out that the dive bomber squadron that I was going to be transferred into – they left the fighter squadron there, the men that was in that, and the rest of us went on up with the ship to the Admiralty Islands at Manus. What a wonderful harbor. We stayed there for quite a while, and we had more fun pulling pranks on any new guys who arrived. We'd tell 'em the equator went through the Admiralty Islands, and we'd tell them they just walk over there about two miles, we'd point over there to these big coconut trees, and we'd tell them they could actually see the equator, a real bright red strip about six to ten foot wide. And more guys got suckered in to going over there and looking for the equator, and it was such a hoot.

But lot of guys drowned; the water had the worst riptide; I was used to the ocean, but this was something else. You could throw a coconut in the surf and the riptide would suck down that coconut, which usually floats, and it would pop up about 100 or 200 yards out. That showed you what it would do to you if you got in that water. A lot of the guys drowned there, 15 or 16, the very first day. After staying there a while, nearly all of us really enjoyed the coconuts and the palm trees, riptide or not.

The natives hated the Japanese and welcomed the American liberators. (Art ©2010 Jack T. Chick LLC)

The natives hated the Japanese, 'coz they killed most of the men, and the women all had their heads shaved, and the Japanese done that to them. Anyway, there was a meeting. There were 10,000 Marines there at that time, and there was a meeting that said that the first plane was going to leave at 3:00 in the afternoon, a DC-3, and they were going to have a muster. And I just stayed in my sack. I mean, it could only fit 16 or 18 Marines out of 10,000. Why even bother showing up? I said, "All you guys are nuts to run up there and stand on that strip in that sun just to hear those names called," and pretty soon some of them started coming back, and they said, "They called your name." I thought they were kidding me, but I got my C-bag and I grabbed my things that I had, and I went up there, and sure enough, I was on the list.

Well, we flew from the Admiralty Islands (New Guinea) to Morotai (Indonesia) and on the way – our destination was Zamboanga, Philippines – the Japanese took back the airstrip where we're supposed to land. We didn't have enough fuel to go back where we came from, so we had to continue going there, and so when we got there we found out the Japanese had the back part where the buildings and the hangar was, but we had control mostly of the airstrip, so we circled around the mountains, and we come right over the buildings and everything, and we landed on the airstrip and went clear down the other end of the airstrip where our troops were and the Army was there, too, and we safely landed there while they shot at us.

Hanging Out with Guerillas

About a week before we had left the Admiralty Islands, I set on a little raised knoll that had the most beautiful harbor, the whole seventh fleet could be held in there, and I watched as the *Pennsylvania* and all these big battleships and cruisers, destroyers and everything just went out of the harbor, took all day for 'em to string out there. Well, on the way from Morotai to the Philippines, we passed over our fleet going up to the Philippines to engage the Japanese Navy there in the Philippines, and as time went on, we got all secured there.

Dann with pet Water Buffalo in Philippines. (Zamboanga 1945)

I was put in ordnance again. I especially liked the Filipino guerillas. I associated with all the Filipinos. I didn't like our mess halls and stuff, so I ate most of the time their food and ate with them, and I got acquainted with some of the Filipino guerillas, and they wanted to go into the mountains and look for a lot of the Japanese that escaped into the mountains. I told them to come down to ordnance, and I furnished them with all the stuff they needed – grenades and everything else, and ammunition. There was six of 'em. So then, when they started going, if I had a day off, I would go with them into the mountains looking for the Japanese, and it was so much fun to be with them. They looked like an armored car almost – they had hand grenades hanging all over them, and belts of ammunition, and some of them had side arms and rifles, some of them had Thompsons, and even Browning Automatic Rifles, and it was really something to see. I got them all the camouflage stuff, and they would go into the mountains and look for the Japanese.

Dann arms the Filipinos to help them hunt down renegade Japanese. (Art ©2010 Jack T. Chick LLC)

The airfield was really secured. Off of a carrier flew our scout bombers, squadron 236. So 24 dive-bombers came and landed there, and it was amazing to watch them. They'd come in there and landed, and that was the squadron that they put me in, squadron 236, and they searched all the canals and channels all around; they had different islands there for Japanese, smaller type vessels, and also they bombed over there – Java, Burma, Indonesia, – all that through there, they bombed, any suspected Japanese installations and stuff, and they even encountered bigger ships of the Japanese in the waters there between the Philippines and Vietnam and the channels there, and we were really proud of our pilots.

Dann on 50-caliber machine gun (with pet dog "Spunky").

I was in charge of one area with the ground defense. 50-caliber machine guns mostly, and some anti-aircraft installations, but I had nothing to do with anything but 50-caliber machine guns, and we had ammunition dumped near us, and we always thought, "Well, boy, if a bomb hits that thing, it will be the last of the whole island almost."

John The Baptist Day

After the island was mostly secured, we were given more time off. I got two days off usually, or I could work someone else's shift; we had worked all kinds of ways. We went up to town one day, and we didn't know this, but the Filipinos have a John the Baptist Day in February, and they throw water on everybody that they don't think is a believer or a Christian, whatever they want to call 'em, but anyway, we was all dressed up in nice. I had a starched, creased khaki uniform on, and we was walking down the street, and they come along and they threw a bucket of water on us, onto my buddy and I. So we found out what it was all about, it was young women that done it, so I said, "Let's go to the base," and we went back to the base and we went down to the motor pool, and our buddy was in charge of the motor pool, and we got a water truck that had a pressure pump on it. They used it on the air strip, but they had two or three, and they had this one that we checked out, it had a pump on it, and a tank full of water, and it had a fire nozzle hose, so we took it and we went downtown and we drove all over, and we'd see a bunch of people we'd just wash 'em away, blowing water on 'em and everything. We had more fun that day doing it, and the Filipinos, they didn't enjoy it that much because it just knocked them down most of the time. But they didn't complain, because it was a religious tradition.

We took the truck back, and the same guy who ran the motor pool was a real character. When a Marine would steal a jeep from the CBs or from the Army, this mechanic would paint 'em and put Marine Corps numbers on 'em for so much money, and he had a jeep brought in one night, and it was General MacArthur's private jeep, and he said, "That one I won't paint!" But we had a sign posted where the Marine airfield was, that read "With the help of God and a few Marines, MacArthur's taken back to Philippines," but they made us take the sign down.

After nearly a half of a year of chasing the Japanese out of the Philippines, the Marines started to receive some imported recreation. Kay Kaiser was one of the entertainers to visit them.

Everybody tried to have a little leisure, and at that time Kay Kaiser and different ones were coming then, 'cause we'd already been there about five months or so. I ended up staying there about 10 months, and I even had the only horse on the whole island. They said the Japanese ate 'em, but they missed this one, and I would ride him, and plus I had a water buffalo, a caribou, and I'd like to take him when I went because he could go through the rice paddies and everything, the water, and he was broke to ride and everything. I called him Toro. But toward the end, I got interested in the cock fights there, and different things, and I had a lot of good friends there, and finally they found out that we were going to go to Okinawa, so they started loading the ships, and they stood there and checked off all the vehicles, and we had nearly all our vehicles loaded that were on the list, and they looked and there was 27 vehicles left there, and they couldn't figure out how they had more. Most of them were ones my buddy had painted, and they just left most of them there. They didn't even take them 'cause there wasn't hardly any more room in the LST (Land-Sea Transport) that we were loading.

The L.S.T. 706 was loaded to the brim. (Art ©2010 Jack T. Chick LLC)

And so finally, the last day came that we would have to be leaving, and there was 15 men that were unaccounted for, a lot of them married the Filipina girls; a lot of them fell in love with them, and they just went and wasn't going to go on the ship, and so I went in the office and I told them that I knew every inch of the mountains, every inch of the rivers, I'd followed the whole course of the Tomaga River clear from the beginning way up in the mountains, a small stream to a big river, and I could find these guys. And then the Colonel looked at me and he said, "Yeah, but who are we gonna send to get you?" He had an idea that I'd never return – 'cause I loved it there.

A Rise in Rank

And what was really funny, just before we left, there was a rate list posted, and I had in my record book that the four years I was not allowed to make any kind of promotion in anything for four years, so I didn't even get excited. All the guys went down there, it was four-o'clock when it was supposed to come out. So one of the guys who knew me said, "You oughta go down and look at that rate list," I says, "Why?" He says, "Just go look." So I went down there and the commanding officer and the Adjutant and the First Sergeant and a bunch of others were standing there in front of this sheet posted on a bulletin board, and so I walked over there and I looked at it, and it was the most beautiful scroll you ever seen, and it had "By the power invested in me as the Commander-in-Chief of the armed forces, I, Franklin Delanor Roosevelt, do promote every private overseas to the rank of PFC." And it had his signature. I wish I'd have took it, as I was the only private in the whole squadron, and it was so funny – the colonel looked at me, he said, "Well, that can't be, because you can't be promoted because it's in your record book that you cannot be promoted," and I said, "Yeah, but you want to go against that? That's the Commander-in-Chief of the armed forces!" So they made me a PFC!

We got ready to leave, and we loaded up everything, and I had monkeys and parrots and stuff, that I gave away to the Filipinos, but this one monkey, Tina, was a green monkey, and it had no tail naturally. It was a tailless monkey, and it was so cute I really wanted to take her, but they wouldn't let us take any pets with us on the ship. So I gave her away, too.

Dann riding "Torro" in Philippines. He had to be given away as well. (Zamboanga 1945)

I spent the day saying goodbye to the friends I had in the Philippines, the Filipino guerrillas, we had such great experiences up there looking for the Japanese, we even went into one abandoned gun bunker that they had at the side of the hill. And we'd all went through that thing and found Japanese invasion money and such, and a few days after, just before we left, we heard the whole place blew up. We had walked all around in there, and they had bombs set up in there, bombs the Japanese had left in the place as booby traps. We were lucky they hadn't gotten us.

Headed for Okinawa Through a Typhoon

Well, they loaded us up, and we headed up the coast for Okinawa on the way to China. What remarkable scenery! We stayed pretty close to the coastline and we saw a lot of beautiful things on our trip there.

When we arrived at Naha, Okinawa, we sat there in the ship and watched them unload other ships. The wind started to pick up. Before evening, real dark clouds appeared. They decided, even though the front part of the ship was beached, to put the anchors down. We watched the wind increase more and more, and we were just below where the airstrip ended on the cliffs above us. The planes took off and landed with this real high cliff against the ocean. We were seeing light planes going down the airstrip – the wind was blowing them down there. Even Quonset huts that weren't anchored down were blowing down and then going off the end of the airstrip and "into the drink" (the ocean).

By this time, the winds had increased to over 130 mph. We decided that we'd better start the engines of the LST to keep it from getting pulled out to sea. But that didn't do any good because high waves were hitting the back of the LST. Finally, one of the anchors broke loose and the ship shifted. As it shifted, it broke the other anchor loose and we started out into the ocean. All of a sudden, we had the engines running, and there were high waves that lifted the back of the ship up out of the water. When the propellers of the ship came down and hit the water, they broke loose. Before we even got out of sight of Naha, we had lost both of our propellers and we lost the rudder that controlled the direction of the ship. An LST is a flat-bottomed ship. We were on our own and drifting out to sea. By the time morning came, the winds were up to

180 mph. There were 40-to-50-foot waves. The LST had 500 lb bombs and 18-foot torpedoes in the hold. Half of the other hold was full of 55-gallon drums of 100-octane gas for our planes.

We didn't know what on earth would ever happen as the ship was tossed to and fro and the waves were coming over the side of the ship. When the ship would turn, it would come over the front of the ship... whatever direction, it would go clear over the deck of the ship. We saw a destroyer escort in the distance. We saw a big wave go completely over it; it turned over on its side and sank.

Dann witnessed another ship sink during the typhoon.
(Art ©2010 Jack T. Chick LLC)

Sleeping in a Crash Truck

One thing I done at night: I sneaked up topside—no one was allowed topside—but I sneaked up on the top deck and went into the top gun turret on the front of the ship to watch the waves. They were so amazing! When two waves would hit each other, they would make a stream straight up in the air 30 or 40 feet. But the phosphorus in the water would light up like neon lights. It was a sight to behold.

Another Marine and I, we started the next night. There was a crash truck on the deck that had six-foot-high wheels on it and a big crane. It was used to haul wrecked airplanes off the runway when they crashed; they called it a crash truck. It had a seven-foot seat and we took turns – one would sleep down on the floor and the other one would sleep on the seat. Well, the third night, we got a warning from the captain. He caught us sleeping in the truck and told us we would be put in the chain locker for the rest of the trip if we were ever caught sleeping in the truck again. The truck was chained; every wheel was chained to the deck of the ship and it was only four feet from the railing. My buddy and I, we thought we couldn't stand it down in the hold. The smell of gasoline and everything else down there would just about kill you. We looked up on topside. It was raining and the wind was blowing worse, but we both decided not to try it, not to go get in the truck.

The next morning we were on the deck where the captain had warned us. He came by and said, "Well, I see you guys are okay today." I said, "Well, yeah, we're alright." He said, "Have you noticed anything different on the deck?" I said, "What do you mean?" I looked around and the truck was gone. During the night with the 200 mph winds and big waves, it had broken loose and had gone overboard. The railing was a four-foot-high railing. Six feet from the truck, it didn't even bend the railing. It just popped right out and went into the ocean. We were thankful that we didn't sleep in it that one night, for sure.

Drifted to Formosa

The next day we lost all contact. Our electricity went out. The captain sent me down into the hold to inspect and see what was going on down there. I could see some of the welded seams in the hold of the ship where all the bombs and everything were. There were six inches of gasoline in among all of the bombs, where the gasoline drums had ruptured with all the tossing about and everything. I came up and reported my find. They put out an order: Anyone caught smoking would be shot and thrown overboard. Our Marine captain went over to the ship captain and looked at the order on the bulletin board and he said, "Who's going to do the executing?" The Navy captain and them kind of glanced around at each other. I was standing there and I said, "Well, sir, if you catch anybody smoking, I'll do the honors of executing them. But one thing I would request is that they hang onto the outside of the ship so that we don't have to throw them overboard after they're shot." They all thought I was so terrible. I grinned and said, "You know what? If anybody strikes a match, none of us has to worry about anything. It'll be the end of us all because the vapor is everywhere, the gas fumes are throughout the entire ship."

Finally, the wind died down, and everything was getting back to normal, except we had no control of the ship, no electricity, none of this was going on. They put a flag on the fantail of the ship. The men were begging and crying to smoke. I never smoked, so I didn't know how much they were really hooked on cigarettes. But anyway, this flag – whenever the flag was going over the ship the opposite direction, they'd put a big plank on the fantail and put some heavy chains on one end of it. It was about 18 feet long and it stuck out there. The men all lined up and they were allowed to smoke one cigarette out at the end of this plank whenever the flag was going to show that the wind was coming from off and blowing the fumes and stuff in the other direction from where they were smoking.

The very first man that slid out on the plank – he got on the end of the plank and he was wiggling around there trying to get his matches and trying to get everything straightened up and he fell off the plank into the ocean. We had no lifeboats and we never thought about tying the guy or putting a rope on him in case he fell. As soon as he hit the water, he was about 20 feet or so from the ship and there was nothing we could do except watch him go out of sight. They immediately gave up letting the men smoke in that condition.

Arrived in China

The seventh day it got calmer and we got up on the bow or whatever of the ship—sometimes it was drifting with the fantail—it was just like a log in the China Sea and there was no way of controlling it. We saw (we couldn't figure out what it was at first) what looked like a little island or something. It turned out it was a whole pod of big whales sleeping on top of the water. We almost bumped into them with the ship because we made no noise. They all just swam off, finally, when they saw the ship. Then, all of a sudden, we saw some mines in the water. We thought, "Oh, no!" The saw one that wasn't even 50 yards from the ship. We got up in the turret. We decided to see if we could see any on a lookout. We had field glasses and stuff; we looked for them. We saw some that we might drift into and we shot at and exploded them. When night came, we didn't have any idea that we had gone through a minefield. Anyway, we drifted clear down to the island: it was Formosa then. A repair ship happened to be there and a repair ship started working right away on the LST. We had to get all of these supplies up there, too. They pumped all of the gasoline out and got everything straightened up in the hold. When we started off again, we were headed for Tsingtao, China on the Shandong Peninsula in the China Sea.

Dann as Head of Shore Patrol, Tsingtao, China. (Dec. 1945)

We finally landed in Tsingtao on November 5, 1945. The airbase was about seven to eight miles from downtown Tsingtao. We had to take all our gear, all our stuff, to the airbase where we were going to stay. The next day, an aircraft carrier brought our planes and they all started arriving: dive bombers, torpedo bombers, and fighters for the airbase were all coming in. The reason that we went to North China was to take back all the Japanese military, and all the Japanese civilians. Japan had conquered the northern part of China years before. Some of these families had already been settled there for years. We took all of them, even the Japanese citizens that were in China. We took them all back to Sasebo, Japan (a big port in the Nagasaki district). After we got all settled down in the airbase there in Tsingtao, I was put in charge of the shore patrol in downtown Tsingtao. It was really unbelievable! Our dollar was up to 4500 to 1 of the Chinese dollars. So you can imagine what the prices of everything were. A dollar was just like having a $1000 bill here almost. You could get all kinds of things. In fact, we had to go check out all the houses of prostitution with the medical officers. We took the medics into there and found out the brothels had bought the young girls and got certificates from the farmers who had sold their daughters. In our money, it was $15 that bought those young girls who later would be prostitutes.

Disarming Communists

The northern boundary of the base was a 10-foot wall that divided Nationalist and Communist China. I got tired of going through the town and I got interested in the Communist side of the wall. I started going over the wall to this town called Song Tou. It was a Communist area. I had no problems. I met people, met soldiers. Everything was fine. I traded with them and all of this. I came back over the wall again. Then I made a mistake: my friend Gil that I usually went on liberty with and everything wanted to go with me, so I took him. When we got there. I guess one Marine never seemed to bother them wandering around and stuff, but two Marines suddenly raised concerns. Two Chinese Communist soldiers pulled their Lugers out of their wooden holsters and were going to arrest us. We were in the hallway of a building when they done this and I told Gil, I said, "I'm going to take the one closest to me, you take the other one. Let's see if we can disarm them." We did. We disarmed both of them and we ran out of the place. About halfway back to the base, we saw a big armored vehicle with a machine gun on top coming down the road. They didn't see us quite yet, I don't think. So we ran and there were two trees, the only two trees in the whole place, and we knew we could never make it out between all of those buildings. So I climbed one tree and he climbed the other tree. I looked over at Gil and his tree was shaking. I said, "Sit still! Sit still! Your tree is shaking!" He said, "I can't help it! I can't help it!" Anyway, they turned around and went out of there. I thought for sure they might strike those trees or something, but they didn't. When they left, we jumped out of those trees and ran just as fast as we could and we got over the wall. That was the last time I ever went over to that place.

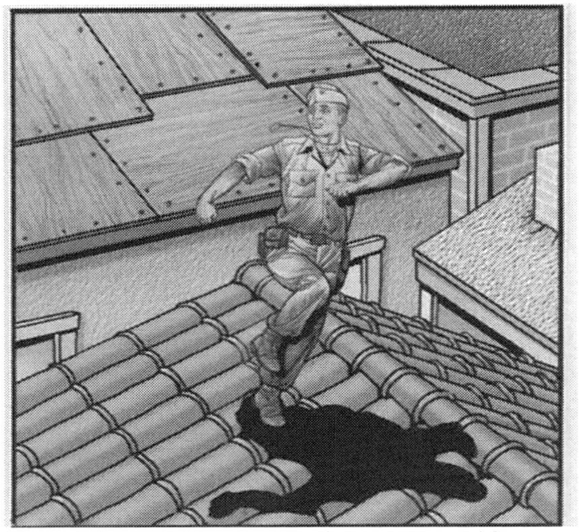

Dann sometimes ran across rooftops to get to and from communist parts of China. (Art ©2010 Jack T. Chick LLC)

The Warehouse Fire

The next couple nights, there were two Chinese Communist soldiers that were stealing stuff out of our warehouse. The guard saw them (they weren't armed or nothing), and he shot and killed both of them. They took their bodies down to our northern gate there and laid them there for the communists to pick up. It wasn't but a week after that and the communists set our warehouse on fire. We had no heat in our barracks and this was winter. It got down to 10 to 20 degrees in the night. I put a blanket around my shoulders, slipped on my shoes and I told the guys, "I'm going to go up there and see what's with the fire. At least I can get warm there." When we got up there, the whole building was on fire – a two-story building about one-half block long. It had everything we had in there: our clothes and everything else we had was in there. It was a warehouse for storing all kinds of materials that we used. As the seven of us were standing there, an officer came up in a jeep with some other officers. They ordered us to go in there and try to get some of that material out of the building. I stood there and refused. I said, "That's got a tiled roof that's been on fire for long enough that it's going to collapse." He wanted my name and serial number and everything. The other guys started going towards the building and I said, "You're all crazy! It would be better to get brig time than to be dead!" Just about then, the whole building collapsed. It exploded and the roof fell in. It was only a two-story building, wasn't even 10 feet high, maybe eight feet high. I looked at this Marine Corps officer and I said, "Sir, would you be thrilled if you had known that we were in there trying to save some flight jackets, or some carbine rifles, or whatever was in there?" They just drove off. That was a big set back for us because we were supposed to get winter clothing and blankets issued out of there (and other stuff), but we didn't get it.

Time in Tsingtao

Tsingtao was really interesting. I went to town five nights a week for the shore patrol. Then I usually went on liberty downtown. One day, we were uptown and here came a parade. They were all banging pans and playing music and singing. I said, "Boy, they must be going to have a party, or they are celebrating something." When we got there, we found out that it was a funeral. And what they do: they even pay people to mourn. The richer you are, the more mourners you can get to cry at your funeral and do all of this stuff. They bury them differently. They sit them on the ground and build kind of a brick thing around them. They don't put them in the ground. This was what they were going to do.

Dann in China with one of the many orphans (1945).

Another time, we went to town and saw all of these people in a big field. We saw them all gathered around – hundreds and hundreds of Chinese. We went down there. I was on shore patrol that day and me and my buddy went down there to see what was going on. When we got down there, they had two Chinese guys tied to a stake. Every person had this little thing that looked like the tool you would use to pick the meat out of walnut shells. That's what it looked like exactly. They would line up and each one would go by and they would prick the men tied there to the stake somewhere. They called it the "Death of a Thousand Knives." Some Nationalist officers came over there to where we were and one of them could speak English. I said, "I think I'll go over there and shoot both of those guys." The Chinese officer said, "You do and you'll be taking their place. This has gone on for a year. They deserve what they're doing to them." Anyway, it was quite an ordeal. I found out the spectators all had little scarves. Every time they joined one of these events, they sewed a little red thing on the khaki scarf showing they had participated in the death of a thousand knives.

Return to States

On a real foggy day, I was in the operations office when they received a call that they needed six dive bombers for an air show in Peking to perform at a planned air show. The operation officer said it was not possible because a heavy fog had settled in and you can't see at all, but the higher ranking officer said once they take off and get above the fog, it would be okay. So being overruled, the six SBD4s took off not far from our base, but they all crashed into a mountain in communist China. They all died and we had a problem to get the bodies out. We got permission to retrieve the bodies, but not the remains of the aircraft. They had picked up most the parts for examination and copying. Later, someone got a clipping out of the newspaper that talked about the 12 Marines who had been killed in a crash in China, but it didn't mention anything about the missing half dozen Douglas SBD dive bombers.

Six SBD4s were flown straight into the fog covered mountain. (Art ©2010 Jack T. Chick LLC)

I got a notice that I was on the list to fly back to the states. I didn't want to go back. I had vowed earlier when I went into the Marine Corps that I'd never come back, but I actually thought it would be because I would be killed by the Japanese or whatever. Anyway, I missed the plane. I didn't show up. I got into quite a bit of trouble. I had a worthless excuse as to why I missed it. The next time, it wasn't long after that, they had another flight and I missed that one. During this time, they had a big inspection. It was two generals and an admiral came to inspect the whole base. We were in the mess hall listing our grievances. Everybody had all kinds of problems: men were getting sent back home ahead of others who had more seniority and stuff like that. A lot of things were going on around there that shouldn't be happening. So the officers, the generals and the admiral decided to stay and take anybody's complaints. During this time, there was a lot of tension around there and I found out when I came back to the barracks—they told me to get my stuff together. Another plane was leaving for Okinawa with 22 men and I was going to be taken down there under guard so they would be sure that I was on the plane.

Dann dodges his ride home. (Art ©2010 Jack T. Chick LLC)

When we got down to the airfield, everybody was lined up there, mulling around. They had the ramp down to load the plane and everything all ready. I saw this Sergeant; everybody liked him and I had known him since the Philippines. I said, "I didn't see your name on the list." He said, "I'm not on the list. I'm just here in case somebody doesn't show up. I'll be the next one that can go." And I said, "You mean to tell me that if someone doesn't show up, you can go?" He said, "Yeah!" I kind of looked over there at these guards that were supposed to be guarding me. They didn't have me handcuffed or anything. They were standing over there just shooting the breeze. I looked at him and said, "What's it worth to you if I disappear?" He said, "50 bucks?" I said, "Suit yourself; whatever you say." He gave me 50 bucks and they started to get on the plane, and everybody mulling around, and I ducked down and went under the ramp where they were loading the aircraft and I went under the belly of the plane. I ran just as fast as I could and zig-zagged through all the planes that were parked on the airstrip. I got clear off and away and hid until the plane took off.

When Dann returned to the barracks, they thought he was dead.
(Art ©2010 Jack T. Chick LLC)

Well, I thought maybe I better, while I'm at it, visit town. So I went to town and when I came back to the base, everybody was absolutely all shook up. I walked in my barracks and the guys said, "What's this? You're supposed to be dead!" Then they found out that this sergeant had taken my place before the take off and crash. They had hit a downdraft and crashed into the cliffs and killed all 22 men aboard the plane. Everybody was mad at me because they loved that guy. The next morning, when they found out that I missed that plane also, they didn't get that excited because they already had orders that the whole squadron and the entire base had to leave within 30 days (all personnel).

We went aboard the *USS General Randall* that was headed for San Diego 11,000 miles away. The *General Randall* was an enormous big ship. We were all assigned—we had chow all hours, day and night, because there were so many men. They had an order on the board: anyone that wanted to get circumcised would be relieved of duty from working. I think there were three hundred and some men who went down to get circumcised. We could tell the ones who got circumcised by the way they walked, and it made us mad that they got out of the work detail. We would come up behind them and get hold of the bottoms of their pants and we would pull their pants up and say, "How are you doing today?" and they would just about pass out or scream. I was lucky enough, being that I'd had the experience in the guard detachment, that I was put on the guard duty on the ship. The ship took almost 26 days to get to San Diego.

Discharged

It finally made it to San Diego. We had trucks, and buses, and stuff to take up to Miramar where most of us would be discharged. At Miramar, we only stayed there about three weeks. Anybody who wanted to have some kind of disability that they thought they had in the service, they had put on the board that they might be delayed 30 to 60 days, if they claimed a disability in the service. So most of the guys had a lot of things wrong and different things. I had some things, but it wasn't really related to the military that happened to me, like freezing in my sinuses. I had completely froze them and other things. But anyway, I got lined up for my discharge. When they handed it to me, it looked different from the others. I looked at it and it said, "other than honorable conditions" and I blew up. They said it was because the brig time that I had done was all hard labor. They should not ever have counted that against me – because I did the hard labor. An officer came over and asked me to step aside. He said, "I'll tell you what. You write to the Marine Corps Institute and tell them your story. I'm positive that they will give you an honorable discharge." I wrote that letter and he was right. I did eventually get an honorable discharge from the Marine Corps.

Dann gets discharged, but his joy turns to anger when he reads it and realizes that his papers were different from the others. (Art ©2010 Jack T. Chick LLC)

When I left Miramar, I went up to see my uncle who had the drugstore in San Dimas. He had a liquor license, since he had beer and all that. They drank a lot. He and my aunt drank every night. I didn't want to stay in the house and he had a good-sized chicken house out back left from the previous owners. I spent a couple days cleaning it all out and everything. I had bought home a bunch of shelter halves (camouflaged canvas tarps) and different things and I made it into a little place to stay. I had it fixed up with all my pictures and all my souvenirs on the wall and everything. Then I went out – I had always wanted a motorcycle again – and I went out and bought a 1945 Harley Davidson. There was enough space to slip between the wall and the house. I could drive my motorcycle right into the backyard up to the door of the chicken house and I could come and go without bothering anybody that much.

Outlaws Motorcycle Club

There weren't many men that had motorcycles at that time. It was 1946 after I was discharged. I would go out at night to the barn dances and the bars. In the daytime, I finally found some more motorcycle guys and they wanted to start a club. We were into hill climbing, so we started a motorcycle club and called it the "Outlaws." This was really different because at the time there wasn't hardly anybody that had motorcycles, except the police officers. I would go up to the mountains and I'd go down to the beach and I'd go to the desert. I'd just go everywhere. I had signed up for what they called the 52/20 club. Instead of giving you $1,000, the military gave you $20 a week for 52 weeks ($1,040.00). Between the six of us in the club, we had different days we got our $20, which kept us all going, because we would loan each other money. We thought we were milking the military out of an extra $40 with that deal, but we were wrong. Because it wasn't too long until one of the club members got killed on his motorcycle. A few weeks after that, another one got killed. The military was keeping all the remainder of the $1,040, so they were milking us. By the end of the 52 weeks, I was the only one not killed! I'd had a pretty bad accident, but at least I was still alive.

Dann, a year after discharge (1948). Scruffy, and riding a motorcycle, getting a job was tough. Thousands of other men were also back from the war looking for work. Then he heard about the Kellogg ranch, and he was soon back in the saddle.

Meeting Esther

It was at this time I met Esther Tieken, my wife-to-be. I didn't know that at the time, though. She liked my motorcycle and liked to go everywhere with me. We had a lot of fun. We went all over the place together.

I got a job on an Arabian horse ranch near us in San Dimas. It was in Pomona. Mr. Kellogg (of Kellogg's cereal fame) started this Arabian horse ranch and they had a little house between the two colleges: Mount San Antonio and it wasn't Cal Poly yet. There was a little house there. It had no utilities but water. They said I could rent that house at $10 a month, but they never did collect the $10 because I did a lot of things back there to help out the ranch. Anyway, I went down to see Esther one day and she said she wasn't going to go with me anymore. I said, "Why's that?" She said, "I'm going to get married." I said, "Oh, okay." I was so dumb. She didn't even have a chance to know anybody else because I was there around her all the time. I turned my motorcycle around after four blocks and I came back. She came out of the house, and I said, "You know, if you're going to get married, I'd like to marry you." She said, "You would?" I said, "Yeah!"

Dann and Esther get married in Las Vegas. (Art ©2010 Jack T. Chick LLC)

I bought a 1933 four-door Ford and we went to Las Vegas and got married there and came back and I took her out to the ranch. All we had was an old table and we sat on orange crate boxes to eat. We had a bedroom set that Esther had bought. We hauled it out there. Different ones on the ranch would give us things. It was pretty funny. We had to open seven gates to get out to the ranch between the pastures and everything. Esther still was working for a lemon packing house. She would take the car to work and I had the motorcycle. There was no sign of anyone else in sight. We lived in kind of a little miniature canyon between the hills; we couldn't see lights of anybody from everywhere. We had about one-fourth of an acre fenced off with the house and the barn and garage and sheds, and all brood mares were always hanging around the fence there. It was really picturesque. I started raising wild geese and ducks as well.

When the Cash Came Rolling In

While at work at the Kellogg Ranch, I did all kinds of jobs. Whenever anyone needed help in a different department, I was often called on to help them. One of my regular jobs was to irrigate the alfalfa on the lower part of the ranch. It had to be flooded between brims. One really foggy morning, I was working on a ditch, and I heard a loud crash from the nearby highway. I took my shovel and went over to see what was going on. I came across an accident scene. An armored Brinks truck was rolled over on its back in the field. It had come through the fence into the flooded alfalfa field, rolled over, and the rear door was busted wide open. Bags of money were strewn all about. As I looked on in wonder, a voice from behind me says, "That's close enough, now drop that shovel!"

I dropped the tool and slowly turned around to see a guard aiming a gun straight at me. The two other guards in the truck were knocked out, but the third one was thrown out with the money. He revived after I passed him, got up and drew his weapon. I explained that I had a Jeep and I could go get help (an offer he quickly accepted). But I confess, when I first saw all those bags of money, I was tempted to dig a hole, bury a bag, and tell the authorities I saw a man run off with a bag toward the highway. I'm thankful now that the guard prevented me from doing that. It would have been stealing, but at the time, I still drank a lot and did stupid things.

As it was, the wreckers came and flipped the truck back on its wheels. They loaded up the bags, and revived the two other guards. They all drove off after thanking me for helping them.

They say money doesn't grow on trees, but that foggy morning, it sure looked like it grew in alfalfa fields!

California Game Breeders

I joined the California Game Breeders Association. It was a lot of fun. It met in Pasadena every month. Walter Brennan and quite a few other people joined. I was already starting to raise plants and do all kinds of other things. I was trading stuff: we'd trade for eggs or we'd trade for ducks. I finally ended up with wood ducks and about ten other varieties of wild ducks and had Canadian honkers and geese, plus fifty-some peacocks, and pheasants and quail. You name it—we had foxes—I spent a lot of my time with them. Mr. Kellogg himself got so interested and when he came out to the ranch, he found out about my little thing. (I had my deer that I was raising and other animals down in the rose garden.) The Kellogg Foundation had a bird sanctuary in Michigan somewhere and he told me that he was going to try to build a bird sanctuary down there where I had all of my stuff by the rose garden. They would give me all the excess birds and stuff from there.

When Mr. Kellogg would come to the ranch, everybody was on the alert. He would just drive back with his chauffeur and his nurse, and he would drive back to see us and he would visit with us for a long time and then he'd just leave. He didn't like the manner in which they were handling the ranch or the way they were doing the Arabian horses that he'd started bringing in from the Middle East and elsewhere. He brought these real beautiful Arabians. He didn't like the way they were treating them. The manager of the ranch, after he had done this about three times, saw me one day and he said, "Why does Mr. Kellogg come over to see you all the time instead of over here? Why does he do that?" I replied, "Because he likes me!" That was a good definition, anyway. Mr. Kellogg was slowly going blind then. Different things happened. The ranch was changing hands and all of this was going on.

On one of my days moonlighting, I met Marlon Brando while landscaping in Hollywood. I mentioned that I worked on the Kellogg Arabian Ranch, and he said he would like to go there sometime. I told him which days I would be there to bathe the Percheron horses, dress them up for the show ring, and put them through their paces with the show wagon. He called and came down to see it. He really loved all the horses and the ranch. He had just finished filming one of his movies, *The Wild One.* No one at the ranch recognized him. He said he was going to Ensenada, Mexico the next weekend and invited me to meet him there. I went and had a good time. We ended up drinking a lot at a nightclub there with some more of his friends.

Marlon Brando (middle) invited Dann (right) for drinks at a nightclub in Mexico after completing *The Wild One* (1954).

I had met another friend of mine that was manager over at the fish and game bird farm in Chino. His name was Mark Halderman. We had a lot of fun together with his wife, Pam. I had these Chukar partridges and I didn't know what to do. They all started laying eggs all over the place. I showed Mark the Chukars and said, "You want those eggs?" And he said yeah, he'd take the eggs and give me something in return for them. That was the actual beginning of the Chukar partridges that the fish and game grew and they got a bunch of them and started releasing them in different areas of the mountains and the deserts and stuff. The population is in the millions now. The original 70 or 80 that they got were from the eggs that I had given them. That was the original bunch of partridges that started the whole thing.

Motorcycle Pains

Sometimes, Esther would visit her folks then come home. I was coming home on my motorcycle and I saw her behind me in the car. I drove ahead of her to open the gates. I'd open the gate, she'd pass through, then I'd pass her and open the next gate. When she came to about the fourth gate, I wasn't anywhere around. She circled back and she saw the headlight of my motorcycle in the orange grove. I had gone around the corner so fast, that I lost control of the motorbike and hit a rock and a couple of trees. I broke both of my hands: one in ten places and the other one in eight places. She went over there and got somebody from the ranch. They took me to the hospital. I had my hands in a big hoop with my fingers all stretched with rubber bands. I stayed that way for almost two months. I couldn't turn a doorknob, I couldn't do any of my things in the bathroom, nothing hardly. I had to depend on others. It was almost like I didn't have any hands at all. Esther would have to open doors and do all of that. I couldn't drive or nothing. It was such an event when I finally got the cast off my hands and they were most pitiful looking, black and blue things you ever saw. I started working in about two weeks. I couldn't turn the key to start a car and I couldn't shift the gears with my hands but I could kind of hold on to stuff when I was working.

Time to Move

After living on the Kellogg Ranch for three years, we found a nice house in a walnut grove next to the Kellogg Ranch farm section. It had two bedrooms and a large bath. We liked it cause there were no more gates to open. Soon after we moved in the house, the owner, Jimmy Biller, harvested the walnuts from a lot of the trees. He told me that I could have any walnuts I could find in this big grove that he had finished harvesting.

One morning, I got up real early to pick some walnuts. I stood outside wondering the best way to do it. This was in 1955 or so. All of a sudden, an earthquake struck and all the trees in the grove shed remaining walnuts like hail in a storm! In two hours, I had two big sacks full. Esther collected three more bags after I left for work. The next day, I got up early to harvest the rest of the walnuts still on the ground. Near the road, I saw some people picking up walnuts also. I hollered to them, and they all ran away, leaving four full sacks behind. I was calling to them to tell 'em to come over where I was, since there were far more there than I could ever gather!

The Buck Stops Here

Dann's favorite buck and bucket destroyer. Circa 1956

We had a pet buck deer. He had pretty big antlers with eight points on each side. I didn't know that much about the time of year when they become aggressive for females and fighting. One day, I went into his pen to feed him, and he attacked me. I had a bucket of grain and I held it up in front of me. His antlers went right through that galvanized bucket! It kind of stunned us both! I dropped the bucket and ran out of his pen. I got Mark to take him and release him somewhere way up in the mountains. So I lost both him *and* the bucket! When I think back at all the times I nearly got killed, the thought of getting done in by a pet deer has to be one of the most embarrassing ways to go!

Off the Wagon

I worked every Saturday and Sunday on the ranch for years. They had nine Percheron horses, French Percherons. On Saturdays, we bathed eight of them and hooked them up to the show wagon with a beautiful brass and leather harness. We took them up to the show ring for the horse show and done all of these different maneuvers in the show ring and everything. They were really beautiful. They weighed anywhere from 1600 to 2200 pounds. The wheel horses were the biggest ones. One of the drivers that came out there on Sundays to drive the horses, he worked for Eastside Beer Distributors delivering beer. He always brought a bunch of quarts of beer out there. We weren't *supposed* to drink while we harnessed the horses or worked them, but I noticed when he climbed up on the wagon, he about fell off of it. Then he made a real tight turn with the horses running fast and the horses all fell over. They all hit the ground. The whole eight of them got all tangled up and fell. We had a heck of a time. We got them all up finally. None of them were hurt. This went on all the time. He'd bring beer out there and that day he really overdone it.

Another thing they had at the ranch – they had horse sales. I would tell some of the people I knew that wanted Arabians about the sales and stuff. They had one horse that I wanted so bad. They wouldn't sell the horse to me. I had to get someone else to buy it. So I got this horseshoer (a farrier) I knew to buy it. It was the first colt horse of Ratez II which was captured from the Germans in Poland and brought over here to the United States by the US Remount. He was there at stud at the Kellogg Ranch at this time. The horseshoer got Ratez and I ended up with him because I got him to buy the horse for me. I saw right away that Ratez was too much of a beautiful blood bay horse for the likes of me. I didn't have the right place to keep him and so I put him up for sale. A man came—MacMillan's in Corona—they owned a whole lot of land and everything. He came and looked at the horse. He wanted it for his daughter. I kind of hesitated and I told him why I was selling the horse. He says, "You want to get in my car and go over to where I'll show you what kind of a place he's got." I got in the car with him and we went over to Corona and down this road to a lavish hillside place. I thought this was a house behind his house. It was a beautiful 24-by-30 stall with all sod in there. It had the most beautiful inside. Then it had a paddock that was about 50-by-40 feet outside with steel fencing. I said, "Sir, you've got yourself a horse." I got a horse trailer and I delivered the horse. About a month later, I read in the paper that a plane had crashed up on San Antonio Mountain. I read and it was Mr. MacMillan, his wife and his daughter. He was taking flying lessons and the instructor told him he could fly solo but not to take anybody with him until he had some more hours. Well, he got so anxious that he took his daughter and his wife and they flew into the mountain and crashed, killing all of them. I never went back over to see what happened to the horse or anything, but that was an awful sad ending for a good beginning.

Finding a Baby... or Two

On weekends, I would work for some of the men on the ranch that was building houses or whatever they were doing. I was taking care of some racehorses for a guy. I was doing anything I could to keep busy and I just got the notion to quit my job and go into business for myself. We bought an acre in San Dimas and I started building a house on it. We moved this old trailer we bought from my landlord, and we moved it on the lot. We lived in there while we started building our house. It took a couple of years to build it. I started landscaping and doing any kind of job – different folks around there would get me to do things for them. As time went by, we finally got the house livable, got rid of the trailer, and we were just kind of coasting along: finishing this and that. One day, out of a clear blue sky, on Mother's Day in 1961, our doctor, Dr. Sellers in San Dimas called. I answered the phone, and he said, "I don't want to talk to you. I want to talk to your wife." We were there playing pool, doing all the things you do, and my wife answered the phone and the doctor said, "Happy Mother's Day, Mother!" My wife said, "Are you drunk?" and he said, "No, I'm not drunk! I just delivered a beautiful baby girl for you." We didn't know this back then, but he had found 1,200 adoption parents for independent adoption of babies. He sure helped a lot of babies that might have otherwise been aborted or abandoned find new, loving families, and he did it in addition to being a doctor. Anyway, he said he was going to come by to take us down there to see it – the baby. I told Esther I had all of these things going on. I had jackasses, and ponies, and horses, and had all of this other stuff. I said, "It's up to you if you want to take on a baby, but I'm not going to have much time for it." Anyway, he came shooting in the driveway and took us down to West Covina Hospital and here was this little baby girl in the incubator: she looked like a doll! She only weighed 4 ½ pounds. My wife kept looking. She looked at me and I said to the doc, "Yeah, but how much is all this going to cost us?" He says, "Well, a dollar down and a dollar a month." I says, "Well, that seems fair." I told Esther, "It's up to you like I said..." She said, "I want her!" So I says, "Okay."

About a week later, they said we couldn't take her until she weighed five pounds. But Dr. Sellers told them in the hospital, he says this guy raises things from babies, all kinds of stuff, and he knows. She was just a little under five pounds. He said, "I'm going to sign her out. You can come and take her home." I named her Dianna Lynn and I was the one most in charge except for the diapers and stuff. I watched her so close. One day, I came in from work and she had her girl friends there handing Dianna back and forth. The doctor had said don't let anybody around her for a month at least, just you folks. It hadn't been a month yet. I picked up the phone and I called Dr. Sellers and I said, "Should anybody be handling this baby besides my wife and I?" He said, "Absolutely not!" I said, "Thank you," and I just took Dianna out and took her back to her little crib. I always said I watched over her like a mama wolf with pups.

Dann with Dianna (one of two adopted daughters).

A lot of times in my working, (back then, I called my nursery *Trader Dann's Nursery and Landscapes*), I would trade a lot of times for stuff they had, for materials or take it off their bill. When I worked for this one man, it was one of the original contractors in California from 1926, Mr. Flint. He liked helping me. I told him I'd knock off half the labor if he helped me. So he did. When I finished the job, he said, "I enjoyed that so much, if you ever want me to help you sometime, I'd gladly help you – whatever you want to pay me." He had a lot of money but he wanted something to do because he was retired. So he helped me. One day, we were working away. He always asked me of the morning, "Anything different? Anything new?" and I'd say, "Nope!" He asked me this one day and I said, "Yeah, can you believe this? Dr. Sellers called and said he had another baby for us. Another girl!" He said, "What did you tell him?" I said, "Oh, no, we can't—we don't want another baby. But, anyway, thanks." He said, "You know what?" I said, "What?" He said, "You don't want to raise that little girl all by herself. I'll tell you what. I know what to do here. You just go get in your truck. Go down there and get your wife and go down there and get that baby."

So I talked to Esther and we decided to just go look. We decided to talk to the doctor and we ended up bringing the little girl home. I named her Pamela Jean. You know that was something else. Here we had two girls already and we had just gotten started good and the first thing we knew I had our house just about finished. Everything seemed to be changing and taking place, and all of a sudden the school district in the city wanted our place for a school site. We wouldn't sell to them because I just had gotten finished and got started with our family. So they took it using "eminent domain", which is what they call it when they condemn your property whether you agree to sell it or not. There's a saying that goes, "you can't fight City Hall", and sure enough, we tried to fight it but lost in court. They gave us so long to move out of there. We bought a place two blocks away and I moved most of the stuff from the old new place to the *new* new place. I was working for myself, we had two new kids, and suddenly a new house—So much had changed! But the biggest change was yet to come.

Met Chick and Saved in a Beer Joint

Dann attended a public appearance by Jack T. Chick giving a Gospel presentation. (Art ©2010 Jack T. Chick LLC)

We started taking the girls to Sunday School, but we didn't go to church. I still was drinking a lot and it was getting out of hand. I figured I didn't want to be the kind of dad that I'd had with these young girls. So I read in the paper that an artist was coming to a church in Pomona to give an art demonstration and to give his testimony and speak. So I got under conviction to just go. I got all dressed up and my wife looked at me and said, "Are you going to the bars already?" I said, "No, I'm going to church." She said, "Well, that's good." So anyway, I went to church. This man had the most beautiful set-up there – drawing as he preached. His name was Jack Chick. As he talked, I realized that was what I needed to do, to change my life and now.

Dann gets "saved" in a bar. (Art ©2010 Jack T. Chick LLC)

When I left the church, I hadn't made any kind of commitment or whatever you want to call it to know the Lord or anything. I just left. I knew all about what needed to be done. I thought that while I was all dressed up, I should visit my favorite beer joint, since they never had seen me well dressed. So I went up to this beer tavern, the Woodshed, and I ordered a beer. I sat there and I looked at that bottle of beer. The owner of the tavern said, "You all right? You feel okay?" I said, "Yeah, I'm sick alright, but in the head, I think." He walked off and I looked at that bottle of beer and I said, "Lord, I want to change my life and I know you're the only one who can help me. I want to receive you. Lord, I'm so ashamed of myself and I'm sorry for all the things I've done. I want to start a new life with you. When I look at this bottle of beer in front of me, I think that's all I am—a container for beer, Lord, and with your help I know I can do it. Lord, I want you to come in my heart, be my Lord and my Savior and my director."

I left the tavern and I went back and I told my wife, "From now on we're going to church with the girls, but we're going to change to this Central Baptist Church here in Pomona.

We started going to the church and I enrolled the girls in a Christian school that the church had. We started going regularly and as time passed by, we got more interested in the things of the Lord.

Started The Tract Ministry

An evangelist came to the church and he gave a talk – a speech – about all the different ways a person can witness for the Lord and all this. I got so interested in the tract ministry and stuff. I talked to him afterwards and he encouraged me more. I went in the church office and they had (generic types filled with text) tracts in Spanish and English and I asked for a hundred of each one. I started giving them out regularly wherever I went. I started putting them on cars (under the wipers). The next week I got more until I got 500 of each and took them to all the shopping centers. I was giving them out and I was really excited about this new way to give out Christian literature with the little gospel tracts. I was really on fire.

Dann starts his tract ministry. (Art ©2010 Jack T. Chick LLC)

Esther and I met some new friends at the church and he had one daughter, named Karen, who was the same age as Dianna. She saw that I liked the little tracts and she said, "I got some tracts I bet you'd like." She had a shoebox of Chick Tracts – all different kinds; different titles, colors and everything. It really attracted me. I thought, "Boy, this is what I really love and like." I started going to the Christian bookstores that had them and I'd buy all I could get. These were much better because they had cartoons that caught your eye, and made you interested in reading them. There was one store that had a big display sign saying "Chick Publications" and I suddenly remembered Chick was also the name of that guy who I first went to hear his testimony (Jack Chick), the artist who drew as he spoke. He was the one that was actually responsible for me, in a way, coming to really know the Lord in a personal way. I asked if he was the same artist who actually drew the tracts and was told he was. I couldn't believe the coincidence, because his tracts were by far my favorite to pass out. They had lots of really good cartoons that kept people reading them. I was also amazed that one man was doing so much to lead people to Christ. He had already made a big impact on my faith not once, but twice (and I would have been even more astounded if I knew how he would continue to encourage that faith in the future)!

I started up to Pomona one day and a man was looking at my station wagon. I had scripture on it and such. I started talking to him and he was the preacher of the country church in Ontario. He invited me to come to the church. My wife and I and the girls went next Sunday. At the church, we met Tom Harris (a Hollywood stunt man) and his wife. We liked the Spanish tracts that she gave me, and later on I found out that Chick printed them in dozens of other languages. I was so grateful to get these because I see a lot of people out here in Southern California who are from the Philippines and China and different places all over, and France and Germany. It was really a joy. I started giving out the foreign tracts, too.

One day I went into Pomona to give my testimony for a short time at a Christian radio station, and when I left the station, the man just before me was Pastor Cass Schribe of the Country Church in Ontario. And he followed me out to my station wagon and he talked to me and invited me to come to the church. It was such a beautiful little church; it was originally a chicken house. The man started the church in his chicken house. He cleaned it all out and everything, and then, later on, they built this Country Church. Well, I enjoyed the services and my family did, too, so we started attending.

Sent to Prison Ministry

While attending that church, I met a chaplain that was in the prison system in Chino as a volunteer chaplain. He also was a Hollywood stunt man and a very interesting person. His name was Tom Harris—the same Tom I mentioned earlier. Eventually, he asked me if I would like to go in the prison with him sometime to see if I would consider being a volunteer chaplain also, like him. Well, it wasn't long after that when I did go in the penitentiary with him, and I just thought *Oh, Lord, this is the place for me!* I really loved it; all those men everywhere in need of Christ, and everyone that knew me said, "Oh, yeah, you've got a captive audience, you sure would enjoy that." I just looked in the eyes of all those sad men and thought that I could be really blessed by going in there to do the Lord's work.

So I went to a meeting and signed some papers, and they placed me 18th on the waiting list to get in there as a volunteer chaplain. Then Tom went in to talk to them on my behalf, and they moved me to the front of the list. About two weeks later I started going in the prison, usually with Tom but sometimes alone. I had free access to go anywhere in the three prison systems I wanted. They had the east side, the west side, and the main building, which they called the Maximum Security Center. That's where most of the inmates were housed that weren't allowed to mingle with the other population. Some chaplains avoided the worst inmates, but I figured if anything, they needed our help more than the others, no matter what they'd done.

Dann ministers to prisoners. (Art ©2010 Jack T. Chick LLC)

I really enjoyed it and I also had services one or two nights a week there from 7 'til 9:00 pm, usually 200 men or so attended those services. Plus, I sponsored groups that came in with music, and they sang and they gave testimonies and tried to deliver the Gospel message to the inmates.

Making Tracts

I kept noticing guys in prison who were former soldiers, bikers, and even cowboys. As helpful as it was to pass out Chick tracts to inmates, I thought it would be even better if I had some that featured the same groups that I had been a part of and so many of the inmates had, too. It might also help them realize how similar they were to me, and how God could improve their lives, like he did mine. After all, I wasn't no better than they were for most of my life. I even served my own time behind bars (in the brig). So I got it in my mind to draw some of my own tracts with stories along those lines, or other things that would be of particular interest for prisoners. I'm not a good artist like Chick is, but I saw how much they enjoyed having pictures and cartoons with the tracts they read, so I decided to copy the Chick tract layout. It was a lot harder than I thought, and took a good deal of time and work, but I'm glad I done it. They came in real handy when some Catholic complained about a Chick tract about the Vatican, and after that one complaint, the prisons I served basically banned ***all*** tracts from Chick Publications, even the ones that had nothing to do with Catholics. But I was still able to pass out my own tracts in there.

Dann started making and distributing his own tracts. (Art ©2010 Jack T. Chick LLC)

I wrote one about an outlaw motorcycle gang entitled *Biker's Last Weekend,* plus another about the future where killers get to pick their own execution *(Choice of Execution),* and one about a cowboy who gets injured really bad but then gets saved *(Cowboy's Last Round-up).* I did one about my life as a cowboy and Marine and all the troubles I had growing up *(Long Way to the Son),* and even one about a homosexual sent to prison for prostitution who finds Jesus and gets saved *(From Carl to Carla to Christ).* That one was drawn by a gay inmate named Rob who found The Lord and became straight. Rob drew several of them (signed R.S.L.) while in prison, and I drew the rest. I also drew a native-American version of *This Was Your Life* (with Chick's permission) to reach my Indian friends. There were 15 or 20 different ones all told. I had them printed using a regular press, with printing plates and everything, usually 1,000 of them at a time. Then I'd hand staple them about a hundred at a time. I wish I kept samples of all of them, but some I completely gave out. It sure made me realize all the work Jack Chick goes through to write and draw so many. I hear he's drawn over 250 different stories, and he's still adding more.

A Cowboy Reunion

The Country Church found out that I was going to the union rescue mission downtown with Cass Schribe and Tom Harris. There was usually from 200 to 250 men there. They had to listen to a sermon before they could go in to eat, and we had these services. So Pastor Cass – I told them down there at the rescue mission about my preacher, and they set up a time period that we could go down there to the union rescue mission and talk to the men. Well, Cass also sang and he was also a Marine like me. He had an inspiring testimony about his life, but more than that, he had really scriptural messages to preach to the men.

The rescue mission used to take men right off of the street, the poor old souls, they'd find them sleeping behind dumpsters or in old cars or under bridges, they'd find 'em just about anywhere, hundreds and hundreds of homeless people all around downtown, and they would take 'em in there. They had volunteer doctors, eye-doctors, dentists, and all kinds of volunteer people, and they would take the person and provide a nice shower and shave if they wanted it. They would also give 'em all clean clothes and stuff. They had rooms there for some of 'em, and even gave some of 'em jobs to work there.

What was pretty funny was one time I come home and I told my wife, "I got so many cowboy shirts and stuff that I can't even wear anymore. I'm gonna take 'em down to the rescue mission." (She bought me cowboy shirts all the time from the thrift shops around here.) So I picked out about 30 or more shirts and other things, and I took 'em down there the next time that we had the services, and I left them where they had the clothes. Well, about three or four weeks later, I had the services there again, so I went down there and when I got up to the pulpit, I almost burst out; I couldn't believe it, there were so many of the men sitting there with my shirts on, they looked like a cowboy reunion! But I praised God that I was able to do this, and it's what everybody should do when they got extra stuff, to try to help others in a worse situation.

We went down quite a few times in the afternoon services. We never had evening services. But about that time I met another volunteer chaplain. His name was Marlin Baker. He was in Mexico with his wife for years and years being a missionary south of the border. They both spoke real fluent Spanish. He was with another missionary couple in Mexico, but his preaching partner (the husband) died, leaving his widow behind, and so did Marlin's wife, making Marlin a widower. I used to tell him, "I'm praying for you. You're such a nice gentleman and such a good person and everything. I'm praying for you to get a wife," and he says, "Well, I'm not quite ready for that." But not long after that I went to the prison, and he comes up to me smiling, and he says, "You're going to be surprised... one of your prayers got answered!" I ask, "which one?" And he said he married his friend's (widowed) wife Shirley. And that was so wonderful, because they were long time friends, and then to know that he remarried someone so special.

Losing Esther

One of the hardest parts about getting old is the fear of death. Not my own death, but the death of others I love. I've had so many brushes with death, I think that the only reason I'm still alive is because the Lord wants me to witness for him. But that means I've had to watch so many of my good friends leave before me. Of all my dearest friends, the most painful one to lose was my wife of 66 years, Esther. She died October 20th, 2010. She put up with me for so many years while I was a drunk, and good for nothing, and I'm thankful she lived long enough to see me get saved and return her love and devotion. She was always supportive of my ministry, too. Although she is gone now, I know she is happy in the arms of the Lord, and I look forward to seeing her again when my turn arrives. Now, when I witness to couples, I often remind men how important their wives are and to show them how they feel while they are still alive, because nobody lives forever, so tell them while you can.

Dann lost his wife of 66 years in 2010.

Other Family Members

My father died in a Veteran's Hospital in Long Beach, Ca, in 1961. He died from throat and lung cancer. He was a chain smoker and alcoholic. I would go down to visit him, and once, while I was there, a Veteran support group came by and gave everyone in the ward (who were all dying from lung related cancers) a carton of Camel cigarettes! He had lived with us in a separate little house (along with his cat) before he got too sick. Before that, he would come a lot for Sunday dinner. He didn't see John Roy too much except to send money to get him out on bail. John Roy served time in three different prisons, mostly on drug related crimes and stolen cars.

John Roy never did give up his drugs, drinking, or going to jail. He died in 1975. There were just two people at his funeral besides my wife and myself. His common law wife, Reba, came up to me after the service and said he was murdered. All I could say was, "It's a lucky thing I didn't kill him." It wasn't a nice thing to say at a funeral, but we fought so much and he threatened my life so many times, it was the honest truth. He once even tried to run me down on my motorcycle. I ended up giving him my burial spot, since my body is being donated *to Loma Linda* hospital upon my death.

My mother got a divorce after she left us, and then remarried within a couple of years to a fellow named Mr. Kimberly, who was a big shot in the railroad business. He had a good job, but my mother spent all his money as fast as he earned it. She ended up with a free pass to go anywhere on the trains for life. She came out to see Esther and me after we got married when we lived on Kellogg's Arabian Horse Ranch in Pomona, Ca. She had become a Christian, at least she said he had, but back then, I wasn't one myself. She didn't stay very long. She acted nice but we never felt close. She never apologized or discussed any of the things she did when she abandoned us.

Dann recalls his mom taking off without the kids—but with everything else. (Art ©2010 Jack T. Chick LLC)

I went to see her again six or seven years later in Nebraska. I stayed there almost a week but ran out of money. I asked her if I could borrow $20 to get back home, but she said, "How do I know you'll ever pay me back?" I had to offer to loan her my gold wedding band before she gave me the money. This, after never paying a dime to any of the people who took care of us all those years, even after she was remarried and had money to help. She just put us out of her mind. She even left all the family photos when she left home. Not the bank account, not the silverware, nor the paintings, or the car, but she left all the family photos.

She died in the 1970s when she was in her 80s. John Roy never bothered to go see her after she left him at age seven.

The Thorn in the Flesh

I went in the prison a lot with Marlin. He was wounded in Korea. He had stepped on a landmine, but he was so humble and sincere, that the men just loved him. I always liked it when I could go with him. About that time, I had such trouble walking 'cause I had a lot of bad accidents with horses and motorcycles and such, that I could barely walk anymore, so I went in and made an appointment and I found out I had to have hip surgery. They gave me a total hip replacement on my left leg. It wasn't long before I could go back into the prison. I was laid up for about six weeks, and during that time I had saved a lot of stuff that I could distribute to the men that we were allowed to give materials to. Well, a little bit after that, I had problems and the doctor I had at that time. He said, "You lift a lot of weights, and that's why you have blood in your stool, you have inner hemorrhoids or something." Over time, it got worse and worse, and I finally went in, and they gave me lots of painful tests, and they found out I had a big malignant tumor in the rectum. So I had to have that all taken care of. They removed my whole back end and sewed me shut back there, and I was presented with a pouch that hangs out my abdomen. If I had of been tested and checked before, I might not have had to go through all this, but I accept it beyond measure because I would have died otherwise, I believe, and I call it my thorn in the flesh.

I had been corresponding with a real nice lady missionary. She had a big ranch in the Mexican Sierras below Douglas, Arizona. Her name was Alice Valenzuela and this big ranch had been in her husband's family for years, and they had a chance to expand it (to over 100,000 acres), but all this time I had been writing to her and sending her Gospel tracts, and she was supporting me some. So I decided I wanted to go down and see her. I went all the way down to Douglas, Arizona and met her, and she took me out to the ranch below Agua Prieta, Mexico, way out in the mountains, beyond any known civilization around there, and the ranch was over 160, or 170 years old, older some of the parts of it. It was just beautiful up there in the mountains, but I didn't stay very long because I had these medical problems and stuff, but I did take her a lot of literature. She would go to all the small villages and try to help the young Mexican women that were pregnant; she had Bible studies and classes. She taught them how to do all kinds of things at home, and she was the most remarkable lady I ever saw. It was quite an experience.

Soon after that trip, I could hardly stand on my other leg (my right leg). So I had another total hip replacement done on that leg. All this time I still collected Chick tracts that I could send to prisons, and send to Marlin. Marlin had moved to Texas, and he had a full-time prison ministry there. You wouldn't believe how this man and his wife and group worked at it. They'd go into jails, prisons, correctional places, had Bible studies and everything, all around Dallas; they go in all these places. God gave me the privilege and honor to be able to support him with Chick tracts through all that time. It's been almost twenty years that I've known Marlin and helped him, and he's still into this, but now he's supported by a missionary group in Long Beach. What a great man.

I met another family that I knew the mother and father years ago. I met them at the Christian businessmen's breakfasts and lunches and stuff, and this family – Paul Miller and his wife, Rebecca – they both speak Spanish real well. They go down into Mexico to two or three towns, and they have a loudspeaker on the back of their truck and they drive around and advertise their services there. They also go on the streets where they live in Hemet with their children and they witness to people on the street and give out tracts. God has allowed me to support them all these years, too, with tracts and other kinds of literature and Bibles. So I keep the post office pretty busy (thank goodness for book rate)!

The Swap Meets

Dann (at left) giving out free tracts in different languages at the Union Rescue Mission on Main Street, Los Angeles, CA.

On weekends, I used to rent spaces at the swap meet near me, and I'd take all my tracts and line them on the table in rows, one after another. People would file by all day long for six or seven hours, and scan all the tables for anything that interested them. I usually had plants for sale and other stuff on my table, but the main attraction was the free tracts. I had 'em in 20 languages at that time (but now Chick prints over 100 different languages). I was getting very involved with the prison ministry back then, so I was real interested when a lady came to me and said she saw a couple at the other end of the swap meet that was always witnessing. They come from El Salvador. I quickly walked to the other end and found them. They sold jewelry. I talked to them and asked them if they would like some of the literature that I had. This was around 2004. And they just went wild over Jack Chick's tracts in Spanish – he had about 40 Spanish tracts, plus comics and books. So the next time I went over there, I said, "You know what? I'm gonna give up my space here in the swap meet, and I'm gonna start giving you guys my tracts." Well, all these years, 10 years, they faithfully go there any time they can, Saturday *and* Sunday, and two other days every week. I'm able to furnish them the tracts, and they also are one of the few that give me donations. So it works out well for both of us. I just think they're a great couple, and so dedicated to the Lord, and so knowledgeable in His Word.

Funeral Friends

Back when Esther was still alive, there were friends of ours that we always went out to eat with, and we seen 'em here and there all the time, and the man drove a bus for people that were crippled and stuff like that. And he had a terrible accident. They think he had a heart attack, but they never did find out for sure. But he ran into a big telephone pole down on the corner with a bus full of them little kids in their wheelchairs and stuff, and it killed him. His wife was listening to the news, and they even mentioned his name, Everett Brady, as killed in the accident. I think that's when she kinda had a stroke or something. But anyway, they had the funeral services, and I gave the eulogy for Everett. I told them how Everett was one of the very few people that wasn't ashamed to be around me. Many people avoid being around me because I often stop talking to them when someone else comes by that needs witnessing. If we went out to eat, I'd witness to the waitresses and the bus boys and what not. It embarrassed people I knew. So most people didn't really care to be around me, but I said, "Everett always did enjoy, no matter what, being with me," and I gave the eulogy.

Well, it wasn't long after that that Marge, his surviving wife, also died. And when I gave the eulogy at her funeral, I mentioned how vital friends were, because as I looked out at the people in the audience, I didn't see anyone that was a regular visitor. Certainly not her two sons or her daughter, they never came by to see her. I mentioned that even in my own life, when things got so bad, and I was so down-trodden as a young person, and set out on a life of destruction, trying to hang myself at nine, or much later, as an adult, expecting the Marine Corps to finish me off, or to die on a speeding motorcycle, during all those times, I still felt friends were one of the best things I had to keep me going. I said, just like Marge lying there in her casket, "My recently passed wife has already found another friend, because she knew and cared about Marge, too." Then I said, "Even when no one else seems to care about you, a friend will sometimes stick closer to you than a brother."

I mentioned at both funerals how beautiful it was to know the Lord as your personal savior and to try to live the Christian life. After the service was over, when we went outside, Marge's grandson Mark came up to me and he was at the funeral of her husband, and he said, "You know, you'll be glad to know after we got back from Granddad's funeral, we decided we oughta start goin' to church." They'd never been in church, and they started going, and they joined a Baptist church down there near San Diego somewhere, and they all got saved and they all got involved in the church, and that made me feel so good to know that someone benefited from what was otherwise a tragedy. I was so thankful that I got involved in giving these eulogies.

A Testimony

One of my favorite places to go in the Chino prison was the day rooms. In there is about 40 to 50 men. One day as I sat at a table with some men, one of the prisoners in there came over to our table and said there was someone in the corner who said if I could tell him where God came from, he would believe in Jesus. I said I would go try to answer his question.

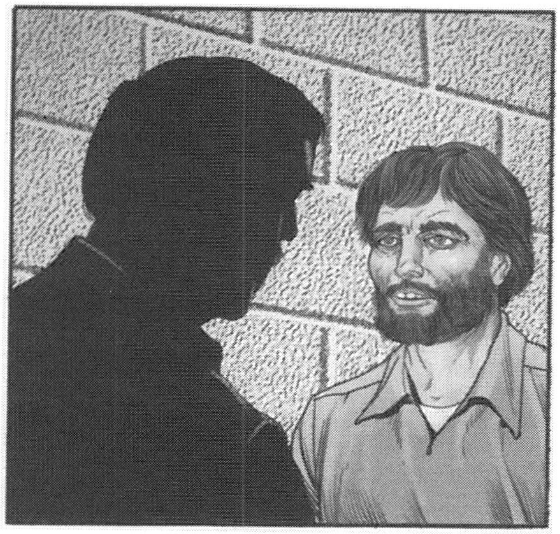

Dann tries to answer a prisoner's question.
(Art ©2010 Jack T. Chick LLC)

I walked over to man and said, "No one really knows for sure but he could tell you just as you are about to be tossed into the lake of fire. For an instant you'll know but God's secret would still be safe because you wouldn't be able to tell anyone what he told you."

Then I said, "Now you also claimed you would believe in Jesus as your Lord and Savior if someone would answer your question, so was that answer I gave you enough to satisfy you as a good reply?" He said it was and he received Jesus that day. I gave him some Chick tracks and a Bible. The men that who were already born again went over with me and after we all prayed, he joined their Bible study. I saw him for the last time as he was going to another prison. I also prayed he would continue in the faith.

Saying Goodbye to Ned

Right now, I have about 10 customers left that I landscape for on a regular basis. Some of them I've had 35 years. And most all the other ones who died I had that many years, too. I had one customer, his name was Ned, and I liked him a lot. But he had to get ready to move into a rest home. I went there one day, and he asked me to really clean up the yard because they were going to try to sell the mobile home once he moved, so he asked me to clean it up as best I could. I spent almost a day really going over the thing, and then I went inside the house to collect, and he asks, "How much do I owe you?" and I says, "Well, Ned, I'd say 80 dollars," and he says, "Oh, no," and I couldn't believe it; all these years we never had a confrontation, but he just hit his hands on the table and he says, "How much did you say?" and I says, "Well, did you go outside and see how much work I done and how nice it looks and everything?" He says, "Yeah, but you say 80 dollars?" and I said, "Well, whatever you think. You just tell me; I don't want to argue with you after all these years," and he says, "I say $180 dollars!" and I said, "What?" He repeated, "I said $180 dollars." I said, "Well, Ned, I don't know what you mean. I said 80, not 180." He kept insisting, "But *I* say $180." So he paid me $180, and he moved to the rest home. It wasn't long after that that he got drastically sick and they put him in the hospital.

Well, here come all of his rich relatives and everybody. They took his car, they went and ransacked his house and everything, his son took over the mobile home, and all of this and that, so I asked 'em, "Did you go over and see Ned?" he was in a town called Covina real close in a hospice, and they said, "Well, we went over there, but he don't know anybody, so we didn't go back," and I said, "Where exactly is he?" and they told me, and I says, "Well, I'll go see to him." And they said, "He didn't even know us!" but I went anyway, and I asked where he was, and he was in a dim room all by himself. He looked like death warmed over. He looked so bad; he was laying there, and I thought he had already passed away. So I got a hold of his hand, and I said, "Ned?" and he opened his eyes and looked at me, and he says, "Dann!" and I said, "Yes sir, I wanted to come over and see you." So we talked a little while, and I said, "Ned, would you like me to pray with you and for you?" He said, "I'd like that; I'd really like that." So I took his hand and I prayed to the Lord, and then I stopped and I says, "Ned, would you like me to pray that the Lord take you to be with your wife, to end this pain and this suffering you're going through; where you'll be where there's no pain or suffering, and with your wife? Would you like me to pray that?" And he said, "I would love you to do that." And he squeezed my hand, and I prayed that the Lord would take his loving arms and just lift Ned and take him away to be with him. And he just was so happy.

Well I left, and I went back the next day and I found out that he died just about three or four hours after I left. The relatives wanted the funeral quick. About the only way they could have it real fast (so they could all get back where they came from), was to have it at the gravesite. And they asked me to give the eulogy at the graves; to say a few things. They emphasized a *few* things. Well anyway, it was kind of drizzling and they had the grave area all covered with a canvas thing, but it had holes in the canvas, and rain was dripping through. I got up and spoke, and I said the 23rd

Psalm, and then I said, "The folks here told me that I wouldn't be able to talk to Ned because he didn't know anybody," and I told the whole story, just like it was, about Ned, and how I praised God that he recognized me, and that he understood what I said and he understood the prayer. And how he was saved in the end.

Meeting Sara Owen

I was contacted by a young lady around 1991 from North Carolina. She had a newsletter called *Christ's Friends United Ministries* at that time. She sent out this newsletter to about 40 people. Well, she found out through Chick's *Battlecry* newspaper about my prison ministry and about my life and everything, so she wrote me a letter and sent me one of her newsletters. She was only 15. We started corresponding, and I started sending her literature to put in her newsletters, and all this time we really had such a neat relationship. She said she was single, and she wanted to get married in this little church out in the country. Well, one of her girlfriends told her, "You've gotta go to church next Sunday, they've got a young guy that started going to the church. You oughta meet him." So Sarah said that she was stuck on this, that she wasn't going to marry anybody unless they could play the fiddle. They went to church, and that girl pointed out this young man, Julian was his name, and the preacher got up and said, "Well, we have a treat for us today; got a young man's gonna play the fiddle for us," and it was Julian. And Sarah told her, "That's the one! I'm gonna marry him!" Well, it sure happened that way, he was really something, and they got married. He was studying to be a Baptist preacher. He finally got ordained, and he got a church and they had 20 acres out in the Smoky Mountains, in the country, and he was building a house and renting a house a little further away. The house was in Virginia, and so they started building the house, and when they got about half way done, they moved into it and started fixing it up. Wasn't long after that that they had a little baby. They named her Corey. And they've had such a great time with that baby and doing things, and I'm thankful to the Lord for all these different ones I meet from afar off. Her little friend Amber Frankas was also delightful. I started writing to Amber, and then eventually the whole family. I started writing to them and sending them literature, 'cause they all distribute tracts and talk to people wherever they can. Even when I would once in a while get German literature, Audrey Francas, the mother, she goes to Germany about every year, so she takes all those tracts with her to give out.

The Word in Their Words

Dann's cameo appearance in the "The Letter" Chick tract. (©1982 Jack T. Chick LLC)

I never knew how much work witnessing with the 100 foreign languages gospel tracts was until about 5 years ago when I really started taking them with me about everywhere I go here in California, to the markets, stores, but most of all, the fruit stands and Farmer's Markets. I've done it so long now that I can almost tell where everybody is from just by looking at them. If in doubt, I hold up a few and say "can you read any of these little books?" One man from Vietnam looked at four that I held up and said, "I can read all of them including English." He asked if he could have each of them. What's really strange is more women than men will take the tracts.

I still help my fellow Chaplain Brother Marlin Baker and his wife Shirley in Texas. I loved it when he was here in California. He was the only Chaplain permitted to go into the woman's prison here in Chino. He now goes full time in most jails and prisons around the Dallas area. I've sent him literature and tracts for over 30 years. That's what keeps me going since I lost my wife, Esther. I praise our Lord

Jesus Christ for all the ones I've been able to help minister all these years.

I hope you enjoyed my story.

A Closing Prayer

Dann also appeared in the "Reverend Wonderful" Chick tract. (©1982 Jack T. Chick LLC)

Heavenly Father, we come to You in the name of Your only begotten Son, our Lord and Saviour, Jesus Christ, and we ask You to bless this book and its readers to Your glory. We pray that it will help lead the lost of this world through the working of the Holy Spirit to the saving knowledge of Jesus Christ our Lord. Even so, come quickly Lord Jesus (Revelation).

– *Cowboy Chaplain Dann*

Afterword (by Kurt Kuersteiner)

As of 2016, Chaplain Dann continues his tract ministry and supplying materials to other prison ministries. Like his friend Jack Chick, Dann Slator is now over 90 years old. When he dies, all his eyewitness memories of The Great Depression, the Dust Bowl, the last of the untamed west, wild horses, World War II, and the unusual people and conflicts he knew growing up, will be gone forever—except those that live on in our memories after reading his story (or seeing it in his comic book and/or hand drawn tracts). His was a hard life, but one also punctuated with amazing natural beauty, dramatic historical events, and a very colorful cast of characters. It was a unique time in America, and indeed, in the world.

The Chinese say it is a curse to live in interesting times. If that's the case, Dann's life was especially cursed. Given his tough beginnings, many brushes with death, and constant encounters with trouble, Dann would have been the last to predict he would wind up becoming a dedicated Christian who devotes so much time and energy witnessing to others. For him, it has been a long journey filled with many mistakes, but with a happy ending that he's thankful for.

If you would like to write Chaplain Dann or contribute to his ministry, you can do so by writing him at this address:

Chaplain Dann Slator, 4400 Philadelphia Street, Space #29, Chino CA 91710-2217.

You can also view most of Dann's hand-drawn tracts on the web by visiting ChickComics.com and scrolling down the alphabetical links (listed along the left side of the page under "Contents") to the section entitled: "Dann, the Tract Man." (Or internet search engine "Cowboy Chaplain Dann.")

The most detailed supplement on Dann's life is the 32 page comic book, *Unwanted*, available through Chick Publications (and on the web at Chick.com). It tells much of Dann's story with beautiful full color art by Fred Carter. Many of Fred's wonderful illustrations were used in this book with permission from Chick Publications, but they are much more dramatic in Chick's full color comics, complete with dialog.

There is also a two-part radio show on *Unshackled* about Chaplain Dann. They are episodes #3331 and #3332, broadcast on Nov. 16th and 23rd of 2014.

It should also be mentioned that you can find several articles about Chaplain Dann in various back issues of *Battlecry* (from Chick Publications). Many of them are also posted in Dann's section at ChickComics.com

Dann's hand drawn and self-published tracts also include many autobiographical details. Although most of them are quite rare (usually only 500 or 1,000 printed at a time), some may eventually turn up on eBay. I have scanned and placed on-line all the tracts I have been able to acquire, and you can view most of them at ChickComics.com.

The following are all the known titles, but Dann remembers making four to six more tracts that he completely gave away and can't recall the names of them. If you encounter any that are not listed here, please email me (Monsterwax@aol.com) so we can include information about them in any future editions of this book, as well as in his section at Chickcomics.com. Here are the known ones:

Biker's Weekend (1983) Art by Dann.

The Burdens (2010) Art by Dann

Choice of Execution (1993) Art by Dann

Cowboy's Last Round-Up (1981) Art by Dann

From Carl to Carla to Christ (1983) Art by "RSL" (Rod). No last name is ever given.

Golden Years (1986) Art by RSL (Rob)

The Loner (1983) Art by Dann but also featuring photos of his wife, Esther

Long Way to the Son (1983) Art by "Rob," (named Rod elsewhere). There is a 24 and a 32 page version of this title, but the 24 page version uses fewer panels of the same art. (The 32 page version uses 62 panels.)

Party Time (No date, circa 1983) Art by "Rod" (Rob/ RSL)

Rail-Roaded (No date, cica 1980s) Art by Dann

The Revenge Seekers (1983) Art by Dann

This Was Your Life (1985) Art by Dann (Native-American version)

Ultimo Hunted De Los Vaqueros (No date, circa 1982) Spanish version of *Cowboy's Last Round-up.* The artist is uncertain, but Dann remembers he was a Mexican inmate in the prison where Dann served, and he drew it unsolicited. (This tract is not reprinted here.) His name was probably "Nachos Jr." the same person who translated words to another tract.

I'm fascinated by all of Dann's tracts (just as I am Jack Chick's), and they are a treasured part of my collection. I appreciate the way they are hand crafted, and that the art is so basic and unsophisticated (similar to the folk artist style of Gradma Moses). I also enjoy the way certain images are pasted over with actual photographs or, in other instances, Fred Carter's illustrations of Dann from various Chick tracts in which Dann was featured. (The juxtaposition of the two different styles couldn't be more dramatic!) The degree of effort he has spent on each tract makes it clear he's obsessed with reaching people with his message, despite his very limited income and all the time and money he must spend writing them, drawing them, printing them, cutting them up and stapling them, and then actually distributing them to a world that will mostly reject them and throw them away. Yet he continues to toil away at it, like Sisyphus, the mythological Greek character who is condemned to repeatedly roll a boulder uphill, only to watch it roll back down again. The irony, of course, is that *that* story was a heathen version of hell, while Dann volunteers to do what he does to get people into heaven.

In appreciation of his determination in that Herculean task, I'd like to conclude this book by reprinting those rare tracts. Let's start with the unusual 32 page version of his life's story, "Long Way To The Son" (scanned and reprinted here for the very first time).

Dann with a funeral hearse he bought as a conversation opener, to help pass out tracts and discuss the afterlife with strangers

Notes: This 1983 autobiographical tract is factual and reveals intimate details of Dann's life. He talks about many of these scenes in this book, and some also appear in the *Unwanted* Crusader comic. It's a lot of personal information to reveal to prisoners, who were the main audience of this tract. The cover states that it was drawn by "Rob," also known as Rod, a prisoner with initials of RSL.

AFTER ALMOST 2 YEARS OF THE DUST STORMS AND NO RAIN THE U.S. GOVERNMENT CAME IN AND GAVE $10 FOR EACH COW. THEY SHOT ALL THE COWS, AND THE HORSES!!
POOR DUGAN AIN'T DEAD YET. HE'S STILL TRYING TO GET UP.
I WONDER WHO'LL TAKE US NEXT?
BILLIONS OF GRASSHOPPERS CAME NEXT. THAT DID IT.
JOHN, THE BOYS' DAD, FOUND A SISTER IN CALIFORNIA THAT WOULD TAKE THE BOYS FOR A WHILE.....
GOODBYE HELMER. WE'LL MISS YOU. DAD SAID THAT WE CAN SEND FOR YOU LATER.
HURRY UP! WE'RE READY TO LEAVE.
WE NEVER SAW HELMER AGAIN HE QUIT EATING AND DIED OF GRIEF.
JOHN ROY SOON GOT INTO TROUBLE AND WAS SENT TO JUVENILE HALL AT 15 YEARS OLD.
BUNN, YOUR UNCLE LOUIE HAS A BIG CATTLE RANCH IN COLORADO. HE WANTS YOU TO GO OUT THERE AND STAY WITH THEM.
I'LL GET TO RIDE HORSES AGAIN AND BE A COWBOY. MAYBE I'LL HAVE MY OWN HORSE!!
LITTLE DID I KNOW THAT I'D BE WORKING 14 HOURS A DAY.
LOUIE'S SON IN-LAW JOE KEPT AFTER BUNN TO KILL LOUIE SO HE COULD TAKE OVER, SO BUNN DECIDED TO GO TO TEXAS. HE TELLS LOUIE HE'S GOING TO LEAVE IN 30 DAYS.
SO YOU'RE GOING TO LEAVE. WELL YOU BETTER THINK TWICE BECAUSE WHEN YOU CONSIDER YOUR OWN MOTHER AND FATHER DIDN'T WANT YOU WHO ELSE WOULD?
I'M GOING NOW

BUNN WALKS OVER THE MOUNTAINS TO A RAILROAD SPUR TO CATCH A TRAIN TO TEXAS.....
I'M BUNN FROM COLORADO. YOU SAID IF I CAME DOWN TO THE MATADORS, YOU'D GIVE ME A JOB. SO HERE I AM READY TO WORK!!
I HEARD YOU HAD A LOT OF TROUBLE WITH BEAL QUEEN THE MARSHALL. PUT YOUR TACK IN THE BACK
THE MATADOR RANCH WAS ONE OF THE LARGEST SPREADS EVER WITH A CHUCK WAGON AND ALL THE REST OF THE OLD TIME STUFF.
YOU'LL BE IN CHARGE OF TRAINING ALL THE COLTS, AND BREAKING THE HORSES AND STALLIONS TO RIDE THEM BUNN.
MONTHS PASSED AND THE ONLY MAIL I GOT WAS FROM A GIRL IN COLORADO WHO BEGGED ME TO COME BACK
DEAR BUNN, I REALLY MISS YOU A LOT. I WISH YOU WOULD GET A JOB NEAR OUR RANCH SO WE COULD SEE EACH OTHER LIKE BEFORE!
I BELIEVE JOSEPHINE REALLY CARES ABOUT ME. I'M HURT BAD RIDING THESE BRONCS. I SHOULD GO SEE A DOCTOR. I'LL QUIT HERE AND GO TO FOXES RANCH!
WANTING TO SURPRISE HIS GIRL, BUNN GOES UNANNOUNCED BUT SHE HAS A VISITOR, A MARRIED MAN FROM TOWN WITH HER.
THAT SETTLES IT! I'M GOING TO TAKE THE JOB WITH NEWCOMB BREAKING RANGE BRONCS.

WITHOUT SAYING ANYTHING TO JOSEPHINE, BUNN LEAVES TO TAKE A JOB BREAKING HORSES FOR MR. NEWCOMB
THIS IS HARDY ROBERTS. HE'LL HELP YOU SADDLE THE BRONCS AND GO OUT WITH YOU IF YOU GET A ROUGH ONE.
SOME OF THE BRONCS ARE ONLY 3 AND 4 YEARS OLD.
ONE DAY, A MONTH OR SO LATER, A BRONC RAN OFF INTO THE ROUGH CEDAR RIDGE AND FELL DOWN IN SOME BOULDERS.....
MY GOD BUNN! ARE YOU CRUSHED UNDER THAT HORSE?
MY LEG HURTS! BUT I'M KIND OF STUCK BETWEEN TWO ROCKS. PULL HIM OFF ME, WILL YA?
I HAD TWISTED MY LEFT LEG AND WAS SORE BUT WAS ABLE TO CONTINUE RIDING BRONCS.
WE'RE GOING TO RUN THE WILD HORSES NEXT WEEK. BRING A FAST HORSE!
I'LL GET RONDO BOSS!
ACROSS THE RIVER IS OPEN LAND
THE HERD OF HORSES ARE RUNNING STRAIGHT FOR A BARBED WIRE FENCE.....
HEAD THEM OFF. THEY'LL HIT THAT FENCE. YOU GOT THE FASTEST HORSE.
COME ON RONDO, STRETCH OUT. WE GOT TO HEAD THEM OFF!

JUST AS BUNN HEADS THE HORSES FROM THE NEW FENCE, RONDO STEPS IN A PRAIRIE DOG HOLE AND ROLLS OVER
I WAS UNCONSCIOUS FOR OVER 2 WEEKS
WHEN I GOT OUT OF THE HOSPITAL I WENT BACK TO UNCLE LOUIE'S RANCH IN BARRELA.....
I PUT CATTLE AND LAND IN YOUR NAME SO THEY CAN'T DRAFT YOU.
WILL THE CATTLE OR LAND EVER BE MINE UNCLE LOUIE? OR IS IT JUST FOR NOW.
I'M JUST DOING IT SO YOU CAN WORK!
1942- A WHILE LATER I GO TO GET THE WEEKLY MAIL AND I DROP THE NEWSPAPER.....
THERE'S MEN DYING THAT SOMEONE LOVES AND NO ONE PERIOD CARES ABOUT ME, I'M GOING TO TRY AND JOIN THE MARINES.
HUNDREDS OF MARINES DIE IN SO. PAC.
I JOINED WITHOUT TELLING ANYONE
THE PAPER CAME AGAIN AND BEFORE I LEFT MY UNCLE SAW A SMALL ARTICLE ABOUT MY JOINING THE MARINES.
YOU GOT TO BE NUTS JOINING THE MARINES. IF YOU WANT TO DIE SO BAD, HERE'S A .38! USE IT HERE SO AT LEAST WE CAN BURY YOU HERE
NO THANKS! I'LL LET THE JAPS DO IT.

THE MARINES ACCEPTED ME ONLY BECAUSE THEY WERE IN NEED OF MEN.....
MOST MEN THAT GET MEDICAL DISCHARGES AREN'T IN AS BAD A SHAPE AS YOU ARE!
BUT I'M ACCEPTED, AINT I SARGE?
TESTS AND X-RAYS SHOWED I HAD FRACTURES OF THE PELVIS, BREASTBONE, SPINE, AND CHEEKBONE
THE FIRST MONTH I WENT TO MANY DIFFERENT SPECIAL SCHOOLS INCLUDING SPECIAL WEAPONS IN SAN DIEGO NEAR THE ZOO IN BALBOA PARK.
HI THERE! HOW YOU DOING PAL? I TOLD YOU I'D COME SEE YOU AGAIN!
AFTER 10 P.M. CURFEW I WENT OVER 3 GUARDED FENCES TO SEE MY NEW FRIENDS FOR 30 STRAIGHT NIGHTS.
ONE NIGHT I WAS REAL TIRED AND DIDN'T NOTICE HIS ARM WASN'T EXTENDED ALL THE WAY...
HELP!! WHAT'S THE MATTER WITH YOU
HE TRIED TO PULL ME INTO HIS CAGE WHEN I GOT FREE I THOUGHT I WAS GOING TO DIE.
I GOT IN TROUBLE AND WENT AWOL THEN I CAME BACK ON MY OWN AND WAS SLAMMED IN THE BRIG TO AWAIT TRIAL.....
KEEP THOSE FACES IN THE FRAME AT ALL TIMES. YOU HEAR ME?
3
4
5
I FEEL SORRY FOR THE SHORT GUYS!
WAITING FOR OVER 30 DAYS, I MADE A BAD MISTAKE.....I ESCAPED!!

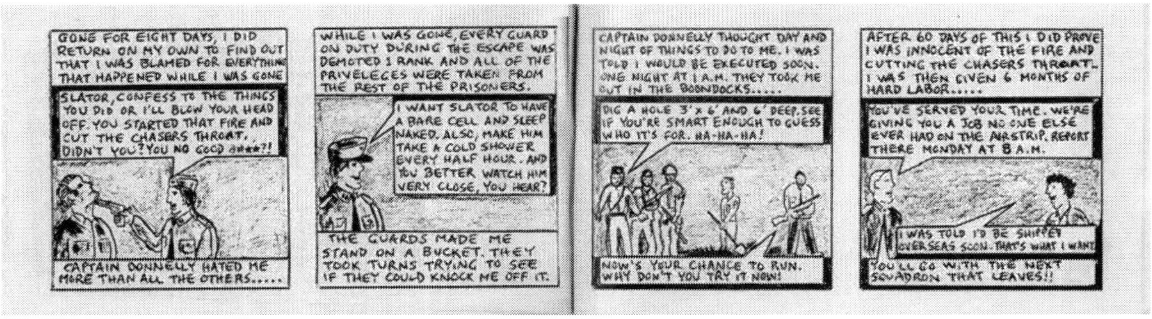
GONE FOR EIGHT DAYS, I DID RETURN ON MY OWN TO FIND OUT THAT I WAS BLAMED FOR EVERYTHING THAT HAPPENED WHILE I WAS GONE
SLATOR, CONFESS TO THE THINGS YOU DID OR I'LL BLOW YOUR HEAD OFF. YOU STARTED THAT FIRE AND CUT THE CHASERS THROAT, DIDN'T YOU? YOU NO GOOD #**?!
CAPTAIN DONNELLY HATED ME MORE THAN ALL THE OTHERS.....
WHILE I WAS GONE, EVERY GUARD ON DUTY DURING THE ESCAPE WAS DEMOTED 1 RANK AND ALL OF THE PRIVELEGES WERE TAKEN FROM THE REST OF THE PRISONERS.
I WANT SLATOR TO HAVE A BARE CELL AND SLEEP NAKED. ALSO, MAKE HIM TAKE A COLD SHOWER EVERY HALF HOUR. AND YOU BETTER WATCH HIM VERY CLOSE, YOU HEAR?
THE GUARDS MADE ME STAND ON A BUCKET. THEY TOOK TURNS TRYING TO SEE IF THEY COULD KNOCK ME OFF IT.
CAPTAIN DONNELLY THOUGHT DAY AND NIGHT OF THINGS TO DO TO ME. I WAS TOLD I WOULD BE EXECUTED SOON. ONE NIGHT AT 1 A.M. THEY TOOK ME OUT IN THE BOONDOCKS.....
DIG A HOLE 3' x 6' AND 6' DEEP. SEE IF YOU'RE SMART ENOUGH TO GUESS WHO IT'S FOR. HA-HA-HA!
NOW'S YOUR CHANCE TO RUN. WHY DON'T YOU TRY IT NOW!
AFTER 60 DAYS OF THIS I DID PROVE I WAS INNOCENT OF THE FIRE AND CUTTING THE CHASERS THROAT. I WAS THEN GIVEN 6 MONTHS OF HARD LABOR.....
YOU'VE SERVED YOUR TIME. WE'RE GIVING YOU A JOB NO ONE ELSE EVER HAD ON THE AIRSTRIP. REPORT THERE MONDAY AT 8 A.M.
I WAS TOLD I'D BE SHIPPED OVERSEAS SOON. THAT'S WHAT I WANT
YOU'LL GO WITH THE NEXT SQUADRON THAT LEAVES!!

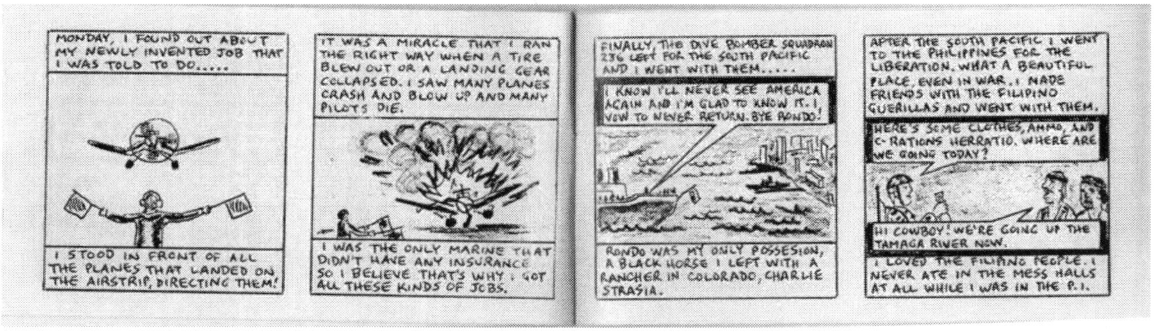
MONDAY, I FOUND OUT ABOUT MY NEWLY INVENTED JOB THAT I WAS TOLD TO DO.....
I STOOD IN FRONT OF ALL THE PLANES THAT LANDED ON THE AIRSTRIP, DIRECTING THEM!
IT WAS A MIRACLE THAT I RAN THE RIGHT WAY WHEN A TIRE BLEW OUT OR A LANDING GEAR COLLAPSED. I SAW MANY PLANES CRASH AND BLOW UP AND MANY PILOTS DIE.
I WAS THE ONLY MARINE THAT DIDN'T HAVE ANY INSURANCE SO I BELIEVE THAT'S WHY I GOT ALL THESE KINDS OF JOBS.
FINALLY, THE DIVE BOMBER SQUADRON 236 LEFT FOR THE SOUTH PACIFIC AND I WENT WITH THEM.....
I KNOW I'LL NEVER SEE AMERICA AGAIN AND I'M GLAD TO KNOW IT. I VOW TO NEVER RETURN. BYE RONDO!
RONDO WAS MY ONLY POSSESION, A BLACK HORSE I LEFT WITH A RANCHER IN COLORADO, CHARLIE STRASIA.
AFTER THE SOUTH PACIFIC I WENT TO THE PHILIPPINES FOR THE LIBERATION. WHAT A BEAUTIFUL PLACE, EVEN IN WAR. I MADE FRIENDS WITH THE FILIPINO GUERILLAS AND WENT WITH THEM.
HERE'S SOME CLOTHES, AMMO, AND C-RATIONS HERRATIO. WHERE ARE WE GOING TODAY?
HI COWBOY! WE'RE GOING UP THE TAMAGA RIVER NOW.
I LOVED THE FILIPINO PEOPLE. I NEVER ATE IN THE MESS HALLS AT ALL WHILE I WAS IN THE P.I.

WE LEFT ZAMBOANGA, P.I. FOR OKINAWA ON OUR WAY TO CHINA. WHEN WE GOT READY TO LEAVE OKINAWA A 180 MPH WIND CAME UP CALLED A TYPHOON. IT BLEW US OUT OF THE NAHA HARBOR.
WE LOST BOTH PROPELLARS AND OUR RUDDER FIRST DAY OUT. WE DRIFTED FOR 18 DAYS WITHOUT CONTROL TO FORMOSA
IN THE HOLE WERE 500 LB. BOMBS AND 100 OCTANE GAS IN BARRELS THAT RUPTURED. I JUST KNEW THAT THIS WAS IT. THERE WAS NO HOPE AT ALL.....
706
DURING THE DAY WE WOULD SPOT SOME MINES THAT BROKE LOOSE BUT WE MISSED THEM. THE WAVES WERE 30 FEET HIGH.
WE HAD L.S.T. 706 REPAIRED AND WENT UP THE COAST OF CHINA TO TSINGTAO ON THE PENINSULA OF SHANTUNG.....
WHERE CAN WE FIND A GOOD PLACE TO TEAR UP? HA, HA, THIS IS FUN! HE CAN'T UNDERSTAND US AT ALL!!
CAMMA SHAW JOE.
WAN TO LOOKA SEE?
THEY UNDERSTOOD US LATER BETTER THAN WE COULD UNDERSTAND THEM!
A LOT OF MARINES WENT BLIND FROM DRINKING THE CHINESE BOOZE AND SOME EVEN DIED! I QUIT.
YOU'RE IN CHARGE OF SHORE PATROL UP TOWN SO MOVE INTO THE GUARD BUILDING IMMEDIATELY.
YES SIR. I KNOW THAT TOWN LIKE THE BACK OF MY OWN HAND. I'D CALL IT GOOD DUTY!
I MISSED 2 PLANES AND 2 SHIPS ON PURPOSE TO KEEP FROM GOING BACK

I WAS GIVEN AN HONORABLE DISCHARGE AND WITH MY BACK PAY AND MUSTERING OUT PAY I BOUGHT A HARLEY MOTORCYCLE.
I LOVE IT HON! MAROON IS MY FAVORITE COLOR. HOW FAST WILL THIS THING GO? LET'S GO TO THE BARN DANCE ON IT TONIGHT!
THE KELLOGG ARABIAN HORSE RANCH HIRED ME. MY DRINKING KEPT GETTING WORSE. THERE WERE MANY SERIOUS ACCIDENTS. IN ONE, I BROKE 26 BONES.....
DR. BASHAM, HOW LONG WILL I HAVE TO WEAR THESE CASTS?
PROBABLY 3 MONTHS. ANYWAY I'D LIKE TO SEE YOU EVEN TRY TO RIDE YOUR BIKE NOW.
I CONTINUED TO DRINK A LOT. MY WIFE HAD TO DO EVERYTHING FOR ME
AFTER 10 YEARS AT THE RANCH I LEFT AND WENT INTO MY OWN BUSINESS DOING LANDSCAPING WITHIN A 100 MILE RADIUS.
DOC SELLERS SAYS HE HAS A BABY GIRL FOR US TO ADOPT.
WHY WOULD HE THINK WE WOULD TAKE A KID. I AINT FIT TO HAVE KIDS!
FIT OR NOT, WE ADOPTED DIANNA AND 1 YEAR LATER DOC GOT US ANOTHER LITTLE GIRL 2 DAYS OLD. WE NAMED HER PAM.
THE GIRLS HAD PETS, PONIES, AND A BEAUTIFUL YARD TO PLAY IN BUT THEIR DADDY WAS STILL A DRUNKARD AND GETTING WORSE.
I CAN'T BELIEVE IT! IT'S 6 A.M. AND I'M HERE IN A BAR... AGAIN!
HI PAL! WANT ANOTHER BREW? YOU SICK OR SOMETHIN'? YOU LOOK A SIGHT!
NO THANKS!
I MADE UP MY MIND TO GO TO CHURCH SOMEWHERE THE NEXT SUNDAY. I WAS AT WITS END!!

I LOOKED IN THE PAPER FOR A CHURCH AND SAW WHERE A MAN, THAT WAS AN ARTIST, WOULD BE AT A CHURCH IN POMONA. HIS NAME WAS JACK T. CHICK
666
THERE WILL BE 7 YEARS OF TRIBULATION THAT THE WORLD HAS NEVER KNOWN!
WOW!! ALL THAT'S IN THE BIBLE??
GOING TO ONE OF MY FAVORITE BEER JOINTS TO PLAY SOME POOL, I ORDERED A BREW.....
YOU KNOW, THAT'S ALL I AM; A CONTAINER FOR THAT DARN BEER WITH LEGS. AND NOT TOO GOOD OF LEGS AT THAT. HELP ME LORD!
DEAR LORD JESUS, FORGIVE ME OF ALL MY SINS AND COME INTO MY HEART AND BE MY LORD AND PERSONAL SAVIOUR.
AS I PRAYED, I REMEMBERED MY BROTHER JOHN ROY'S FUNERAL WHERE ONLY 4 PEOPLE CAME. HIS LIFE WAS A NIGHTMARE. HE SPENT OVER 14 YEARS IN PRISON AND FINALLY DIED A HEROIN ADDICT AND DRUNKARD AT 50 YEARS OLD.
HE LOOKS SO MUCH LIKE ME IT COULD BE ME! I'VE GOT TO CHANGE BEFORE IT'S TOO LATE, BUT HOW CAN I DO THIS? WHO COULD HELP ME?
WHEN I FINISHED PRAYING I KNEW WHO I HAD BEEN SEARCHING FOR AND ALSO THE ONLY ONE THAT COULD HELP ME CHANGE MY LIFE
I WENT TO CHURCH TODAY AND ASKED JESUS TO FORGIVE ME FOR MY SINS AND HELP ME STOP DRINKING
WELL, I'M SURE YOU CAN STOP IF YOU REALLY MEAN WHAT YOU SAID. MAYBE ALL OF US CAN START GOING TO CHURCH EVERY SUNDAY.

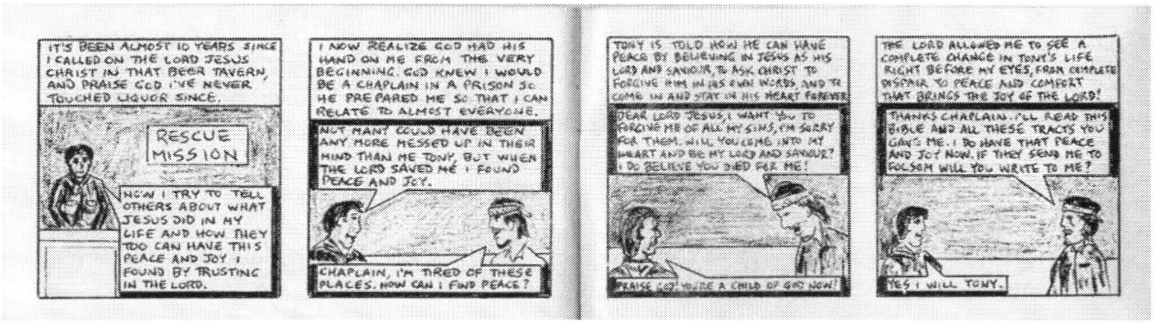
IT'S BEEN ALMOST 10 YEARS SINCE I CALLED ON THE LORD JESUS CHRIST IN THAT BEER TAVERN, AND PRAISE GOD I'VE NEVER TOUCHED LIQUOR SINCE.
RESCUE MISSION
NOW I TRY TO TELL OTHERS ABOUT WHAT JESUS DID IN MY LIFE AND HOW THEY TOO CAN HAVE THIS PEACE AND JOY I FOUND BY TRUSTING IN THE LORD.
I NOW REALIZE GOD HAD HIS HAND ON ME FROM THE VERY BEGINNING. GOD KNEW I WOULD BE A CHAPLAIN IN A PRISON SO HE PREPARED ME SO THAT I CAN RELATE TO ALMOST EVERYONE.
NOT MANY COULD HAVE BEEN ANY MORE MESSED UP IN THEIR MIND THAN ME TONY, BUT WHEN THE LORD SAVED ME I FOUND PEACE AND JOY.
CHAPLAIN, I'M TIRED OF THESE PLACES. HOW CAN I FIND PEACE?
TONY IS TOLD HOW HE CAN HAVE PEACE BY BELIEVING IN JESUS AS HIS LORD AND SAVIOUR, TO ASK CHRIST TO FORGIVE HIM IN HIS OWN WORDS, AND TO COME IN AND STAY IN HIS HEART FOREVER
DEAR LORD JESUS, I WANT YOU TO FORGIVE ME OF ALL MY SINS, I'M SORRY FOR THEM. WILL YOU COME INTO MY HEART AND BE MY LORD AND SAVIOUR? I DO BELIEVE YOU DIED FOR ME!
PRAISE GOD YOU'RE A CHILD OF GOD NOW!
THE LORD ALLOWED ME TO SEE A COMPLETE CHANGE IN TONY'S LIFE RIGHT BEFORE MY EYES, FROM COMPLETE DISPAIR TO PEACE AND COMFORT THAT BRINGS THE JOY OF THE LORD!
THANKS CHAPLAIN. I'LL READ THIS BIBLE AND ALL THESE TRACTS YOU GAVE ME. I DO HAVE THAT PEACE AND JOY NOW. IF THEY SEND ME TO FOLSOM WILL YOU WRITE TO ME?
YES I WILL TONY.

MY BROTHER, JOHN ROY, DID MENTION TO ME, WHEN WE WERE OUT DRINKING, THAT HE WISHED WE COULD CHANGE, BUT WE HAD NO ONE INTERESTED IN US AT ALL TO TALK TO US.
ARE YOU A CHAPLAIN? CAN YOU HELP ME? I JUST HAVE TO TALK TO SOMEONE!
YES SIR. THAT'S WHAT WE ARE HERE FOR. TELL ME, HOW CAN I HELP YOU NOW?
WHEN YOU SEE ANY OF US ON THE TIERS OR ANY OTHER PLACE JUST REMEMBER, WE DO CARE ABOUT YOU.
ONE CHAPLAIN HAS BEEN COMING INTO C.I.M. FOR OVER 30 YEARS! HE'S THE ONE WHO ENCOURAGED ME TO BE A CHAPLAIN. RIGHT TOM?
LET'S GIVE ALL THE GLORY TO THE LORD. GOD LOVES US IN SPITE OF OURSELVES!
(I WAS KNOWN AS GUNN AS A BOY)
IF I HAD SUCCEEDED IN DESTROYING MYSELF LIKE THE TIME WHEN I TRIED AS A BOY AND MANY OTHER TIMES I WOULDN'T BE HERE NOW DOING WHAT I LOVE TO DO IN THIS PRISON. LIFE IS SO SHORT AT ITS LONGEST COMPARED TO OUR ETERNAL LIFE. THE MOST IMPORTANT OF ALL THINGS IS TO KNOW THAT YOU HAVE SALVATION AND ETERNAL LIFE IN THE LORD JESUS CHRIST AS YOUR ONLY SAVIOUR. WON'T YOU PUT YOUR TRUST IN HIM TODAY? WHY IN HEAVEN'S NAME WOULD YOU PUT IT OFF ANY LONGER...
NO NEED TO SUFFER AT ALL IN THE NEXT WORLD, DO IT NOW.
I THANK EVERYONE WHO TOOK THE TIME TO READ THIS TRACT ABOUT PARTS OF MY LIFE. I'D LIKE TO CLOSE THIS IN PRAYER.
DEAR LORD, BE WITH US ALL AS WE PASS THROUGH THIS WORLD.
LORD, PLEASE HELP US TO BETTER UNDERSTAND YOUR WORD, THE HOLY BIBLE. THANK YOU FATHER. IN THE NAME OF JESUS CHRIST I PRAY. AMEN.

Notes: Another 1983 tract. It was drawn by Dann, except for the cover, which was drawn by a prisoner named Anderson. Anderson redrew most of the entire tract, but then got released before finishing it (making his incomplete art useless). The fictional plot features Dann's adopted daughters, Pam and Dianna.

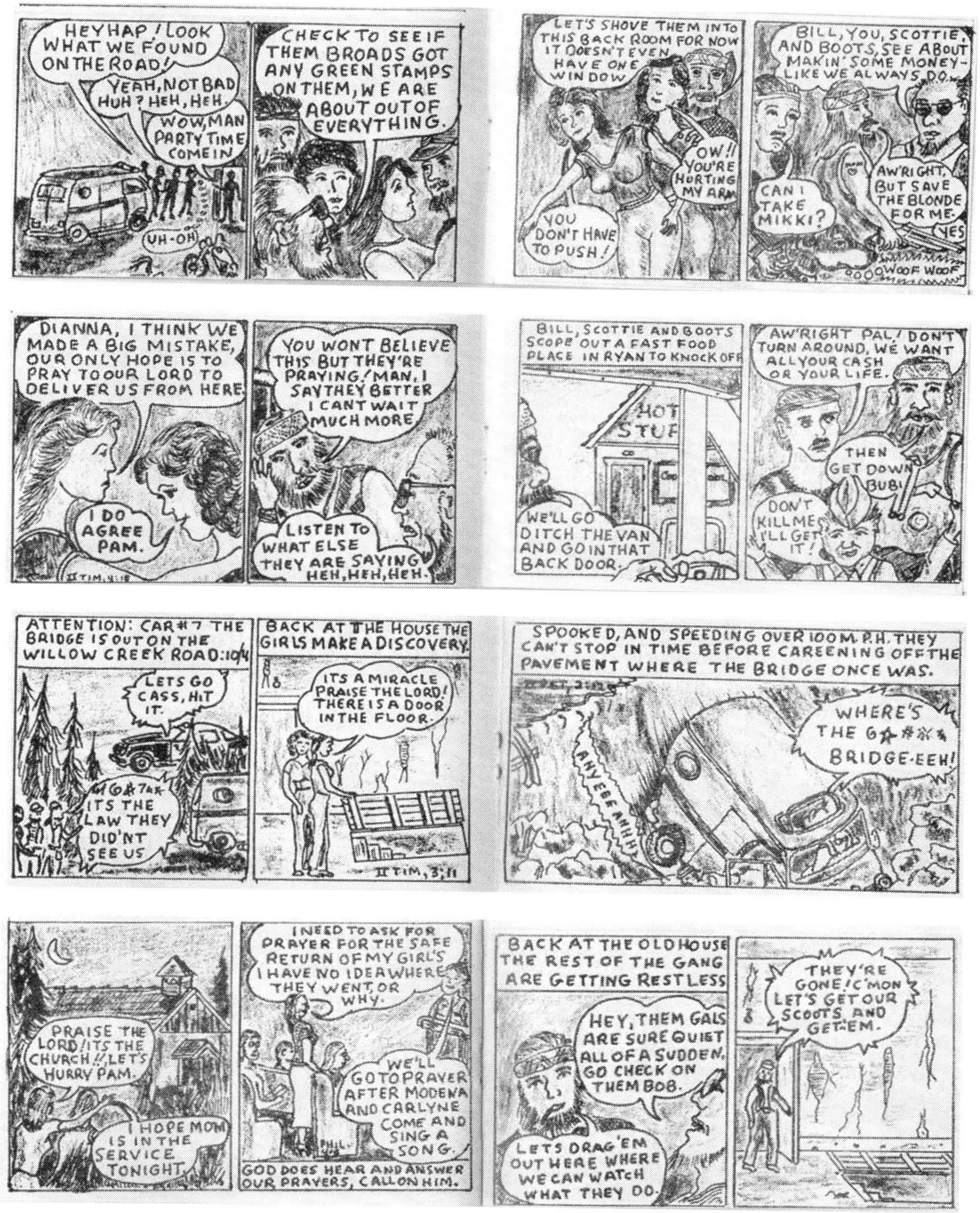
HEY HAP! LOOK WHAT WE FOUND ON THE ROAD!
YEAH, NOT BAD HUH? HEH, HEH.
WOW, MAN PARTY TIME COME IN
UH-OH
CHECK TO SEE IF THEM BROADS GOT ANY GREEN STAMPS ON THEM, WE ARE ABOUT OUT OF EVERYTHING.
LET'S SHOVE THEM INTO THIS BACK ROOM FOR NOW IT DOESN'T EVEN HAVE ONE WINDOW
OW!! YOU'RE HURTING MY ARM
YOU DON'T HAVE TO PUSH!
BILL, YOU, SCOTTIE, AND BOOTS, SEE ABOUT MAKIN' SOME MONEY-LIKE WE ALWAYS DO.
CAN I TAKE MIKKI?
AW'RIGHT, BUT SAVE THE BLONDE FOR ME.
YES
OOOWOOF WOOF
DIANNA, I THINK WE MADE A BIG MISTAKE, OUR ONLY HOPE IS TO PRAY TO OUR LORD TO DELIVER US FROM HERE
I DO AGREE PAM.
II TIM. 4:18
YOU WONT BELIEVE THIS BUT THEY'RE PRAYING! MAN, I SAY THEY BETTER I CANT WAIT MUCH MORE
LISTEN TO WHAT ELSE THEY ARE SAYING HEH, HEH, HEH.
BILL, SCOTTIE AND BOOTS SCOPE OUT A FAST FOOD PLACE IN RYAN TO KNOCK OFF
HOT STUF
WE'LL GO DITCH THE VAN AND GO IN THAT BACK DOOR.
AW'RIGHT PAL! DON'T TURN AROUND, WE WANT ALL YOUR CASH OR YOUR LIFE.
THEN GET DOWN BUB!
DON'T KILL ME! I'LL GET IT!
ATTENTION: CAR #7 THE BRIDGE IS OUT ON THE WILLOW CREEK ROAD: 10-4
LETS GO CASS, HIT IT.
ITS THE LAW THEY DIDN'T SEE US
BACK AT THE HOUSE THE GIRLS MAKE A DISCOVERY.
ITS A MIRACLE PRAISE THE LORD! THERE IS A DOOR IN THE FLOOR.
II TIM, 3:11
SPOOKED, AND SPEEDING OVER 100 M.P.H. THEY CAN'T STOP IN TIME BEFORE CAREENING OFF THE PAVEMENT WHERE THE BRIDGE ONCE WAS.
WHERE'S THE G✱#✱✱ BRIDGE-EEH!
ANYEEE AHHH
PRAISE THE LORD! ITS THE CHURCH!! LET'S HURRY PAM.
I HOPE MOM IS IN THE SERVICE TONIGHT.
I NEED TO ASK FOR PRAYER FOR THE SAFE RETURN OF MY GIRL'S I HAVE NO IDEA WHERE THEY WENT, OR WHY.
WE'LL GO TO PRAYER AFTER MODENA AND CARLYNE COME AND SING A SONG.
GOD DOES HEAR AND ANSWER OUR PRAYERS, CALL ON HIM.
BACK AT THE OLD HOUSE THE REST OF THE GANG ARE GETTING RESTLESS
HEY, THEM GALS ARE SURE QUIET ALL OF A SUDDEN, GO CHECK ON THEM BOB.
LETS DRAG 'EM OUT HERE WHERE WE CAN WATCH WHAT THEY DO.
THEY'RE GONE! C'MON LET'S GET OUR SCOOTS AND GET-EM.

THE GIRL'S WENT INSIDE GO IN ACE THEY DON'T KNOW YOU SEE WHATS UP.
O.K. BUT HIDE MY BIKE OVER BEHIND THOSE TREES, I'LL COME OUT AS SOON AS I CAN.
INSIDE THE CHURCH A MAN WHO WAS RAISED A COWBOY IS GIVING HIS TESTIMONY, HE IS ALSO A CHAPLAIN IN THE CHINO PRISON
PRAISE, GOD!! SISTER AUSTIN, HERE COMES PAM AND DIANNA IN NOW.
ACE SLIPS IN AND SITS DOWN ALONE, UNKNOWN TO ANYONE IN ALL THE EXCITEMENT.
LET'S PRAY, FATHER WE THANK YOU IN THE NAME OF JESUS, FOR PROTECTING THE AUSTIN GIRLS, AND FOR BRINGING THEM BOTH BACK TO US TONIGHT SAFELY. AMEN
JESUS CHRIST, DIED FOR EVERYONE AND FOR EVERY SIN ANYONE EVER COMMITTED, AND HE LOVES US ALL, BUT HE HATES SIN.
MAN I CANT BELIEVE I AM IN HERE, I HOPE IT DONT LAST VERY LONG.
IF YOU ARE JUST RELIGIOUS AND ARE TRUSTING IN THAT ONLY BEWARE! YOU MUST PUT YOUR COMPLETE FAITH IN JESUS CHRIST AS YOUR VERY OWN PERSONAL SAVIOR, ONLY JESUS CHRIST CAN FORGIVE YOU OF YOUR SINS. AFTER YOU ARE FORGIVEN TRY NOT TO, "SIN," ANYMORE
GOD WANTS YOU!
CASS AND LARRIE ARE CHECKING AROUND TOWN FOR THE REST OF THE GANG.
LET'S GO IN THE COUNTRY CHURCH AND TAKE A LOOK IN THERE.
HOLY CATZ #@! LET'S SPLIT WE CAN LEAVE ACES BIKE HERE.
CASS, YOU WAIT AT THIS DOOR, I'LL GO INTO THE BACK ENTRANCE!
COUNTRY CHURCH OF ONTARIO
I JUST HOPE THAT EVERYTHINGS IS O.K. INSIDE LARRIE
INSIDE THE CHURCH THE SERVICE CONTINUES
I HAD NO REAL PEACE UNTIL I TURNED MY LIFE OVER TO MY LORD AND SAVIOR, JESUS CHRIST. IS THERE SOMEONE OUT THERE THAT WANTS WHAT I HAVE? COME FORWARD, REMEMBER JESUS CHRIST LOVES YOU, IS THERE SOMEONE? "PRAISE GOD!"
MY NAMES ACE AND I'M TIRED OF THE WAY I LIVE, I WANT TO ACCEPT JESUS CHRIST AS MY SAVIOR.
THE MEN WHO WERE IN THE VAN ARE THE ONES WHO HELD UP THE HOT STUFF CAFE, THEY ARE ALL DEAD, MAY GOD HAVE MERCY ON THEM WE TRIED TO STOP THEM.
DIANNA DO YOU OR PAM HAVE ANYTHING TO TELL CASS?
YES, MOTHER, WE HITCHHIKED A RIDE WITH THE MEN IN THE VAN, PLUS THEY KIDNAPED US, WE PRAYED FOR JESUS TO DELIVER US FROM THEM PRAISE, GOD HE DID, FORGIVE US MOTHER WE ARE TRULY SORRY.
CASS I'D LIKE YOU TO MEET ACE HE CAME FORWARD TONIGHT.
DO I KNOW YOU ACE?
YES, CASS MY REAL NAME IS TOM HARRIS YOU TRIED YEARS AGO TO TELL ME ABOUT THE LORD, WHEN I THINK I COULD OF DIED LIKE MY BIKER PALS AND GONE TO HELL, BUT, NOW I KNOW IF I DIED I'D GO TO HEAVEN
ROM. 6:23
DANN, NOW THAT I AM SAVED, WHAT SHOULD I DO?
START READING YOUR BIBLE EVERY DAY
TOM DON'T EVER FORGET, GOD LOVES US IN SPITE OF OURSELVES.
I BELIEVE THAT ALSO.

Notes: Dann's most recent tract story is from 2010. It's actually his rough storyboard, but it was never redrawn because inmates seemed to enjoy it as it was. It was probably never released in tract form either, as many prisons started to forbid the use of staples in the binding (since they are used by inmates to make tattoos). So instead, Dann printed it on 11 x 17" sheets and distributed it that way.

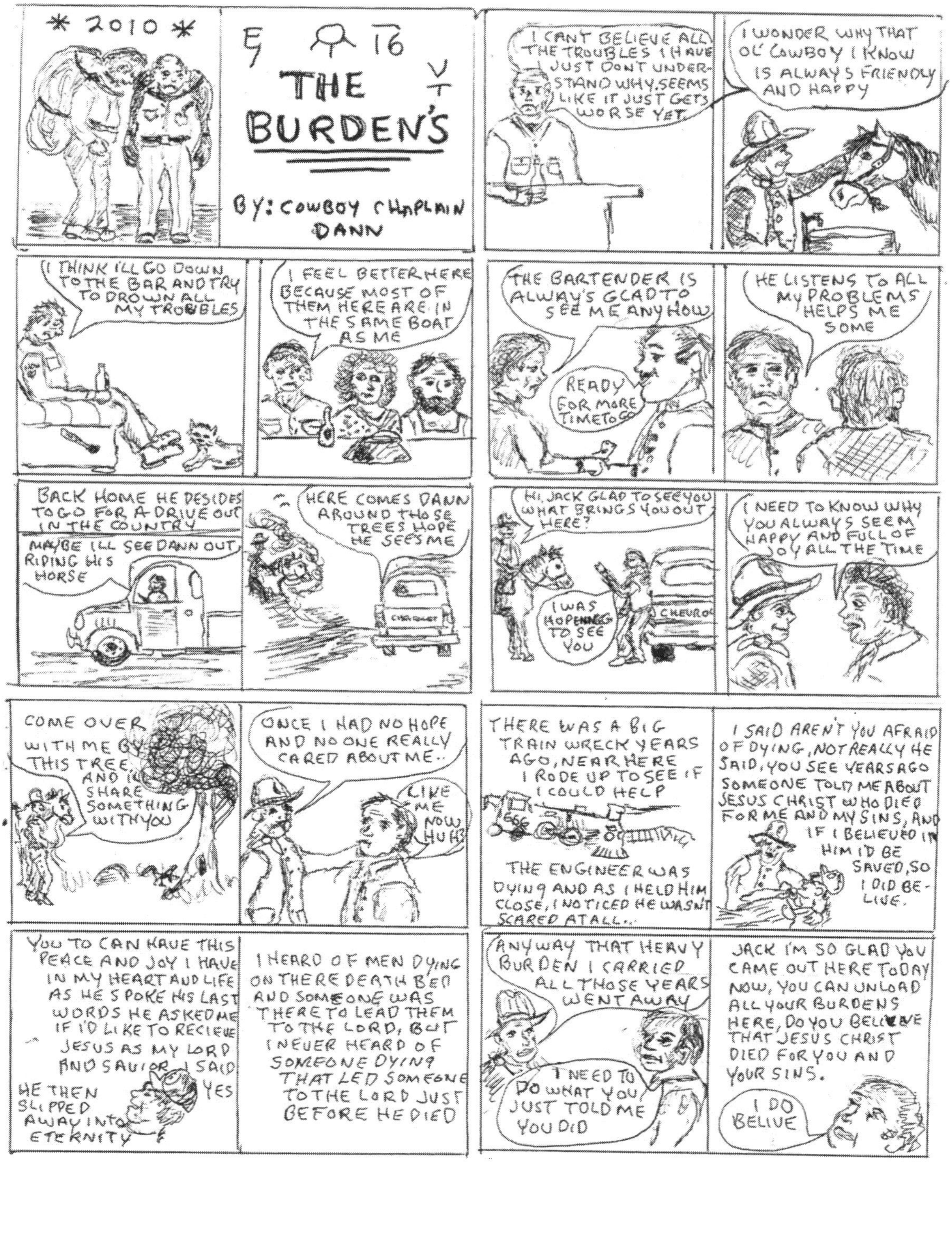

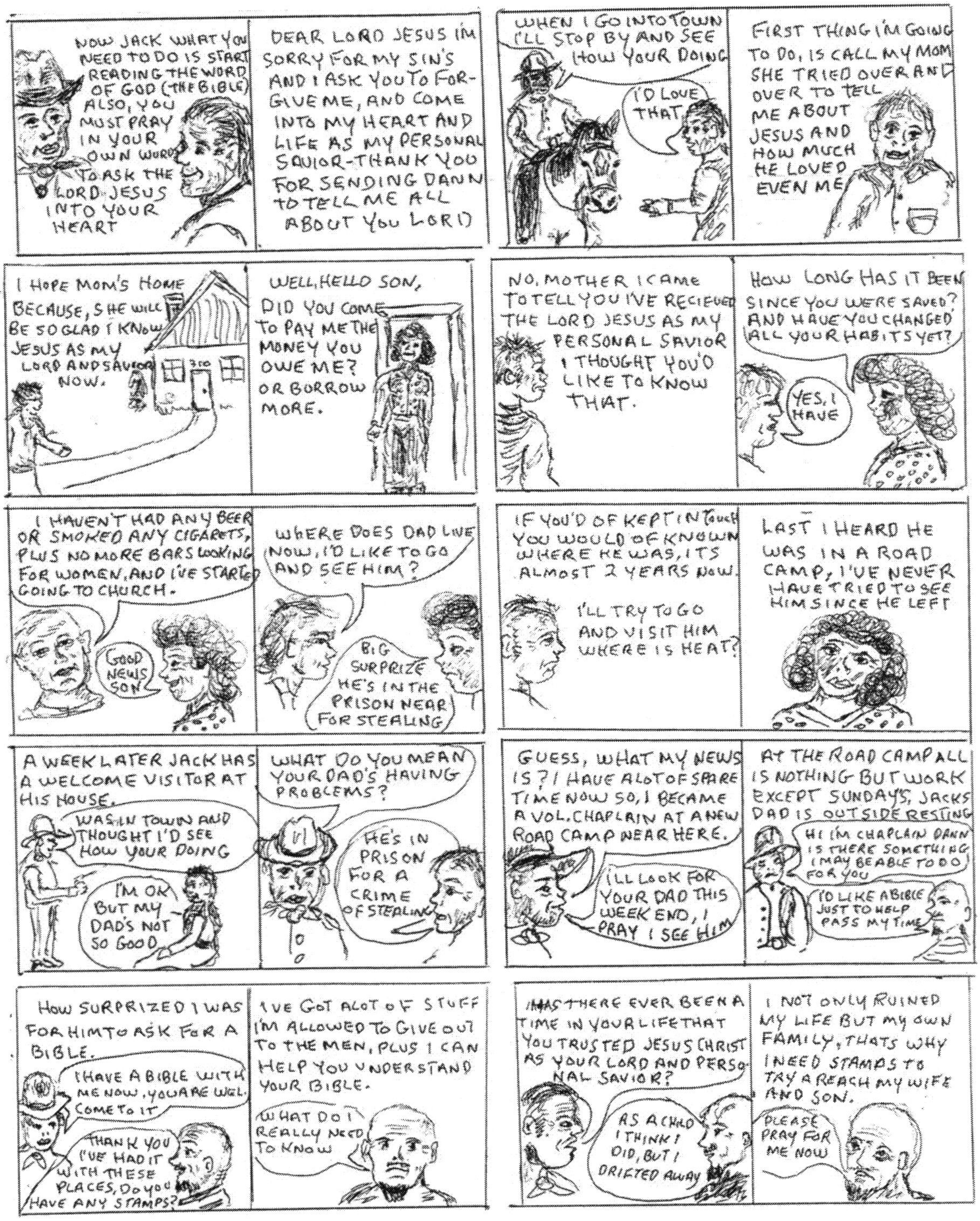
NOW JACK WHAT YOU NEED TO DO IS START READING THE WORD OF GOD (THE BIBLE) ALSO, YOU MUST PRAY IN YOUR OWN WORDS TO ASK THE LORD JESUS INTO YOUR HEART
DEAR LORD JESUS I'M SORRY FOR MY SIN'S AND I ASK YOU TO FOR-GIVE ME, AND COME INTO MY HEART AND LIFE AS MY PERSONAL SAVIOR-THANK YOU FOR SENDING DANN TO TELL ME ALL ABOUT YOU LORD
WHEN I GO INTO TOWN I'LL STOP BY AND SEE HOW YOUR DOING
I'D LOVE THAT
FIRST THING I'M GOING TO DO, IS CALL MY MOM SHE TRIED OVER AND OVER TO TELL ME ABOUT JESUS AND HOW MUCH HE LOVED EVEN ME
I HOPE MOM'S HOME BECAUSE, SHE WILL BE SO GLAD I KNOW JESUS AS MY LORD AND SAVIOR NOW.
WELL, HELLO SON, DID YOU COME TO PAY ME THE MONEY YOU OWE ME? OR BORROW MORE.
NO, MOTHER I CAME TO TELL YOU I'VE RECIEVED THE LORD JESUS AS MY PERSONAL SAVIOR I THOUGHT YOU'D LIKE TO KNOW THAT.
HOW LONG HAS IT BEEN SINCE YOU WERE SAVED? AND HAVE YOU CHANGED ALL YOUR HABITS YET?
YES, I HAVE
I HAVEN'T HAD ANY BEER OR SMOKED ANY CIGARETS, PLUS NO MORE BARS LOOKING FOR WOMEN, AND I'VE STARTED GOING TO CHURCH.
GOOD NEWS SON
WHERE DOES DAD LIVE NOW, I'D LIKE TO GO AND SEE HIM?
BIG SURPRIZE HE'S IN THE PRISON NEAR FOR STEALING
IF YOU'D OF KEPT IN TOUCH YOU WOULD OF KNOWN WHERE HE WAS, ITS ALMOST 2 YEARS NOW.
I'LL TRY TO GO AND VISIT HIM WHERE IS HE AT?
LAST I HEARD HE WAS IN A ROAD CAMP, I'VE NEVER HAVE TRIED TO SEE HIM SINCE HE LEFT
A WEEK LATER JACK HAS A WELCOME VISITOR AT HIS HOUSE.
WAS IN TOWN AND THOUGHT I'D SEE HOW YOUR DOING
I'M OK BUT MY DAD'S NOT SO GOOD
WHAT DO YOU MEAN YOUR DAD'S HAVING PROBLEMS?
HE'S IN PRISON FOR A CRIME OF STEALING
GUESS, WHAT MY NEWS IS? I HAVE ALOT OF SPARE TIME NOW SO, I BECAME A VOL. CHAPLAIN AT A NEW ROAD CAMP NEAR HERE.
I'LL LOOK FOR YOUR DAD THIS WEEK END, I PRAY I SEE HIM
AT THE ROAD CAMP ALL IS NOTHING BUT WORK EXCEPT SUNDAYS, JACKS DAD IS OUTSIDE RESTING
HI I'M CHAPLAIN DANN IS THERE SOMETHING I MAY BE ABLE TO DO FOR YOU
I'D LIKE A BIBLE JUST TO HELP PASS MY TIME
HOW SURPRIZED I WAS FOR HIM TO ASK FOR A BIBLE.
I HAVE A BIBLE WITH ME NOW, YOU ARE WEL-COME TO IT
THANK YOU I'VE HAD IT WITH THESE PLACES, DO YOU HAVE ANY STAMPS?
I'VE GOT ALOT OF STUFF I'M ALLOWED TO GIVE OUT TO THE MEN, PLUS I CAN HELP YOU UNDERSTAND YOUR BIBLE.
WHAT DO I REALLY NEED TO KNOW
WAS THERE EVER BEEN A TIME IN YOUR LIFE THAT YOU TRUSTED JESUS CHRIST AS YOUR LORD AND PERSO-NAL SAVIOR?
AS A CHILD I THINK I DID, BUT I DRIFTED AWAY
I NOT ONLY RUINED MY LIFE BUT MY OWN FAMILY, THATS WHY I NEED STAMPS TO TRY A REACH MY WIFE AND SON.
PLEASE PRAY FOR ME NOW

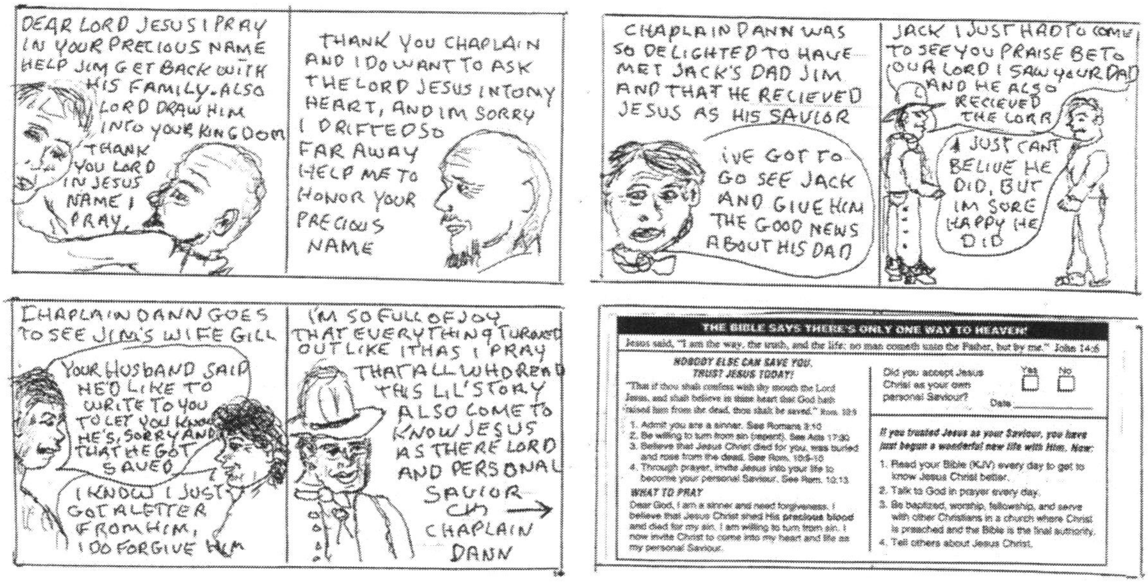

Notes: This 1999 story looks like another rough draft storyboard that wasn't redrawn, but printed on two 8.5 x 14" sheets (or one double-sided sheet). Perhaps the inflammatory comments about other religions (especially the Catholics) limited the distribution and efforts to produce it. Whatever the reason, it is fortunate that a copy survived because it's a true classic, reminiscent of Jack Chick's *The Last Generation*--but even more graphic and over the top. The person who converts at the end is icing on the cake!

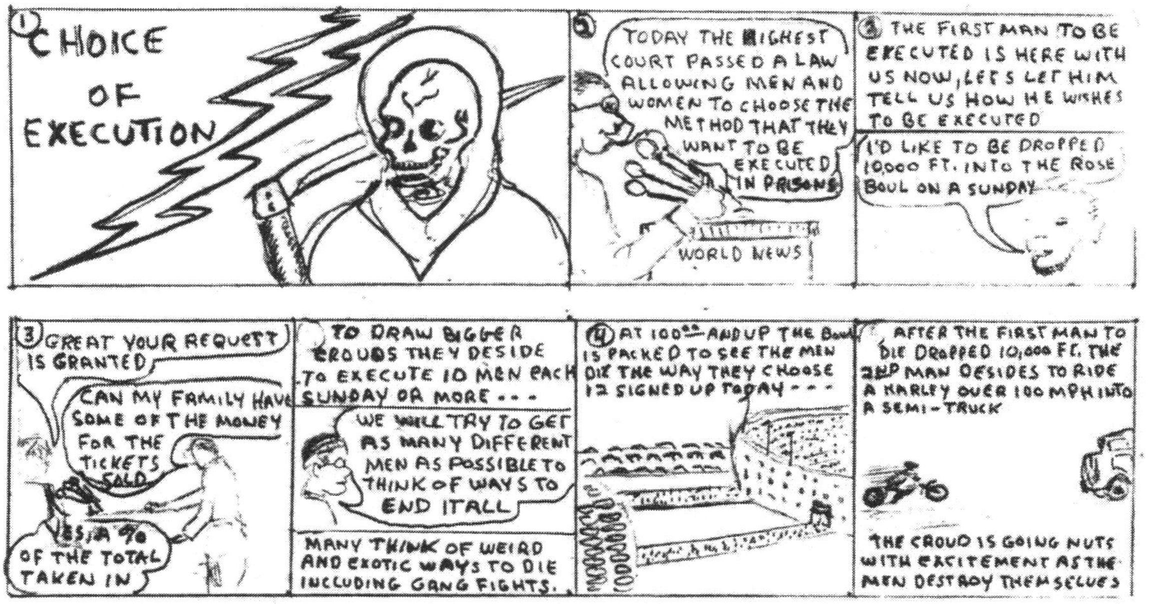

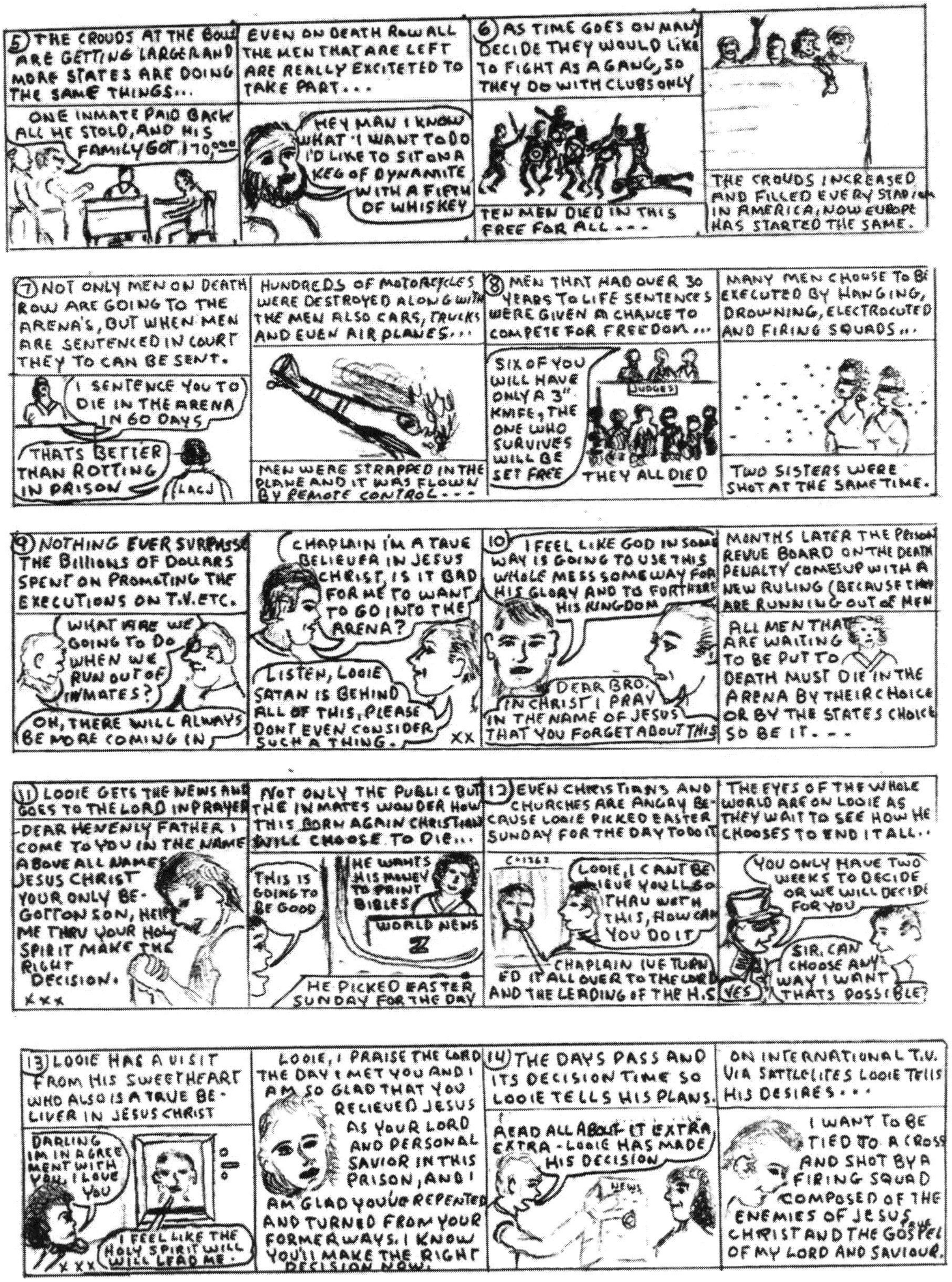

5 THE CROWDS AT THE BOWL ARE GETTING LARGER AND MORE STATES ARE DOING THE SAME THINGS...
ONE INMATE PAID BACK ALL HE STOLD, AND HIS FAMILY GOT 170,000
EVEN ON DEATH ROW ALL THE MEN THAT ARE LEFT ARE REALLY EXCITETED TO TAKE PART...
HEY MAN I KNOW WHAT I WANT TO DO I'D LIKE TO SIT ON A KEG OF DYNAMITE WITH A FIFTH OF WHISKEY
6 AS TIME GOES ON MANY DECIDE THEY WOULD LIKE TO FIGHT AS A GANG, SO THEY DO WITH CLUBS ONLY
TEN MEN DIED IN THIS FREE FOR ALL...
THE CROWDS INCREASED AND FILLED EVERY STADIUM IN AMERICA, NOW EUROPE HAS STARTED THE SAME.
7 NOT ONLY MEN ON DEATH ROW ARE GOING TO THE ARENA'S, BUT WHEN MEN ARE SENTENCED IN COURT THEY TO CAN BE SENT.
I SENTENCE YOU TO DIE IN THE ARENA IN 60 DAYS
THATS BETTER THAN ROTTING IN PRISON
LACJ
HUNDREDS OF MOTORCYCLES WERE DESTROYED ALONG WITH THE MEN ALSO CARS, TRUCKS AND EVEN AIRPLANES...
MEN WERE STRAPPED IN THE PLANE AND IT WAS FLOWN BY REMOTE CONTROL...
8 MEN THAT HAD OVER 30 YEARS TO LIFE SENTENCES WERE GIVEN A CHANCE TO COMPETE FOR FREEDOM...
SIX OF YOU WILL HAVE ONLY A 3" KNIFE, THE ONE WHO SURVIVES WILL BE SET FREE
JUDGES
THEY ALL DIED
MANY MEN CHOUSE TO BE EXECUTED BY HANGING, DROWNING, ELECTROCUTED AND FIRING SQUADS...
TWO SISTERS WERE SHOT AT THE SAME TIME.
9 NOTHING EVER SURPASSES THE BILLIONS OF DOLLARS SPENT ON PROMOTING THE EXECUTIONS ON T.V. ETC.
WHAT ARE WE GOING TO DO WHEN WE RUN OUT OF INMATES?
OH, THERE WILL ALWAYS BE MORE COMING IN
CHAPLAIN I'M A TRUE BELIEVER IN JESUS CHRIST, IS IT BAD FOR ME TO WANT TO GO INTO THE ARENA?
LISTEN, LOOIE SATAN IS BEHIND ALL OF THIS, PLEASE DONT EVEN CONSIDER SUCH A THING.
XX
10 I FEEL LIKE GOD IN SOME WAY IS GOING TO USE THIS WHOLE MESS SOME WAY FOR HIS GLORY AND TO FURTHER HIS KINGDOM
DEAR BRO. IN CHRIST I PRAY IN THE NAME OF JESUS THAT YOU FORGET ABOUT THIS
MONTHS LATER THE PRISON REVUE BOARD ON THE DEATH PENALTY COMES UP WITH A NEW RULING (BECAUSE THEY ARE RUNNING OUT OF MEN
ALL MEN THAT ARE WAITING TO BE PUT TO DEATH MUST DIE IN THE ARENA BY THEIR CHOICE OR BY THE STATES CHOICE SO BE IT...
11 LOOIE GETS THE NEWS AND GOES TO THE LORD IN PRAYER
DEAR HEVENLY FATHER I COME TO YOU IN THE NAME ABOVE ALL NAMES JESUS CHRIST YOUR ONLY BEGOTTON SON, HELP ME THRU YOUR HOLY SPIRIT MAKE THE RIGHT DECISION.
XXX
NOT ONLY THE PUBLIC BUT THE INMATES WONDER HOW THIS BORN AGAIN CHRISTIAN WILL CHOOSE TO DIE...
THIS IS GOING TO BE GOOD
HE WANTS HIS MONEY TO PRINT BIBLES
WORLD NEWS
HE PICKED EASTER SUNDAY FOR THE DAY
12 EVEN CHRISTIANS AND CHURCHES ARE ANGRY BECAUSE LOOIE PICKED EASTER SUNDAY FOR THE DAY TO DO IT
LOOIE, I CANT BELIEVE YOU'LL GO THRU WITH THIS, HOW CAN YOU DO IT
CHAPLAIN I'VE TURNED IT ALL OVER TO THE LORD AND THE LEADING OF THE H.S.
THE EYES OF THE WHOLE WORLD ARE ON LOOIE AS THEY WAIT TO SEE HOW HE CHOOSES TO END IT ALL..
YOU ONLY HAVE TWO WEEKS TO DECIDE OR WE WILL DECIDE FOR YOU
SIR, CAN I CHOOSE ANY WAY I WANT THATS POSSIBLE?
YES
13 LOOIE HAS A VISIT FROM HIS SWEETHEART WHO ALSO IS A TRUE BELIVER IN JESUS CHRIST
DARLING IM IN AGREEMENT WITH YOU, I LOVE YOU
I FEEL LIKE THE HOLY SPIRIT WILL LEAD ME.
XXX
LOOIE, I PRAISE THE LORD THE DAY I MET YOU AND I AM SO GLAD THAT YOU RECIEVED JESUS AS YOUR LORD AND PERSONAL SAVIOR IN THIS PRISON, AND I AM GLAD YOU'VE REPENTED AND TURNED FROM YOUR FORMER WAYS. I KNOW YOU'LL MAKE THE RIGHT DECISION NOW.
14 THE DAYS PASS AND ITS DECISION TIME SO LOOIE TELLS HIS PLANS.
READ ALL ABOUT IT EXTRA EXTRA - LOOIE HAS MADE HIS DECISION
NEWS
ON INTERNATIONAL T.V. VIA SATTELLITES LOOIE TELLS HIS DESIRES...
I WANT TO BE TIED TO A CROSS AND SHOT BY A FIRING SQUAD COMPOSED OF THE ENEMIES OF JESUS CHRIST AND THE GOSPEL OF MY LORD AND SAVIOUR.

15) WHAT A SHOCK TO THE WORLD TO HEAR SUCH A STATEMENT ON T.V.
AND WHO DO YOU CONSIDER TO BE HIS ENEMIES AND WHY?
XXX
FIRST OF ALL THE MORMON GROUP OF L.D.S. IS ONE OF CULTS. THAT DOES TEACH WRONG ABOUT WHO JESUS CHRIST REALLY WAS AND THEY PUT MOST OF THEIR FAITH IN JOSEPH SMITH AND THE BOOK OF MORMON, ALSO THEY TEACH YOUR SAVED MOSTLY BY GOOD WORKS.
16) NEXT IS THE JEHOVAHS WITNESSES WHO ALSO TRUST IN A MANS WRITINGS - HIS NAME IS PASTOR RUSSELL AND JUDGE RUTHERFORD PLUS THEY TAKE MANY SCRIPTURES OUT OF CONTEXT LIKE THEY SAY THE 144,000 JEWS IN REV. ARE JEHOVAHS WIT. ALSO THEY KEEP SETTING A TIME FOR JESUS RETURN TO EARTH - THEY ALSO DENY THERE IS A LITERAL HELL -
SO WHAT YOU WANT IS A PERSON REPRESENTING EACH OF THESE GROUPS TO BE IN YOUR FIRING SQAD
YES SIR AND THERE IS MANY MORE
XXX
17) AS LOOIE CONTINUES HE NAMES MORE FALSE RELIGIONS INCLUDING....
SPIRITUALISM / UNITY
BAHA'ISM (BAHA'U'LLAH)
ZEN BUDDHISM
HUMANISM / LIBERALISM
CHRISTIAN SCIENCE
SEVEN DAY ADVENTIST
ROSICRUCIANISM
UNITARIANISM - UNIVERSALISM
XXX
AS LOOIE THE TRUE BELIEVER CONTINUES TO NAME MORE AND MORE FALSE RELIGIONS THE PEOPLE WHO ARE INTO THESE CULTS CALL IN TO THE T.V. STATION TO VOLUNTEER TO BE ON THE FIRING SQUAD
I'VE BEEN A MORMON ALL MY LIFE AND IM ALSO A EXPERT SHOT WITH A RIFLE, CAN I COME AS A MEMBER OF THE SQUAD?
18) NOW THERE IS SOMETHING NO ONE HAD FIGURED ON TWO MEN WHO ALSO ARE BORN AGAIN BELIEVERS WANT TO BE PUT ON CROSSES ALSO BESIDE LOOIE, JOE AND DAN...
YOU BOTH WANT TO DO THIS WELL YOU CAN.
PRAISE GOD
XXX
THE WHOLE WORLD IS ALL EXCITED ABOUT THE FIRST CHRISTIANS TO FIND THE LORD JESUS CHRIST AS THEIR SAVIOR (IN PRISON TOO)
YOU HAVE PICKED OVER 200 DIFFERENT ENEMIES SO FAR
IM A ATHEIST CAN I ALSO JOIN THE FIRING SQAD?
YES, SIR AND THERE IS MORE
19) I'VE SAVED THIS ONE UNTIL THE LAST - SINCE IT IS THE MOST KNOWN AND MOST POWERFULL IN ITS WEALTH, ALSO HAS OVER 1 BILLION BLIND FOLLOWERS.
IT'S THE ROMAN CATHOLIC INSTITUTION
OF ALL THE REST OF THE FALSE RELIGIONS AND CULTS NAMED SO FAR THIS ONE HAS CAUSED MORE DISTURBANCE BY FAR
WE JUST GOT A CALL FROM THE POPE AT THE VATICAN AND HE DEMANDS AN EXPLAINATION
XXX
20) EXPLAINATION OF THEIR BELIEFS
① SOURCE OF AUTHORITY ROMAN CATHOLIC CHURCH
② THE GODHEAD ORTHODOX
③ HUMAN NATURE AND SIN ORTHODOX
④ WAY OF SALVATION ONLY FOUND IN R.C. CHURCH
⑤ THE FUTURE. ORTHODOX X FOR DOCTRINE of PURGATORY
COMPARED TO CHRISTIANITY BEING BORN AGAIN
① SOURCE of AUTHORITY THE BIBLE (GODS HOLY WORD)
② THE GODHEAD (TRINITY) FATHER SON AND HOLY SPIRIT
③ HUMAN NATURE AND SIN - SIN ENTERED THE WORLD BY ADAMS FALL, ALL MEN ARE SINNERS
④ WAY OF SALVATION - MAN IS SAVED BY GRACE THROUGH FAITH IN THE VICARIOUS ATONEMENT AND SHED BLOOD OF THE LORD JESUS
21) THIS WHOLE UNIVERSAL T.V. SPECIAL IS CAUSEING MORE UPROAR THAN ANYTHING BEFORE ITS TIME.
AS FOR THE FUTURE AFTER THE DEATH OF A TRUE BELIEVER IN JESUS CHRIST WE BELIEVE IN A LITERAL HELL AS THE BIBLE TEACHES, AND A LITERAL HEAVEN FOR THE REDEEMED THAT BELIEVE JESUS SHED HIS BLOOD ON THE CROSS FOR THEIR SINS AND THAT HE AROSE AGAIN TO CONQUER DEATH
THE FIRING SQUAD IS GETTING READY FOR EXECUTION ON EASTER SUNDAY, OVER 500 DIFFERENT CULTS REPRESENTED
ITS THE POPES PLANE HE'S COME TO JOIN THE FIRING SQUAD
THOSE BORN AGAIN CHRISTIANS WILL BE DISINTIGRATED TOMMORO
22) FINALLY THE T.V. PROGRAM GOES OFF THE AIR...
YOU KNOW LOOIE I'D LIKE YOU TO PRAY FOR ME, I DONT WANT TO TAKE PART IN YOUR EXECUTION, I WANT TO BECOME A CHRISTIAN NOW THAT I SEE HOW ALL THESE OTHER FALSE RELIGIONS HAVE DECIVED MOST OF THE WORLD, WHAT MUST I DO TO BECOME A CHRISTIAN.
LOOIE, TELLS PAUL TO BOW HIS HEAD AND ADMIT HE IS A SINNER (ROM 3:23) TO REPENT (LUKE 13:5) THEN TO BELIEVE JESUS DIED FOR HIM ROM 10:9 AND THEN ASK JESUS TO COME INTO HIS HEART AND BE HIS PERSONAL SAVIOUR. ASK JESUS TO BE LORD OF HIS LIFE. ROM-12 1-2
THANK YOU LORD IN JESUS NAME
23) EASTER SUNDAY AND MILLIONS WATCH AT THE ARENA AND ON INTERNATIONAL T.V AS THE FIRING SQUAD OF OVER 500 GET READY TO EXECUTE THESE 3 BORN AGAIN BELIEVERS IN JESUS CHRIST THE LORD....
COME HITHER
READY AIM
WHAT HAPPENED TO THE MEN ON THE CROSSES ARE GONE YET ALL THE FIRING SQUAD IS LEFT - EXPLAINATION ON BACK
24)
AT JESUS SECOND COMMING HE WILL APPEAR IN THE SKY, AND ALL WHO TRULY BELIEVE IN HIM AS THEIR PERSONAL LORD AND SAVOUIR WILL BE CAUGHT UP TO MEET HIM, AND SHALL BE WITH HIM FOREVER IN ETERNITY -

Notes: This tract has the earliest date (1981). Dann's art is very rough, but he gets to relate some cowboy memories and include his favorite horse, Rondo. The cover features brands from the ranches he worked for, like "50" from the Matador, bar sixteen (the Jimmy Fox ranch) and F cross bar (the Louie Cortese ranch).

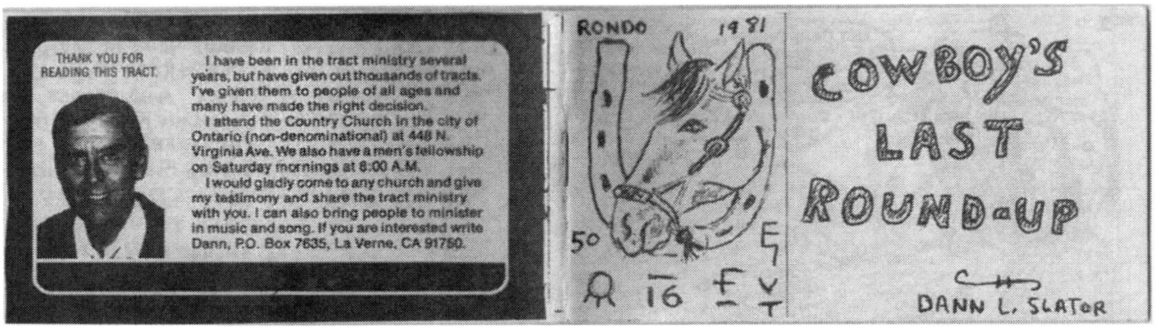

"RONDO"
16
BOY YOU COULDN'T PAY ME ENOUGH TO RIDE THAT BLACK OUTLAW HORSE.
OH GOD HELP ME — OHHH! MY
NO ONE CAN NOW

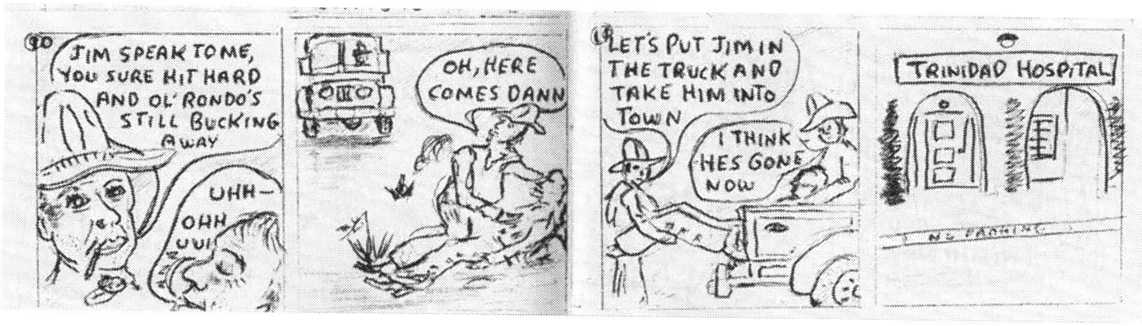
JIM SPEAK TO ME, YOU SURE HIT HARD AND OL' RONDO'S STILL BUCKING AWAY
UHH- OHH UUI
OH, HERE COMES DANN
LET'S PUT JIM IN THE TRUCK AND TAKE HIM INTO TOWN
I THINK HES GONE NOW
TRINIDAD HOSPITAL

YOU HAVE A VISITOR HIS NAME IS DANN, DO YOU WANT TO TALK TO HIM?
YES, SEND HIM IN NOW DOC.
I GUESS YOUR MAD BECAUSE I RODE OL' RONDO, I'M SORRY I DONE SUCH A DUMB THING NOW.
JIM I'M NOT MAD AT YOU I'M JUST GLAD YOU DIDN'T GET KILLED, DID YOU READ ANY OF THE TRACTS I LEFT FOR YOU?
NO
BACK AT THE RANCH
JOHN I SEEN JIM TODAY HE IS BETTER NOW.
HOPE YOU DIDNT PREACH TO HIM ABOUT HELL AND DAMNATION

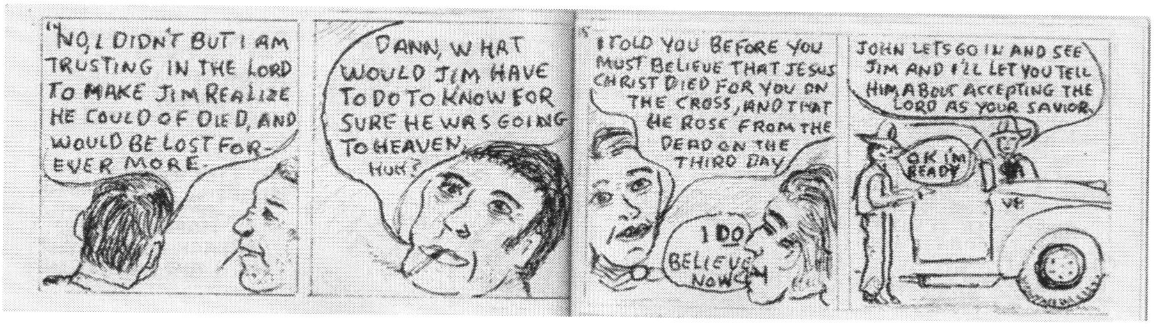
"NO, I DIDN'T BUT I AM TRUSTING IN THE LORD TO MAKE JIM REALIZE HE COULD OF DIED, AND WOULD BE LOST FOR-EVER MORE.
DANN, WHAT WOULD JIM HAVE TO DO TO KNOW FOR SURE HE WAS GOING TO HEAVEN, HUH?
I TOLD YOU BEFORE YOU MUST BELIEVE THAT JESUS CHRIST DIED FOR YOU ON THE CROSS, AND THAT HE ROSE FROM THE DEAD ON THE THIRD DAY
I DO BELIEVE NOW
JOHN LETS GO IN AND SEE JIM AND I'LL LET YOU TELL HIM ABOUT ACCEPTING THE LORD AS YOUR SAVIOR.
OK I'M READY

16
DANN, I CAN'T BELIEVE HOW GOOD IT IS TO KNOW MY SINS ARE FORGIVEN
YEA, JOHN AND WHEN YOU DO SIN ASK JESUS TO FORGIVE YOU
AND DONT SIN ANYMORE
JIM, GUESS WHAT I ALSO BELIEVE THE THINGS DANN HAS BEEN TELLING US ABOUT JESUS
I READ THE TRACTS HE LEFT ME
17
I MAY NOT UNDERSTAND ALL THAT'S IN THOSE BOOKS BUT, I SURE AIN'T TAKING ANY MORE CHANCES. I WANT TO BE SAVED TOO..
JIM I AM SO HAPPY FOR YOU - PRAISE GOD. AND THE DOCTOR SAID WE CAN TAKE YOU BACK TO THE RANCH
DANN, JIM AND JOHN ALL WENT BACK TO WORK-

18
HEY, JIM WHO IS THE NEW COWBOY OUT IN THE ROUND CORRAL?
OH, HE MUST BE THE NEW HIRED HAND FROM NEW MEXICO.
WHOA, YOU #Z@% OUTLAW
19
OH BOY WE HAVE GOT TO START PRAYING FOR THIS NEW MAN SO HE CAN HAVE THE PEACE WE HAVE
YOU GUYS SURE HAVE SOME SNAKY HORSES HERE - MY NAME IS CLEMENTE ANYONE GOT SOME WHISKY?

20
JIM JUST GOT OUT OF THE HOSPITAL, AND NONE OF US DRINK LIQUOR
I CAN SEE THIS PLACE IS DEAD
WEEK'S LATER IN THE BUNKHOUSE . . .
CLEMENTE HAVE YOU EVER GONE TO CHURCH?
I DID WHEN I WAS A BOY
21
DANN, I'VE GOT TO TELL YOU SOMETHING, I KNEW JIM A LONG TIME AGO, I KNOW HE DON'T REMEMBER ME. HE WAS A MEAN HOMBRE, NOW I CAN SEE HOW HE HAS CHANGED
AND I HAVE DECIDED TO TRY AND CHANGE MY WAYS SO I CAN ENJOY MY LIFE MORE, I MAY EVEN CONSIDER BECOMING A CHRISTIAN SOON.

22
CLEMENTE, IF YOU HAVE THE LEAST DESIRE TO BECOME A CHRISTIAN DO IT NOW.
I WOULD LIKE TO KNOW WHAT I MUST DO.
FIRST ADMIT YOUR A SINNE THEN ASK GOD IN JESUS NAME TO FORGIVE YOU. NOW PRAY FOR JESUS TO COME INTO YOUR HEART TO STAY.
DEAR JESUS COME INTO MY HEART TO STAY
23
WELL RONDO I GUESS WE WILL MOVE ON TO ANOTHER RANCH AND SEE WHAT THE LORD HAS FOR US
THANK YOU FOR TAKING TIME TO READ THIS LIL' STORY AND PLEASE, IF YOU HAVE NEVER EVER CONSIDERED YOUR SOUL'S FINAL RESTING PLACE - DO SO NOW ASK JESUS CHRIST TO COME INTO YOUR HEART AND BE YOUR LORD AND SAVIOR.

Notes: This 1983 tract contains one of Dann's most policaly incorrect and outlandish plots: A gay prisoner is saved and becomes straight. However unbelievable, it is a true story, drawn by the artist/ prisoner that it happened to. His name is Rod (seriously!) and his initials are RSL. He also drew several other tracts for Dann, but this one was all about Rod. Dann's image is often cut and pasted in from various Chick tracts.

LISTEN CARLA. MY NAME'S BRUISER AND FROM NOW ON YOU'LL GO OUT WITH ME AND ONLY ME! GOT IT?
S...S...SURE BRUISER!
YOU'RE NOT GOOD ENOUGH FOR ANYTHING YOU !!&*??**! GET OUT OF MY SIGHT!!
I JOHN 3:8
THERE MUST BE SOMEONE OUT THERE WHO WILL LOVE ME WITHOUT WANTING SOMETHING IN RETURN!
ROM. 5:8
HOW ABOUT A DATE SAILOR?
SURE, HOW MUCH?
$20 — THAT WAS EASY!

SAY GOOD LOOKING, HOW ABOUT A DATE?
WHAT WILL I GET FOR ALL MY MONEY?
WELL, $20 FOR AN HOUR IN BED WITH ME ALONE.
YOU'RE UNDER ARREST FOR SOLICITATION!!
I'M A POLICEMAN!
PUT HER IN WITH THE ANIMALS. THAT SHOULD QUIET THEM DOWN. HA-HA-HA!
LOOK GUYS! AINT SHE CUTE? WATCH ME! I GET HER FIRST.

AIN'T YOU BRUISER'S OLD LADY??
YES I AM. WHY?
DON'T WORRY MOMMA. MY LAWYER KNOWS THE JUDGE PERSONALLY. HE CAN GET YOU OUT OF HERE REAL QUICK!
GEE! THANKS A LOT!!
JER. 7:8
YOU HAVE BEEN FOUND GUILTY. DO YOU HAVE ANY THING TO SAY BEFORE I SENTENCE YOU?
NO YOUR HONOR!
GAL. 6:7
I HEREBY SENTENCE YOU TO THREE YEARS IN THE STATE PRISON. I HOPE YOU LEARN YOUR LESSON!!

I CAN'T BELIEVE IT! THREE YEARS! HE'S JUST PICKING ON ME BECAUSE I'M GAY!
NOW CARLA'S ON HIS WAY TO.....
.....PRISON!!!
STATE PRISON
CARLA MAKES MANY INSTANT "FRIENDS"
WE CAN HAVE SOME GOOD TIMES TOGETHER YOU SEXY THING YOU!
OH GOD HELP ME!
I LOVE YOU!
I LOVE YOU MORE!!
I WANT YOUR BODY!
SAY MOMMA! COME OVER HERE
ROM. 2:12

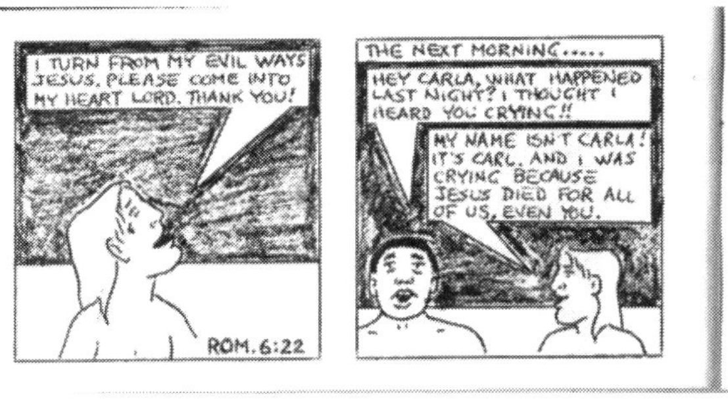

YOU TOO CAN ACCEPT JESUS AS YOUR SAVIOUR AND LORD. BY BELIEVING THAT HE* DIED FOR ALL OUR SINS AND BY TRUSTING IN HIM, WE CAN REPENT FROM OUR SINS AND HAVE ETERNAL LIFE. WON'T YOU ACCEPT HIM NOW BEFORE IT'S TOO LATE? HE REALLY DOES LOVE YOU.

* JOHN 3:16

Notes: This 1986 tract was drawn by Rod (RSL) and features a guard who asked to be included in a tract. But when prison officials got angry about it, Banks denied it, so Dann blotted out his name in later copies.

RON KNOWS BILL HAS A BIG SAFE, SO HE ASKS IF HE CAN PUT SOME OF HIS THINGS IN IT FOR SAFE KEEPING...
THANKS, BILL! I'M SO GLAD YOU'LL KEEP IT UNTIL WE GET BACK FROM THE VACATION.
NO PROBLEM!
UNKNOWN TO BILL, THE THINGS ARE STOLEN RARE COINS AND JEWELRY.
THAT'S THE NICEST CAMPER I'VE EVER SEEN! I'M GLAD I'M GOING WITH YOU. HOPE WE CAN GO FISHING IN COLORADO.
ARRIVING AT A BEAUTIFUL LAKE IN COLORADO, THEY DECIDE TO GO FISHING BEFORE THEY DO ANYTHING.
BILL, I KEEP THINKING OF WHAT THAT CHAPLAIN SAID AT THE FUNERAL. WOW!! I'VE GOT A BITE!
IT'S A BIG ONE! REEL IT IN SLOW. DON'T LOSE IT!
IN ALL OF THE EXCITEMENT, BANKS SEES HOW BIG THE FISH ON HIS LINE IS AND HAS A HEART ATTACK...
WHAT A PLACE TO HAVE THIS HAPPEN. I DON'T KNOW WHAT TO DO. RON, CAN YOU TALK? SAY SOMETHING TO ME.
HOW DO I KNOW WHERE I'M GOING IF I SHOULD DIE?

BILL DOES NOT KNOW HOW TO ANSWER HIS DYING PAL, BUT RON TRIES TO TALK MORE WHILE IN SUCH PAIN...
BILL, OH, MY CHEST! I'VE GOT TO TELL YOU ABOUT THAT... OH MY GOD!... STUFF IN YOUR SAFE, OOOH! AH!!
RON! RON! RON! HE'S GONE!
AFTER RON IS TAKEN AWAY, BILL AND ANN DECIDE TO MOVE ON TO TEXAS...
I WONDER WHAT RON PUT IN OUR SAFE. HE TRIED TO TELL ME ALL ABOUT IT.
OH! JUST A BUNCH OF PAPERS AND STUFF. DON'T WORRY ABOUT IT.
BACK IN BREA, SOME MEN ARE PLANNING A BREAK-IN AT BILL'S HOUSE...
HEY, RON! I KNOW NOBODY'S AROUND HERE. I SCOPED IT OUT FOR A WEEK.
LET'S CHECK IT OUT. MAYBE THERE'S A CAR IN THE GARAGE. WE CAN FILL IT UP AND TAKE THAT, TOO. HA-HA-HA!
MAN, RON! THERE'S A SAFE BEHIND THIS PICTURE. IT MUST BE LOADED!! WOW!
LET'S LOAD THE CAR FIRST, THEN WE'LL BLOW THIS BABY AND SPLIT.
CHUCK, THE OTHER MAN, HAS FOUND A FALSE CLOSET FULL OF FIREARMS.

ALL LOADED, THEY'RE READY TO TRY TO GET INTO THE BIG SAFE...
WHAT A HAUL! MAN! WE CAN GET A LOT FOR THIS CAR AT THE CHOP-SHOP.
INSIDE GARAGE
NOT WANTING TO MAKE ANY NOISE, THEY TRY OTHER WAYS. THEY DON'T KNOW THE SAFE HAS A SILENT ALARM.
IT'S CUTTING THE METAL NOW. IT WON'T BE LONG! GO CHECK OUT FRONT, RON!
IT'S ABOUT OPEN. I CAN'T WAIT TO SEE
HIDDEN OUTSIDE THE PLACE IS AN ARMY OF POLICEMEN WAITING FOR THEM TO COME OUT...
I HEARD SOMETHING. MUST BE THE BURGLARS. WATCH THAT DOOR, BUT STAY OUT OF SIGHT. OKAY?
WHEN I SEE THAT DOOR OPEN I'LL LET YOU KNOW YOU MOVE UP AND BLOCK THE DRIVE. IT'S OPENING!! MOVE IN NOW!

IT'S THE COPS!! WHAT IN THE #¢!?* ARE WE GOING TO DO?
STOP THE CAR! GET OUT ONE AT A TIME!
THEY ALL SURRENDER WITHOUT ONE SHOT BEING FIRED AND ARE TAKEN TO THE POLICE STATION.
AT THE STATION, WHILE GOING THROUGH ALL THE LOOT, THEY RECOGNIZE THE COINS AND OTHER THINGS STOLEN BEFORE...
YOU SAY ALL THIS STUFF IN THE CAR CAME OUT OF THAT SAFE IN THE HOUSE?
IT SURE DID!!
KNOWING THAT THE STOLEN GOODS CAME FROM KRUZE'S SAFE, HE IS UNDER SUSPICION.
BACK IN TEXAS AT ANOTHER LAKE, BILL AND ANN PREPARE TO GO FISHING. BILL TELLS ANN TO USE RON'S FISHING BOX AND TACKLE, ETC.
NO WONDER RON DIDN'T HAVE MUCH MONEY ON HIM. LOOK HERE! LOTS OF BUCKS.
WHERE THE ?#!¢ WOULD HE GET THAT KIND OF DOUGH?
ANN TELLS BILL ABOUT THE PRETTY NECKLACE RON GAVE HER
MAYBE IT'S SOME OF BETTS STUFF, SHE WAS SEEING OTHER MEN. I KNOW THAT FOR SURE
I DON'T LIKE HIM GIVING YOU THINGS LIKE THAT. WE SHOULD GO HOME NOW.

AS SOON AS THEY GET BACK, THE POLICE NAB THEM AND TAKE THEM IN FOR QUESTIONING...
THAT NECKLACE AND EVEN THE MONEY YOU HAVE IS STOLEN. WE'LL HAVE TO HOLD BOTH OF YOU.
THIS IS CRAZY! RON BANKS GAVE IT TO ME.
LOCK 'EM UP—NO BAIL!!
BILL RECEIVED 3 YEARS FOR HAVING STOLEN PROPERTY. ANN GOT 2 YEARS PROBATION.
I DID MY BEST AS YOUR LAWYER, BUT BEING THAT RON DIED, WE HAVE NO OTHER PROOF. I'LL KEEP IN TOUCH.
DON'T BOTHER YOU JERK! I CAN'T BELIEVE THIS!
BILL HAS GROWN A FULL BEARD FOR HIS TRIP TO C.I.M.
NEVER IN A MILLION YEARS WOULD BILL BELIEVE HE WAS AN INMATE WHERE HE WAS ONCE AN OFFICER...
PUT HIM IN MADRONE FOR NOW. I'LL SEE HIM LATER ON.
R.C.C. WATCH OFFICE
I HEAR YOU WORKED IN THIS PLACE ONCE. I SAY YOU SHOULD KNOW THE RULES THEN. JUST KEEP THEM AND WE'LL GET ALONG.
607
I'VE HAD IT WITH EVERYONE. JUST LEAVE ME ALONE. NOBODY CARES!

A FEW WEEKS LATER, BILL IS MOVED TO PALM HALL
THEY LEFT ONE OF THE LITTLE BOOKS THAT COWBOY CHAPLAIN MADE UP. WONDER WHAT IT SAYS??!!
I BET HE'S NOT AROUND ANYMORE. HE WAS REALLY PECULIAR.
AS BILL READS THE TRACT, HE FINDS OUT THAT THERE IS SOMEONE WHO CARES...
DEAR LORD, IT SAYS HERE THAT YOU DIED FOR ME. I DO BELIEVE THAT YOU DID, AND I'M SORRY FOR ALL MY SINS. COME INTO MY HEART AND FORGIVE ME. I WANT YOU FOR MY LORD AND SAVIOUR. HELP ME FIND THE PEACE AND JOY YOU PROMISED.
HELLO SIR. IS THERE ANYTHING YOU MAY WANT THAT I MIGHT HAVE FOR YOU? HEY, I LIKE YOUR BEARD.
I JUST ASKED JESUS TO BE MY SAVIOUR AND LORD. AM I SAVED AND FORGIVEN?
PRAISE GOD, YOU ARE! GLORY!
BILL ASKS THE CHAPLAIN TO PRAY WITH HIM ABOUT HIS SITUATION WITH RON...
IF YOU CAN SAY BEFORE GOD ALMIGHTY THAT YOU ARE NOT GUILTY, I'LL PRAY WITH YOU AND FOR YOU IN THE NAME OF JESUS.
GOD AS MY WITNESS, I AM INNOCENT!

DEAR LORD, THIS MAN JUST RECEIVED YOU AS HIS SAVIOUR, AND HE ASKED ME TO PRAY IN JESUS' NAME TO HELP HIM PROVE HE IS NOT GUILTY AS CHARGED. HELP HIM IN ALL WAYS AS HE NOW BELONGS TO YOU. AMEN!
THANK YOU!
ONE OF THE THREE MEN THAT BROKE INTO BILL'S SAFE HAS VOLUNTEERED SOME INFORMATION TO THE POLICE...
THAT GUY, RON BANKS, WORKED WITH US AND RAN OUT ON US, TOO. HE TOOK ALL THE LOOT ON OUR LAST JOB. THAT GUY, BILL, AIN'T GUILTY AT ALL!
BOY! HAVE WE GOT SOME EXPLAINING TO DO, AND HOW!
BILL'S WIFE HAS COME TO VISIT HIM AND TALKS TO A MAN WHO IS ALSO VISITING AN INMATE IN THE PRISON THROUGH THE M-2 PROGRAM...
YOU MEAN TO TELL ME YOU DON'T EVEN KNOW THIS MAN YOU'VE COME TO SEE?
OH! I CONSIDER IT A REAL HONOR TO DO THIS. THAT'S HOW I FOUND THE LORD AS MY SAVIOUR.
LARRY TALKS SOME MORE AND GIVES ANN SOME TRACTS TO READ.
CHAPLAIN DANN HAS RETURNED AFTER A WEEK TO MINISTER TO BILL. BILL HAS A SURPRIZE WAITING FOR HIM...
HEY! YOU SHAVED OFF YOUR BEARD. I LIKED IT. ANYWAY, HOW'S IT GOING WITH YOUR PEACE AND JOY? ARE YOU READING YOUR BIBLE?
YOU DON'T KNOW ME FROM BEFORE. I'M GLAD. I DO HAVE PEACE AND JOY SINCE I'VE TURNED MY LIFE OVER TO JESUS CHRIST.

WHILE THEY VISIT, A CALL COMES FROM THE WATCH OFFICE THAT BILL HAS A VISITOR TODAY...
I KNEW YOU THE FIRST TIME I SAW YOU. I JUST NEVER MENTIONED IT. THE MAIN THING IS THAT YOU'RE A NEW MAN IN CHRIST.
MY WIFE'S HERE TODAY. SHE SURE NEEDS THE LORD AND A LOT OF PRAYER. CAN WE PRAY?
ANN TELLS OF CHUCK'S CONFESSION ABOUT RON'S ACTIVITIES. BILL WILL BE OUT THIS WEEK.
I'M GLAD TO HEAR ALL OF THIS, BUT IF IT HADN'T BEEN FOR RON, I DON'T THINK I'D EVER HAVE FOUND THE LORD AS MY SAVIOUR, ANN.
I TALKED TO A MAN IN M-2, AND I WANT TO KNOW MORE.
NOBODY EVER CLAIMED THIS MONEY, SO AFTER WHAT WE PUT YOU THROUGH, WE DECIDED TO GIVE IT TO YOU. ALL $12,000. HOPE YOU'LL FORGIVE US.
WE DO, CAPTAIN.
BILL TELLS THE CAPTAIN HOW JESUS FORGAVE THOSE WHO CRUCIFIED HIM...
BILL AND ANN DECIDE TO CONTINUE THEIR VACATION IN THE CAMPER...
ANN, I'M SO HAPPY YOU ACCEPTED JESUS AS YOUR SAVIOUR THIS MORNING IN CHURCH. WE'LL TAKE HIM WITH US ON VACATION.
I AGREE WITH YOU HONEY. IF IT WASN'T FOR RON, I DOUBT WE EVER WOULD BE SAVED.

Notes: The only surviving copy of this 1983 tract was missing half the first page (but I reconstructed the outside cover with the same photo). Dann's image is often cut and pasted over with Chick tract illustrations or actual vintage photos. So is his wife, Esther. Cruel cowboy pranks were real, but the story is all fiction.

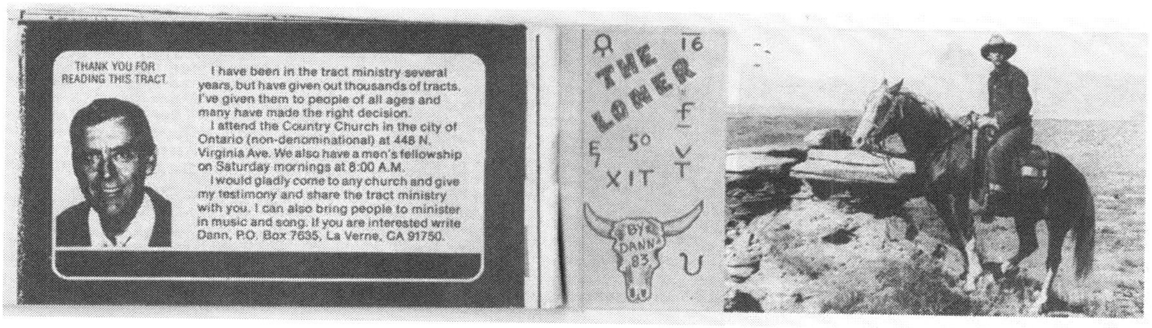

8)
WENDY PUT SOME RUM OR SOMETHING IN HIS DRINK, LETS GET HIM DRUNK.
HE DON'T SUSPECT A THING AT ALL HAHA
A FEW HOURS LATER ITS TO LATE FOR DANN TO REALIZE HE WAS DRINKING SPIKED DRINKS
WANT ONE MORE AND THEN I'LL LET YOU MAKE LOVE TO ME FOR 20.00 HONEY
I FEEL SO DUMB AM I DRUNK? DID YOU PUT SOMETHING IN MY DRINKS? I GOT TO GO NOW.
9)
FOOL AROUND WITH MY SISTER WILL YOU I'LL SHOW YOU NOT TO TRY THAT AGAIN
I NEVER SAID NOTHING TO HER ALL SHEE AUGG OHH
LET'S DUMP HIM OUT HERE, HE'S BLEEDING BAD, ANYONE FINDS HIM THEY WILL THINK A CAR HIT HIM. SHORTY

10)
WELL, SHORTY HE DIDN'T SHOW UP LAST NIGHT, THAT'S GOOD
I HOPE SO ANYWAY
50
DAD THAT IS A HAT ON THE ROAD MUST BELONG TO SOMEONE
I'LL STOP AND WE WILL HAVE A LOOK AROUND ESTHER IM GLAD WE TOOK THE BACK ROAD
11)
HE IS STILL ALIVE MUST OF GOT THROWN OFF A HORSE, DO YOU KNOW HIM?
THAT'S THE NEW BRONC RIDER I JUST HIRED.
LATER DANN IS AWAKE
NO WAY AM I GOING TO THE HOSPITAL BUT I KNOW TWO OTHERS THAT ARE GOING
PLEASE DON'T TALK LIKE THAT, COME ON BACK TO THE RANCH WITH US.

12) ESTHER HAS JUST FINISHED BIBLE COLLEGE AND HAS DECIDED TO WITNESS TO DANN
DANN IF YOU HAD DIED BACK IN THE PASTURE DO YOU KNOW IF YOU WOULD GO TO HEAVEN?
YOU KIDDING HOW WOULD ANYONE KNOW THAT FOR SURE?
YOU CAN KNOW FOR SURE, AS SHE TELLS MORE
THE HOLY BIBLE IS WHERE IT IS WRITTEN THAT WE MAY KNOW, IN JOHN 3-16 IT SAYS- FOR GOD SO LOVED THE WORLD THAT HE GAVE HIS ONLY BEGOTTEN SON THAT WHOSOEVER BELIEVETH IN HIM SHOULD NOT PERISH, BUT HAVE EVERLASTING LIFE.
ALSO READ 1-JOHN - 5-9 THRU-13
13) MEANWHILE LARRY AND SHORTY ARE WORKING THE BRONCS
TURN YOU HAMMER-HEAD OR I'LL GET MAD
SHORTY PICKED THE WRONG ONE FOR SURE THIS DAY...

14)
ESTHER, I ONCE YEARS AGO WENT TO CHURCH BUT, I'VE DRIFTED SO FAR THAT I BELIEVE GOD WOULD NEVER CARE ABOUT ME ANYMORE.
ALL YOU HAVE TO DO IS ASK GOD IN JESUS NAME TO FORGIVE YOU, HE WILL THEN YOU MUST TURN FROM YOUR SIN AND TRY NOT TO SIN ANYMORE.
LATER
ESTHER HOW IS DANN DOING? IS HE UP AND ABOUT NOW? CAN HE WORK YET?
YES, DAD HE'S O.K. NOW AND HE IS RESTING I JUST WAS TELLING HIM ABOUT CHRIST. I BELIEVE HE WILL ACCEPT JESUS AS HIS PERSONAL SAVIOR.
15) MIKE GOES OUT TO THE MEN TO TALK TO THEM ABOUT SAT. NIGHT UP TOWN...
YOU MEN GET YOUR TACK ALL TOGETHER AND I'LL TAKE YOU INTO TOWN MONDAY AND YOU BOTH ARE FIRED
I WONDER WHAT THAT'S ALL ABOUT DO YOU SUPPOSE SOME ONE TALKED OR IS HE JUST SORE AT US.
NO ONE COULD KNOW ABOUT DANN MUST BE SOMETHING ELSE.
50

16 DANN WAKES UP AND FINDS OUT ESTHER IS STILL WITH HIM...
I FEEL LIKE LIKE, I WANT TO ACCEPT JESUS AS MY LORD AND SAVIOR NOW, PRAY WITH ME
PRAISE GOD, LETS DO IT NOW BOW YOUR HEAD.
I'LL PRAY FIRST THEN YOU PRAY WHAT EVER YOU FEEL IN YOUR HEART JUST PRAY TO THE LORD LIKE YOU TALK TO ME.
THANK YOU I AM READY TO DO THIS AS I AM TIRED OF MY OLD LIFE.
17 SHE BEGINS PRAYING FOR THE LORD TO SEE THE NEED THAT DANN HAS IN HIS LIFE FOR REPENTANCE
DEAR LORD, I ASK YOU TO HEAR THIS PRAYER AND BLESS HIM WITH YOUR HOLY SPIRIT NOW.
DEAR JESUS FORGIVE ME OF ALL MY SINS, I AM SO SORRY.
AND LORD I WANT TO CHANGE MY LIFE SO I CAN HAVE PEACE AND JOY LIKE ESTHER HAS. I DO BELIEVE YOU DIED FOR ME, AND ARE COMING AGAIN FOR ME, HELP ME LIVE A CHRISTIAN LIFE FROM NOW ON.
THANK YOU LORD JESUS FOR SAVING DANN'S SOUL I LOVE YOU LORD. AMEN.

18 NEXT MORNING MIKE TALKS TO DANN SLATOR.
TODAY I AM TAKING ROCKY AND SHORTY IN-TO TOWN I FIRED BOTH OF THEM FOR WHAT THEY DID TO YOU WENDY TOLD ME ALL ABOUT IT.
OATS
MIKE LET ME TALK TO THEM FIRST BEFORE YOU GO. YOU REALLY NEED THEM BOTH AROUND HERE
GO AHEAD BUT AFTER WHAT THEY DID TO YOU, I DON'T UNDERSTAND WHY YOU CARE WHAT HAPPENS TO THEM TWO.
19
I WANT YOU TWO TO KNOW THAT I DONT HOLD ANY GRUDGE TO YOU GUYS FOR WHAT YOU DID TO ME.
WE ARE SORRY BUT WE CANT BE-LIEVE YOU FORGIVE US NOW.
MIKES DAUGHTER TOLD ME ALL ABOUT JESUS CHRIST AND HOW HE DIED FOR OUR SINS, AND HOW HE FOR-GAVE THEM THAT CRUCI-FIED HIM ON THE CROSS, SO I FOR-GIVE YOU GUYS.
I LIKE ESTHER ALOT TOO DANN.
I ALMOST BE-CAME A CHRISTIAN ONCE MYSELF.

20 THE MEN DECIDE TO GO AND TALK TO ESTHER AND FIND OUT MORE ABOUT JESUS CHRIST, SHE IS HALTER BREAKING A YOUNG COLT...
SHE REALLY DOES KNOWS THE BIBLE AND I'D LIKE TO KNOW MORE MYSELF
DANN IS THAT WHAT CHANGED YOU? YOU ARE SO DIFFERENT THAN BEFORE
ESTHER COULD YOU SPARE A LITTLE TIME WITH US NOW? WE NEED YOU
WHY YES WHAT IS IT
21 THEY DECIDE TO GO INTO THE PATIO TO TALK AND LISTEN TO GOD'S WORD
I AM SO GLAD TO SEE YOU ARE ALL PALS AGAIN NOW WHAT WAS IT YOU WANTED
TELL US ABOUT THE LORD JESUS.
I WANT TO HEAR MORE
SHE TELLS THEM THAT THE LORD LED A SINLESS LIFE HERE ON THIS EARTH, AND WHEN HE WAS REJECTED HE THEN WAS CRUCIFIED. HIS SHED BLOOD ON THE CROSS WAS FOR US.
THE GOOD PART IS THAT IF WE BELIEVE IN HIM, WE WILL SPEND ALL ETERNITY WITH HIM IN HEAVEN.

22 OUT IN THE CORRAL MIKE IS WONDERING WHERE EVERYONE IS.
I'D BETTER GO SEE WHAT IS UP,
I HOPE THAT THERE IS NO MORE TROUBLE.
BACK IN THE PATIO MIKES DAUGHTER IS STILL TALK-ING WITH THE HIRED HANDS.
LARRY AND SHORTY WOULD YOU BOTH LIKE TO ACCEPT JESUS CHRIST AS YOUR SAVIOR NOW?
YES I WOULD
ME TOO
PRAISE GOD, LETS ALL BOW OUR HEADS
23 MIKE WALKS UP AS LARRY AND SHORTY SURRENDER THEIR LIVES TO THE LORD. WHAT A PRECIOUS MOMENT, HOW ABOUT YOU, ARE YOU WILLING TO DO THE SAME JUST JOIN US IN PRAYER AND ASK THE LORD JESUS TO FORGIVE YOU OF YOUR SINS AND COME INTO YOUR HEART AND BE YOUR LORD AND SAVIOR, AND YOU'LL NEVER BE ALONE AGAIN.
PRAISE GOD AND THANK YOU LORD FOR MY SALVATION ALSO.

Notes: Rod (RSL) drew this circa 1984 tract for Dann, and the cover sports a photo of Dann having drinks with Marlon Brando. (Brando middle, Dann far right.) He met Brando in 1954 and joined him at a Mexican night club to drink. The plot demonstrates that even Christians can be bad sinners—but can get saved again.

DAVID'S MOM DOLLY, IS REALLY WORRIED ABOUT HIM NOT COMING HOME.....
BOB, I WISH WE HAD HANDLED THIS DIFFERENTLY.
I'M TAKING HIS CAR AWAY. I'LL SHOW HIM A THING OR TWO!
THE PARTY REALLY STARTS TO HEAT UP WHEN THE FINAL FEW GUESTS SHOW UP.....
HEY DAVE! HAVIN FUN? COME ON AND DANCE WITH ME.
TURN UP THE MUSIC WHAT A JAM!
ARE YOU IN THESE MOVIES?
I SURE AM. I'M THE STAR!!
OKAY GANG, MOVIE TIME. GRAB A SEAT AND GET COMFORTABLE.
ROXIE'S VACATION
I'M GLAD I CAME. HAVE MISSED A LOT!
LOOKS LIKE ROXIE IS MAKING HER MOVE ON DAVID.
DAVID IS SURPRISED TO SEE THAT IT'S A DIRTY MOVIE AND THAT ROXIE IS NUDE.....
I SHOULD GO HOME NOW. I BET MY MOM AND DAD ARE REALLY WORRIED ABOUT ME BY NOW.
I REALLY DON'T LIKE MAKING THE MOVIES BUT I LIKE THE MONEY. LET'S HAVE A DRINK HONEY.
OKAY, ONE. THEN I HAVE TO SPLIT.

WHILE ROXIE GOES TO PUT ON SOMETHING MORE COMFORTABLE, SUE MAKES HER MOVE.....
DAVE, WHILE YOUR WAITING FOR HER, LET'S TAKE A SPIN IN YOUR CAR. I'LL MAKE YOU FEEL BETTER.
SOUNDS LIKE A GOOD IDEA. HERE, YOU DRIVE.
DAVID'S DAD HAS FINALLY GONE TO BED BUT HIS MOTHER STAYS UP TO PRAY FOR DAVID.....
LORD, I PRAY IN JESUS' NAME, HELP MY SON UNDERSTAND THAT HE MUST NOT STRAY FROM YOU. PLEASE LORD, HELP HIM WHEREVER HE IS. AMEN!
SUE DRIVES TO A BEAUTIFUL HILLTOP OVERLOOKING THE OCEAN NEAR THE BEACH.....
DAVE, DO YOU THINK THAT TANYA HAS A BETTER FIGURE THAN ME? DON'T I TURN YOU ON AT ALL?
YEAH. SURE YOU DO BUT I'VE NEVER DONE IT WITH ANYONE.
DAVE, YOU'RE GOING TO BE ALL MINE. I'M CRAZY ABOUT YOU! KISS ME AGAIN.
I PROMISE I'LL BE MORE FUN NEXT TIME. CAN I MAYBE SEE YOU TOMORROW SOMETIME?

AT 5 A.M. DAVID DRIVES INTO THE GARAGE AT HOME. HIS MOTHER IS STILL WAITING!
DAVID, PRAISE GOD YOU'VE COME HOME. I PRAYED FOR YOU.
I'M REALLY SORRY. FORGIVE ME.
IS THAT DAVID?
YOU GIVE ME THOSE CAR KEYS AND GO RIGHT TO YOUR ROOM! WE'LL TALK ABOUT THIS LATER. YOU SMELL LIKE A TRAMP.
DAVID SAID HE'S SORRY SO JUST CALM DOWN. I'M SURE HE HASN'T DONE TOO MUCH WRONG.
ROBERT AND DOLLY GO TO CHURCH WITHOUT WAKING DAVID UP TO GO WITH THEM.
MY CAR IS GONE. I CAN'T BELIEVE MY DAD WOULD DO THIS! WHAT CAN I DO JEFF?
YOUR OLD MAN HAS HAD IT WITH YOU. WHY DON'T YOU COME AND STAY WITH US? I'LL COME AND PICK UP YOU AND YOUR STUFF NOW WHILE THEY'RE OUT AT CHURCH.
AFTER CHURCH, DAVID'S MOM TALKS TO PASTOR MAYS ABOUT WHAT HAPPENED AT HOME THE PREVIOUS NIGHT.
..... SO I TOOK HIS CAR OVER TO SOMEONE'S HOUSE FOR NOW.
I LOVE YOUR SON. LET ME GO HOME WITH YOU AND TALK TO HIM!
OH THANK YOU MIKE. I PRAYED THAT YOU WOULD COME TO SEE DAVID. WE LEFT HIM SLEEPING.

JEFF AND SUE HAVE ALL THE STUFF LOADED AND DAVE IS ALL READY TO SPLIT.
MAN, WHAT A NICE TRUCK. WHO'S THIS BELONG TO?
SUE BOUGHT IT FROM A GUY NAMED DOUG.
I FEEL GOOD ABOUT MOVING OUT OF MY PARENTS' HOUSE. NOW I CAN DO WHAT I WANT!
MY GOD PASTOR MAYS. HE'S GONE. HE MOVED OUT. WHERE COULD HE GO? WHY?
THERE'S A NOTE ON THE BED MIKE. PLEASE READ IT.
YOU BOTH SHOULD HAVE CALLED ME ABOUT THIS. NO TELLING WHAT HE'S DONE.
PASTOR MAYS PICKS UP THE NOTE AND BEGINS TO READ.....
DEAR MOM, I KNOW I MUST GO ON MY OWN FOR A WHILE. I'M NOT GOING FAR AND I'LL CALL EVERY ONCE IN A WHILE.
P.S. TELL DAD HE CAN KEEP MY CAR. I DON'T EVER WANT TO SEE IT AGAIN. YOUR SON, DAVID.
DAVID HAS A ROOM TO HIMSELF BUT SUE IS RIGHT THERE TO HELP HIM GET SETTLED IN HIS NEW ROOM.
WHAT'RE WE GOING TO DO TONIGHT
IT'S PARTY TIME AGAIN BUT WE CAN GO OFF SOMEWHERE ELSE IF YOU WANT TO AND DON'T MIND MY MINI-TRUCK.

BACK AT DAVID'S HOUSE, PASTOR MAYS IS STILL WITH BOB AND DOLLY TRYING TO HELP.....
I'LL TALK TO RANDY. HE'S YOUR SON'S BEST FRIEND. IF WE DON'T HEAR FROM DAVID IN A FEW DAYS I KNOW RANDY WILL GO LOOK FOR HIM ON HIS MOTORCYCLE. I'M SURE DAVID IS OKAY. WE'LL JUST REMEMBER HIM IN ALL OUR PRAYERS.
JEFF AND THE REST ARE LIVING IT UP AT THE PARTY WITH SOME NEWCOMERS.....
JEFF, WHERE'S SUE TONIGHT?
I GUESS SHE TOOK DAVID FOR A RIDE.
FOR A RIDE IS RIGHT. IS HE REALLY ONE OF THOSE SO CALLED BORN AGAIN CHRISTIANS?
YES, BUT HE WAS FORCED INTO IT.
SUE HAS GONE TO THE SAME PLACE THEY WERE SATURDAY NIGHT. SHE BROUGHT SOME BOOZE.
I HAVEN'T STOPPED THINKING OF YOU DAVE. DO YOU THINK OF ME? HAVE A DRINK WITH ME.
I THINK OF YOU A LOT SUE. YOU'RE VERY NICE. I'D LIKE A DRINK!!
TIME PASSES AND THE BOTTLE EMPTIES. SUE CAN'T WAIT ANY LONGER. SHE GOES FOR DAVID.
DAVE DARLIN', CAN'T YOU TELL I WANT YOU TO MAKE LOVE TO ME? WHY DON'T YOU? IS IT SOMEONE ELSE? WHO IS IT?
NO. THERE'S NO ONE ELSE. I JUST DON'T WANT TO GO ANY FURTHER THAN WE HAVE. CAN WE LEAVE NOW? I'D REALLY LIKE TO.

SUE GETS MAD AND HAS HAD A LOT TO DRINK. SHE TAKES OFF LIKE A BAT OUT OF HADES.
YOU STUPID #@?!!#! I'LL TAKE YOU HOME FASTER THAN YOU'VE EVER WENT!
YOU DON'T HAVE TO GO NUTS!! LET ME DRIVE SUE.
THE LITTLE TRUCK GAINS SPEED AS IT COMES TO A SHARP CURVE BY THE SHORE.....
HANG ON! I'VE LOST CONTROL!!
OH, LORD FORGIVE ME AND SAVE US
THE TRUCK GOES OFF THE CLIFF DOWN ONTO THE BEACH AT LOW TIDE. BOTH ARE STILL INSIDE!!
NEXT MORNING, JEFF CALLS DAVID'S MOM AND DAD TO SEE IF DAVID HAS GONE BACK HOME.....
AS FAR AS WE KNOW, HE WENT SOMEWHERE WITH MY COUSIN SUE. SHE NEVER CAME HOME EITHER. I'LL LOOK FOR THEM.
I JUST KNOW SOMETHING'S HAPPENED. I'LL CALL SOME OTHERS TO HELP LOOK FOR THEM TOO.

HONEY, GO SEE RANDY AND TELL HIM ABOUT DAVID. I HAVE A FEELING HE CAN FIND HIM. I JUST KNOW HE HURT AND LAYING SOMEWHERE!
YES DEAR, I SHOULD HAVE AT LEAST SPOKEN TO HIM BEFORE I TOOK HIS CAR FROM HIM. WE WILL FIND HIM. DON'T WORRY. HE'LL BE OKAY.
AS RANDY LOOKS FOR DAVE AND SUE, HE FINDS SOMETHING.
SKID MARKS!! I PRAY IT'S NOT WHAT I THINK DOWN IN THE SURF. PLEASE LORD.
AT THE BOTTOM HE FINDS THE CRUNCHED TRUCK. DAVID IS STILL ALIVE. SUE HAS DIED!
RANDY STOPS A PASSING CAR TO GET A HELICOPTER TO RUSH DAVID TO THE HOSPITAL.
SUE IS TAKEN TO THE MORGUE.
DAVID IS GOING TO BE OKAY AND HIS PARENTS VISIT HIM WITH HIS OTHER FRIENDS, EVEN JEFF.....
DAVE, SUE HAD NO RELATIVES EXCEPT ME. DO YOU THINK YOU COULD GET YOUR PASTOR TO SAY A FEW WORDS FOR HER FUNERAL?
I'M SURE HE WILL. YOU CAN COUNT ON IT. I REALLY LIKED SUE A LOT. TOO BAD SHE'S GONE!
I WISH I HAD WITNESSED TO HER!

THE FUNERAL HOME IS PACKED WITH YOUNG PEOPLE.
AS FAR AS ANYONE KNOWS, THIS BEAUTIFUL YOUNG LADY NEVER KNEW THE PEACE AND JOY OF KNOWING THE LORD JESUS CHRIST AS HER VERY OWN PERSONAL SAVIOUR.
MIKE THEN READS JOHN 3:16 AND TELLS HOW EVERYONE CAN BE FORGIVEN OF THEIR SINS AND BE BORN AGAIN.
TANYA, I'M SO GLAD YOU CAME. YOU'RE A VERY DEAR FRIEND AND I HOPE TO SEE YOU MORE.
DAVE, I'M SORRY FOR THE STINKIN' LIFE I'VE LEAD SO FAR. I WAS NEVER HAPPY WITH THE MATERIAL STUFF I HAD. I WANT TO ASK JESUS TO FORGIVE ME OF ALL MY SINS AND BE MY SAVIOUR. CAN I DO THAT NOW?
YOU JUST DID. LET'S PRAY.
EVERYONE IS VERY HAPPY SINCE MANY RECEIVED CHRIST AS LORD AND PERSONAL SAVIOUR.
DAVID, I'M PRAYING THAT YOU WILL NEVER BACKSLIDE AGAIN AND WILL GET MORE INTO THE WORD OF GOD
I'M STARTING A BIBLE STUDY FOR ALL THE YOUNG PEOPLE THAT WERE SAVED TODAY. EVEN JEFF IS GOING TO COME.
SON, WE ARE THANKFUL THAT SO MANY ACCEPTED JESUS AND THAT YOU'RE COMING HOME.
THANKS DAD! BUT NOW I GOT A SHOCK FOR YOU I WANT TO GET INTO THE PRISON MINISTRIES LIKE UNCLE DANN AND GRANDPA TOM!
I THINK THAT'S GREAT DAVID!!

Notes: This undated tract (probably 1980s) features Dann art and his character helping prisoners. Any inmate reading it would probably wish Dann's prayers would have similar results for them!

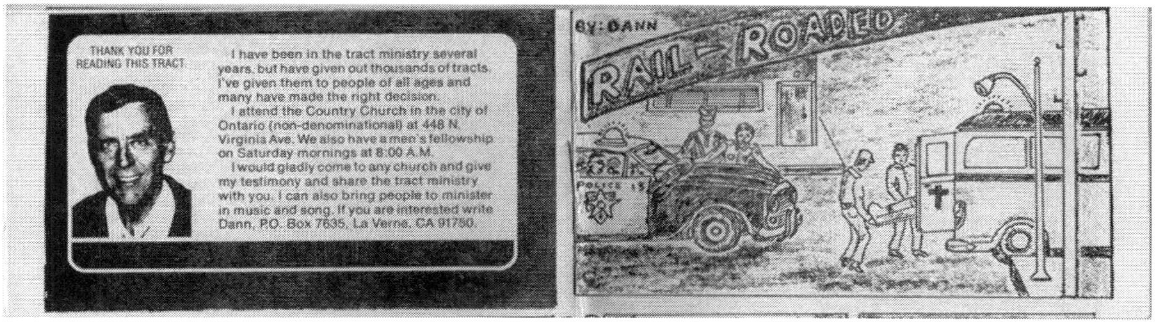

JIM SAID NEXT TIME YOU'LL BE BLOWN AWAY! YOU BETTER LISTEN.
WAPPP!!
OH, LORD, HELP ME. OHHAWW.
JACK HAS ENOUGH TIME TO GRAB MARTY'S KNIFE TO TRY AND DEFEND HIMSELF.
LET'S BEAT IT WE DON'T WANT TO DO HIM IN YET.
I HEAR YAH.
OHHH
HURRY UP!! LET'S GET THE C#3C# OUT OF HERE MAN.
DAD, I THINK YOU KILLED THAT MAN, IT'S ALL YOUR FAULT, I TOLD YOU NOT TO MESS WITH JIM.
WAIT! OHHH I'M DYING.

YOUR OWN GIRL SAY'S THAT YOU STARTED THE WHOLE MESS, SO YOU COME WITH US NOW.
TRY THIS ON FOR SIZE, EH.
DUE TO THE TESTIMONY OF JACK'S GIRL HE COMES BEFORE JUDGE MARION.
YOU HAVE BEEN FOUND GUILTY AS CHARGED, YOUR SENTENCE IS 10 YEARS IN PRISON
JUDGE MARION
OH!! LORD WHY?
GOOD!! DAD CAN'T BUG ME NO MORE
THAT'S SOME STORY JACK, LOOKS LIKE YOU WERE RAILROADED FOR SURE,
HEY, MIKE TELL CHAPLAIN DANN THE GREY GOOSE JUST PASSED.
I'M SURE HE SAW IT, JUST MEAN'S MORE MEN TO VISIT RIGHT CHAP?
YES, OFFICER NOLAN AND TELL MARY TO PRAY FOR ME AS WELL AS THOSE NEW MEN.

THREE MONTHS LATER JACK IS ALL SETTLED IN HIS CELL, IN CHINO, C.I.M.
DONT ANYONE EVER COME TO SEE US? I NEED ALOT OF STUFF
ONCE IN A WHILE ONE OF THE CHAPLAINS DOES, HERE COMES ONE NOW.
CHAPLAIN DANN IS ON HIS ROUNDS TO VISIT MEN
CAN I HELP YOU IN SOME WAY?
I NEED A STAMP AND A PEN.
I SURE COULD USE ALOT OF HELP, AND WOULD YOU HAVE A KING JAMES BIBLE WITH YOU?
JACK OPENS UP HIS LIFE TO CHAPLAIN DANN, HE TELLS HOW HE WAS RAILROADED, AND ABOUT HIS GIRL LYNN.
WHAT I REALLY WANT IS TO HAVE YOU PRAY WITH ME I NEED TO FIND SOME PEACE.
MEANWHILE LYNN IS WITH JIM AT A WILD PARTY WHERE ANYTHING GOES, LATE INTO THE NITE.
DRINK UP LET'S HAVE A BLAST!!
"I'M" SICK!
I DON'T THINK LYNN SHOULD DRINK ANYMORE LOOK AT HER NOW, SHE'S USING DRUGS TOO.

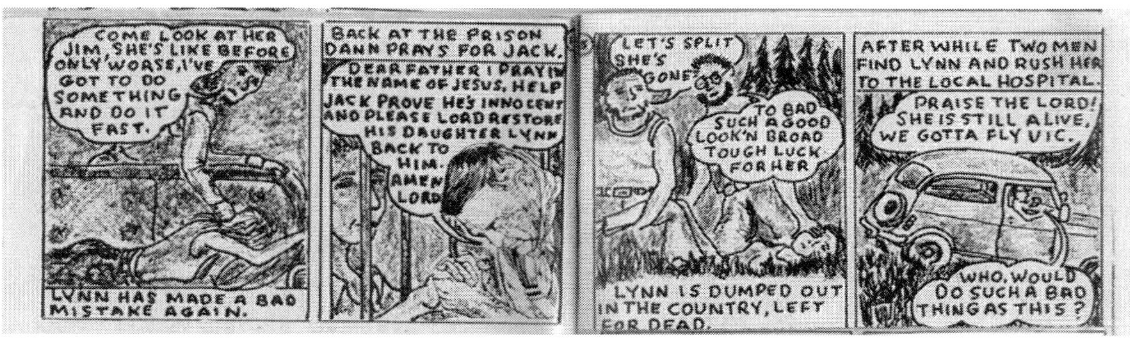
COME LOOK AT HER JIM, SHE'S LIKE BEFORE ONLY WORSE, I'VE GOT TO DO SOMETHING AND DO IT FAST.
LYNN HAS MADE A BAD MISTAKE AGAIN.
BACK AT THE PRISON DANN PRAYS FOR JACK.
DEAR FATHER I PRAY IN THE NAME OF JESUS, HELP JACK PROVE HE'S INNOCENT AND PLEASE LORD RESTORE HIS DAUGHTER LYNN BACK TO HIM. AMEN LORD.
LET'S SPLIT SHE'S GONE
TO BAD SUCH A GOOD LOOK'N BROAD TOUGH LUCK FOR HER
LYNN IS DUMPED OUT IN THE COUNTRY, LEFT FOR DEAD.
AFTER WHILE TWO MEN FIND LYNN AND RUSH HER TO THE LOCAL HOSPITAL.
PRAISE THE LORD! SHE IS STILL ALIVE, WE GOTTA FLY VIC.
WHO, WOULD DO SUCH A BAD THING AS THIS?

YOU SAY THAT A MAN CALLED JIM DID THIS TO YOU, AND THAT YOU AND HIM FRAMED YOUR OWN DAD?
YES, SIR, MY DAD WAS ATTACKED BY THOSE TWO MEN HE SENT.
BUT, I HEARD YOU TESTIFY THAT IT WAS YOUR DAD THAT STARTED IT ALL.
I LIED. AND I AM READY TO TELL THE TRUTH I'M SORRY.
THE POLICE GO INTO ACTION FAST...
LOOKS LIKE THEY GOT ALL THREE OF THEM.
I GOT THIS ONE, HOW ARE YOU DOING WITH THAT ONE?
OH!, HE'S O.K. JUST HAD TO TAP HIM, I JUST FOUND ALL THE DRUG'S, WEAPON'S

RODRIGUEZ, GO GET JACK CHECK OUT OF PALM HALL, HE'S GOING HOME.
O.K. SGT. I HEARD HIS DAUGHTER CLEARED HIM, I LIKE THAT KIND OF GOOD NEWS.
JACK HAS ALREADY GOT THE WORD FROM THE CHAPLAIN WHO PRAYED WITH HIM ONE TIME.
I DON'T EVER WANT TO LOSE CONTACT WITH YOU, AND I'D LIKE TO MEET YOUR DAUGHTER SOMETIME.
I STILL CAN'T BELIEVE THIS, PRAISE THE LORD!!
NEXT DAY LYNN COMES TO TAKE HER DAD HOME.
DAD, I'M SORRY I LOVE YOU VERY MUCH, PLEASE FORGIVE ME.
I DO, LYNN AND I WANT TO COME BACK HOME WITH YOU.
THANK YOU NOLAN AND YOU TO MARY FOR HELP'NG MY DAUGHTER LYNN, AT THE GATE, SO-LONG.
I'M ALWAYS GLAD TO HELP ANYONE, ESPECIALLY A CUTE GIRL LIKE YOU HAVE

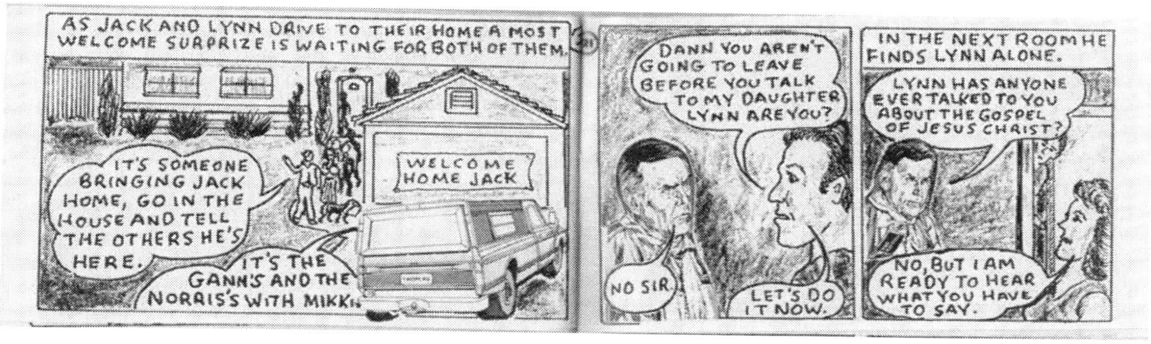
AS JACK AND LYNN DRIVE TO THEIR HOME A MOST WELCOME SURPRIZE IS WAITING FOR BOTH OF THEM.
WELCOME HOME JACK
IT'S SOMEONE BRINGING JACK HOME, GO IN THE HOUSE AND TELL THE OTHERS HE'S HERE.
IT'S THE GANN'S AND THE NORRIS'S WITH MIKKI.
DANN YOU AREN'T GOING TO LEAVE BEFORE YOU TALK TO MY DAUGHTER LYNN ARE YOU?
NO SIR.
LET'S DO IT NOW.
IN THE NEXT ROOM HE FINDS LYNN ALONE.
LYNN HAS ANYONE EVER TALKED TO YOU ABOUT THE GOSPEL OF JESUS CHRIST?
NO, BUT I AM READY TO HEAR WHAT YOU HAVE TO SAY.

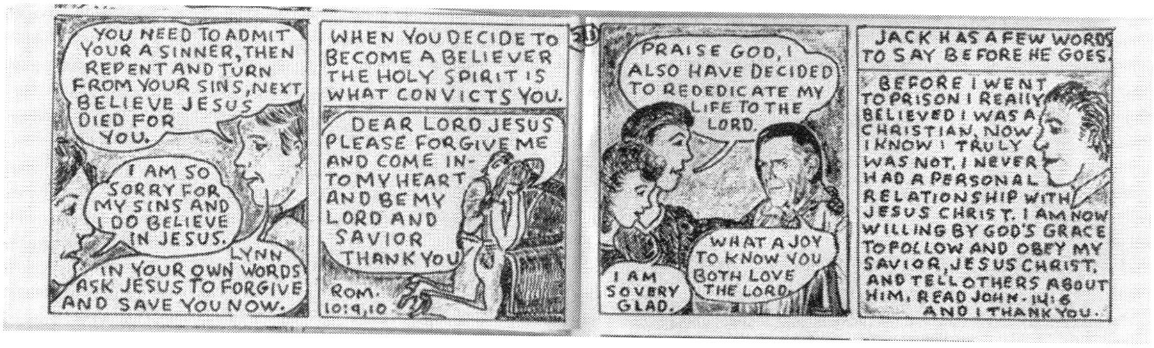
YOU NEED TO ADMIT YOUR A SINNER, THEN REPENT AND TURN FROM YOUR SINS, NEXT BELIEVE JESUS DIED FOR YOU.
I AM SO SORRY FOR MY SINS AND I DO BELIEVE IN JESUS.
LYNN IN YOUR OWN WORDS ASK JESUS TO FORGIVE AND SAVE YOU NOW.
WHEN YOU DECIDE TO BECOME A BELIEVER THE HOLY SPIRIT IS WHAT CONVICTS YOU.
DEAR LORD JESUS PLEASE FORGIVE ME AND COME INTO MY HEART AND BE MY LORD AND SAVIOR THANK YOU
ROM. 10:9,10
PRAISE GOD, I ALSO HAVE DECIDED TO REDEDICATE MY LIFE TO THE LORD.
I AM SO VERY GLAD.
WHAT A JOY TO KNOW YOU BOTH LOVE THE LORD.
JACK HAS A FEW WORDS TO SAY BEFORE HE GOES.
BEFORE I WENT TO PRISON I REALLY BELIEVED I WAS A CHRISTIAN, NOW I KNOW I TRULY WAS NOT, I NEVER HAD A PERSONAL RELATIONSHIP WITH JESUS CHRIST. I AM NOW WILLING BY GOD'S GRACE TO FOLLOW AND OBEY MY SAVIOR, JESUS CHRIST, AND TELL OTHERS ABOUT HIM, READ JOHN-14:6 AND I THANK YOU.

Notes: Dated 1983, only 500 11 x 17" uncut sheets of this story with Dann art were made and given to inmates. Dann's horse, Rondo, is pasted into this tract, along with Dann's image from various Chick tracts.

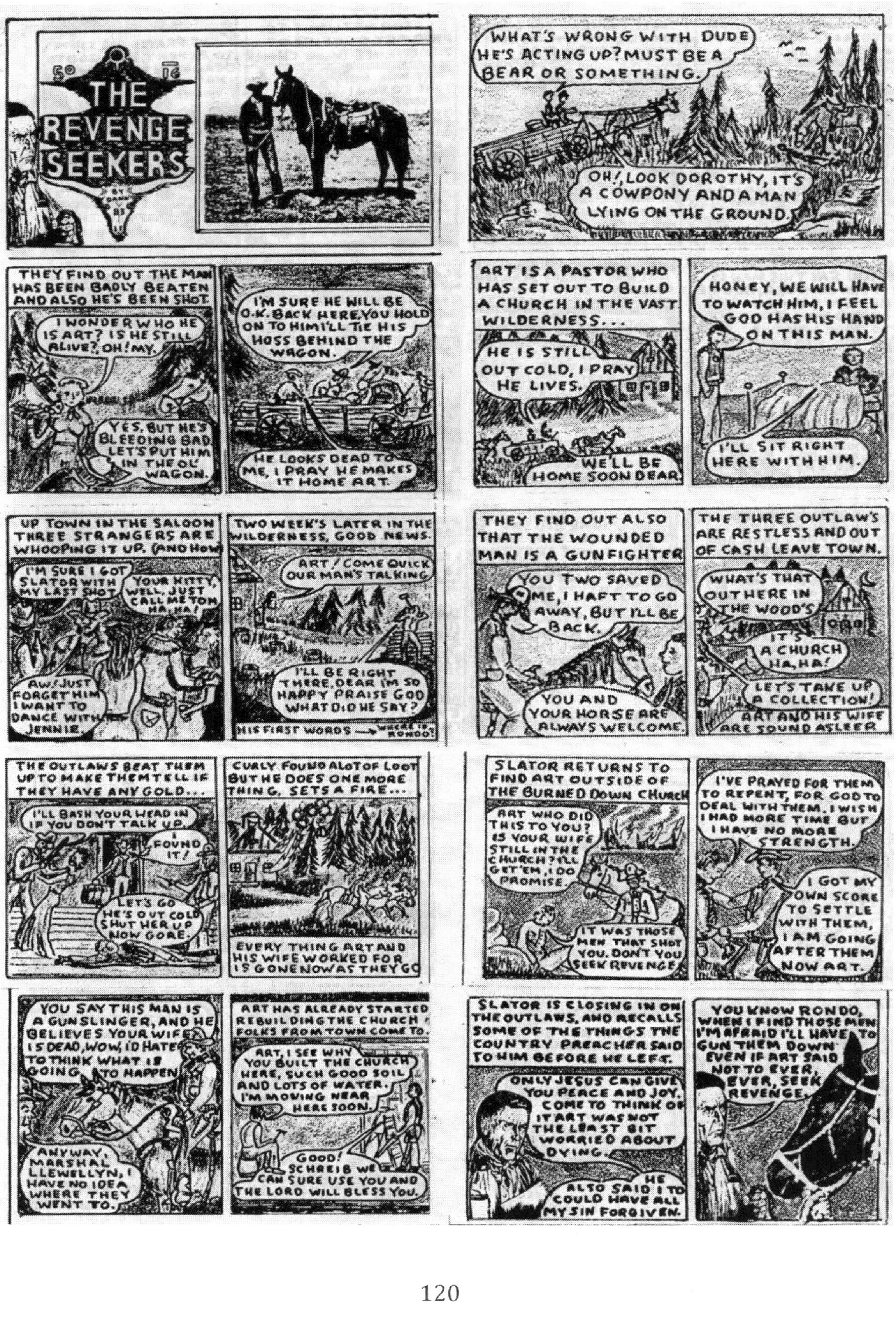

CURLY AND HIS MEN GO ON THE WRONG TRAIL AND THEY ARE IN THE DESERT.
WE'D BETTER FIND WATER SOON MY HOSS CAN'T GO MUCH MORE.
I KNOW YOU DID WRONG TORCHING THE CHURCH
WHY DID YOU BURN THAT CHURCH DOWN? I BET THAT'S WHY WE ARE IN THE FIX WE'RE IN, I'LL NEVER MAKE IT.
WE STILL HAVE A HORSE AND ALL THE LOOT BOB.
LOOK! OVER THE HILL TREES, I BET WATER IS NEAR, IT BETTER BE I'VE HAD IT.
IF I EVER GET OUT OF THIS, I'LL NEVER ROB ANYONE AGAIN.
THAT WAS A NICE LIL' HOSS, RONDO THEY CAN'T BE TO FAR AWAY.
SLATOR FINDS THE WATERHOLE AND A SMALL CAMPFIRE IS BURNING NEAR...
WELL, RONDO, IT LOOKS LIKE WE FOUND OUR OUTLAWS, WE'LL STAY RIGHT HERE UNTIL DARK THEN I'LL SLIP UP ON THEM, YOU ARE SOME HOSS, THE BEST.
THE MEN FIND WATER JUST IN TIME AS THE ONE HORSE LEFT IS ABOUT GONE
MAN! I CAN'T BELIEVE THIS, IT LOOKS LIKE THE END OF THAT #!!N DESERT
I DON'T KNOW ABOUT YOU BUT I SAY THANKS TO GOD FOR THIS WATER HOLE.
LATER BY THE CAMP-FIRE THE MEN LOOK THRU THE LOOT AGAIN.
HERE'S THAT OL' COOT'S BIBLE, HOW DID WE MISS CHUCKIN' IT AWAY? WOW MORE GOLD JEWELRY IN A LIL' BOX.
MY OL' AUNT NORMA IN TEXAS READ THE BIBLE TO ME, I REMEMBER THE 23RD PSALM AND JOHN, 3/16 OR 3/3 I FORGET NOW.
CURLY, IS STILL GOING THRU THE LOOT, HE FINDS AN OLD GOLD LOCKET HE TRYS TO OPEN IT.
OH! MY GOD WHAT HAVE I DONE? THIS IS MY OWN SISTERS LOCKET, AND HERE IS MY MAMA AND PAPA'S PICTURE I JUST CAN'T BELIEVE IT.
CURLY RAN AWAY FROM HOME AS A BOY.
THE MEN ARE DUMB FOUNDED TO REALIZE WHAT THEY HAVE DONE...
YOU ACT LIKE YOU KNOW SO MUCH, WHAT DOES IT SAY ABOUT THE FORGIVENESS OF SIN? CAN WE EVER BE FORGIVEN OF OUR SINS BOB?
IT SAYS RIGHT HERE, THE WAGES OF SIN IS DEATH: BUT THE GIFT OF GOD IS ETERNAL LIFE THROUGH JESUS CHRIST OUR LORD. ROM: 6/23
AS THE MEN READ MORE OF GODS INSPIRED WORD THEY FIND MORE VERSES.
I REALLY KNEW THE BIBLE ONCE, I HAD TO GO TO SUNDAY SCHOOL WHEN I WAS A YOUNG BRAT.
WHAT'S A PERSON TO DO THAT'S SORRY FOR THEIR SIN?
I FOUND JOHN 3:16, I'LL READ IT.
FOR GOD SO LOVED THE WORLD, THAT HE GAVE HIS ONLY BEGOTTEN SON, THAT WHOSOEVER BELIEVETH IN HIM SHOULD NOT PERISH, BUT HAVE EVERLASTING LIFE.
THAT MUST MEAN ALL OF US BOB!
BACK AT THE CHURCH SITE A MIRACLE HAS HAPPENED...
YOU, SAY YOUR WIFE FELL THROUGH THE UN-FINISHED FLOOR INTO THE CELLAR AND THAT SAVED HER.
YES, MARSHAL LLEWELLYN, AND THE MAN THAT IS HUNTING THEM IS A GUNSLINGER.
THE MEN ARE WORRIED ABOUT GOING BACK ACROS THE DESERT AGAIN...
THAT'S THE LAST OF THE MEAT WE'D BETTER GET A DEER TODAY.
I'M KINDA GLAD WE ARE GOING BACK.
ME TOO GORE.
SLATOR IS WELL HID AND HAS BEEN LISTENING TO EVERY WORD, THEN WHAT A SHOCK AS HE WATCHES.
CURLY, I HAVEN'T PRAYED FOR YEARS BUT I'D LIKE TO.
I THINK IT'S A GOOD IDEA GORE ASK GOD TO HELP US GET BACK O.K.
AS SLATOR LISTENS HE CAN'T UNDERSTAND THE THING'S HE IS HEARING, MUCH LESS WHAT HE SEES.
DEAR FATHER, GOD WE THANK YOU FOR THIS BIBLE AND WE ASK YOU TO FORGIVE US, AND HELP US CROSS THE DESERT. I PRAY FOR OUR SOULS SAKE, AMEN.
I'LL WAIT TILL DAY-LIGHT AND CORNER THEM. WHAT'S WITH THIS BIBLE STUFF.
BACK AT THE CAMP WE HAVE A CHANGED THREE THEY HAVE DECIDED TO GO BACK TO RETURN THE LOOT.
WHAT WORRY'S ME IS DID MY SIS' DIE IN THAT FIRE, OR HER HUSBAND? WHAT IF THEY DID? WHAT WOULD WE DO THEN?
I HAVE A FEEL'N THAT THEY ARE O.K. IF NOT WE'LL SEPERATE AND TAKE OFF FOR THE HIGH COUNTRY.
SLATOR, WAITS IN THE NARROW GAP PERFECT FOR HIS ADVANTAGE.
HOLD IT! DON'T MOVE OR YOUR ALL DEAD MEN, GET OFF THE HORSE AND DROP YOUR GUNS.
WE'LL DO AS YOU SAY WE WERE GOING TO GO BACK.

Notes: Last but not least, Dann's 1985 version of Chick's most famous tract, *This Was Your Life.* Dann follows Chick's script panel for panel. Normally, this would be a copyright infringement, but Chick gave his permission. Dann's biggest change was making the tract specifically for Native Americans. (Chick provided his own Native American tract in 2000 with *The True Path.*) This story was printed in both tract form and 11 x 17" sheets. Rondo's photo and Dann's Chick tract appearance both make it into this story.

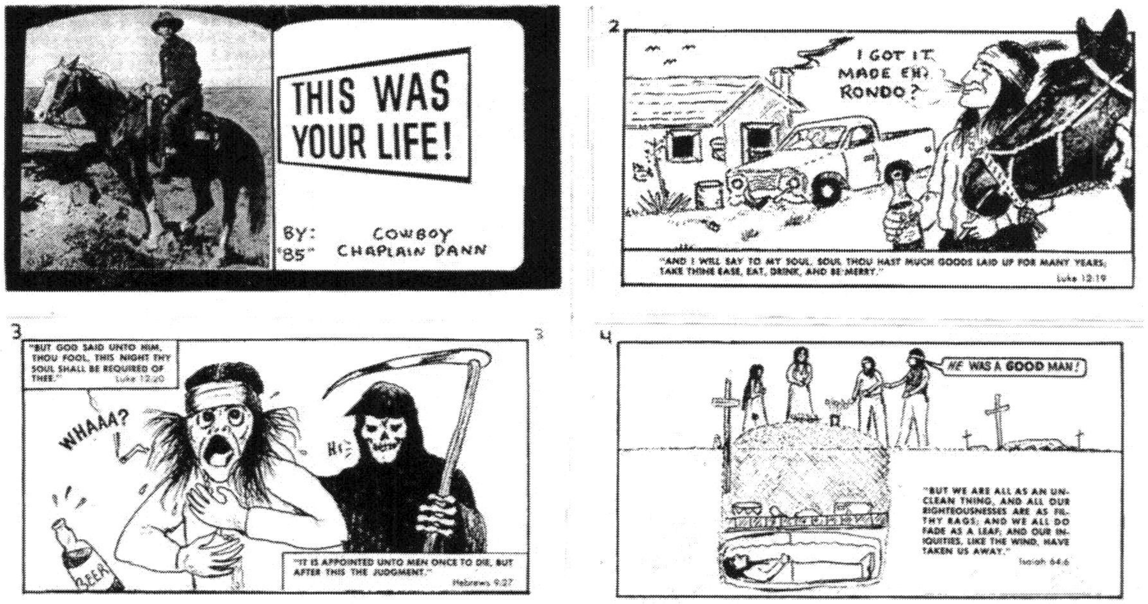

5
"MARVEL NOT AT THIS: FOR THE HOUR IS COMING, IN THE WHICH ALL THAT ARE IN THE GRAVES SHALL HEAR HIS VOICE," John 5:28
ARISE!
"AND SHALL COME FORTH; THEY THAT HAVE DONE GOOD, UNTO THE RESURRECTION OF LIFE; AND THEY THAT HAVE DONE EVIL, UNTO THE RESURRECTION OF DAMNATION." John 5:29
6
JUDGEMENT?-- HERE ON EARTH!- I'VE ALWAYS SAID THAT!
BUT YOU DON'T UNDERSTAND, HEAVEN AND HELL ARE
COME, YOU HAVE AN APPOINTMENT!
WILL ANYONE ELSE BE THERE ?
OH YES, QUITE A NUMBER !
7
THERE IS YOUR DESTINATION !
I SIMPLY REFUSE TO BELIEVE THIS IS HAPPENING TO ME !
Will you spend eternity with Christ or Satan?
8
NOW LOOK! I'VE LIVED A REAL GOOD LIFE! I WAS NO DIFFERENT THAN ANYONE ELSE !
EVERYTHING HAS BEEN RECORDED !
NEXT !
"AS IT IS WRITTEN, THERE IS NONE RIGHTEOUS, NO, NOT ONE:" Romans 3:10
9
"For God so loved the world (THAT'S YOU), that he gave his only begotten Son, (JESUS) that whosoever believeth in him should not perish (IN THE LAKE OF FIRE), but have everlasting life (IN HEAVEN)." John 3:16
"AND I SAW THE DEAD, SMALL AND GREAT, STAND BEFORE GOD; AND THE BOOKS WERE OPENED: AND ANOTHER BOOK WAS OPENED, WHICH IS THE BOOK OF LIFE: AND THE DEAD WERE JUDGED OUT OF THOSE THINGS WHICH WERE WRITTEN IN THE BOOKS, ACCORDING TO THEIR WORKS." Revelation 20:12
10
REVIEW HIS LIFE!
YES LORD!
THIS WAS YOUR LIFE!
11
LOOK - THAT'S ME AS A BABY! DOES THIS MEAN THAT EVERYTHING I'VE EVER DONE IS GOING TO BE REVIEWED ?
"FOR THERE IS NOTHING HID, WHICH SHALL NOT BE MANIFESTED." Mark 4:22
12
HAW HAW - HEY GUYS, THIS IS THE DIRTIEST STORY I'VE EVER HEARD. IT GOES LIKE THIS--
NO! STOP! (GASP) NOT THAT STORY- NOT HERE !
"BUT I SAY UNTO YOU, THAT EVERY IDLE WORD THAT MEN SHALL SPEAK, THEY SHALL GIVE ACCOUNT THEREOF IN THE DAY OF JUDGMENT." Matthew 12:36
UMMM NICE!
I REMEMBER DOING THAT--BUT NO ONE SAW ME!
"BUT I SAY UNTO YOU, THAT WHOSOEVER LOOKETH ON A WOMAN TO LUST AFTER HER HATH COMMITTED ADULTERY WITH HER ALREADY IN HIS HEART." Matthew 5:28
13
FALSE ACCUSER
DECEIT
DISOBEDIENT TO PARENTS
PRIDE
THEFT
LIES
HATER OF GOD
WHOREMONGER
BACKBITER
WHISPERER
ENVY
UNMERCIFUL
HYPOCRISY
WHY DIDN'T SOMEONE WARN ME ABOUT ALL THIS ?
I SENT MY SERVANT, DANN, TO YOU TO GIVE YOU ONE LAST CHANCE ... AND YOU LAUGHED AT HIM IN CONTEMPT.
"FOR THERE IS NOTHING COVERED, THAT SHALL NOT BE REVEALED; AND HID, THAT SHALL NOT BE KNOWN." Matthew 10:26
14
WAIT! LOOK - THAT'S ME IN CHURCH SEE-- I WASN'T SO BAD!
"FOR GOD SO LOVED THE WORLD, THAT HE GAVE HIS ONLY BEGOTTEN SON, THAT WHOSOEVER BELIEVETH IN HIM SHOULD NOT PERISH BUT HAVE EVER LASTING LIFE!"
Z Z Z
*I COR. 15:1-3 **I PETER 1:18,19 †ACTS 1:9-11 & ROM. 8:34
"THAT IF THOU SHALT CONFESS WITH THY MOUTH THE LORD JESUS, AND SHALT BELIEVE IN THINE HEART THAT GOD HATH RAISED HIM FROM THE DEAD, THOU SHALT BE SAVED." ROMANS 10:9
I COULDN'T CARE LESS- WHAT TIME IS IT ?

15

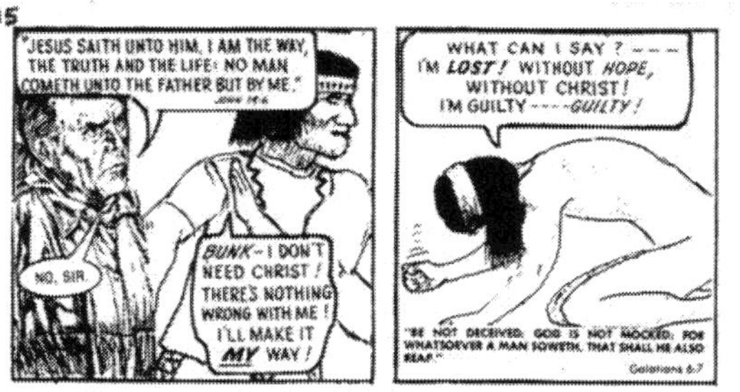

16

17

18

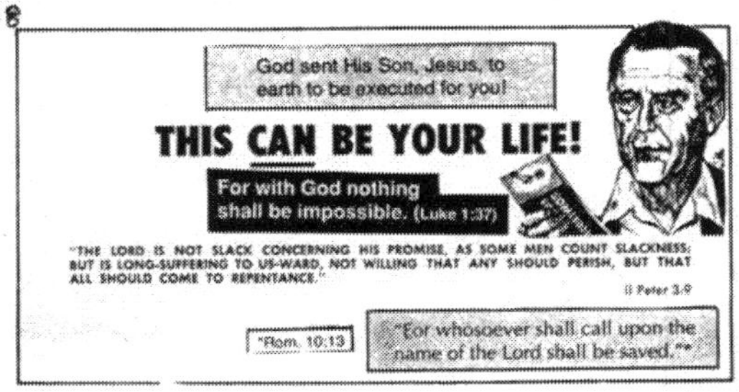

19

20

21

22

23

THE BIBLE SAYS THERE'S ONLY ONE WAY TO HEAVEN.

Jesus said, "I am the way, the truth, and the life: no man cometh unto the Father, but by me." (John 14:6)

NOBODY ELSE CAN HELP YOU.

"For there is one God, and one mediator between God and men, the man Christ Jesus." (I Timothy 2:5)

"For by grace are ye saved through faith; and that not of yourselves: it is the gift of God: not of works, lest any man should boast." (Ephesians 2:8-9)

WHAT YOU MUST DO:

PRAY TO GOD IN YOUR OWN WORDS:

1. **ADMIT** you are a sinner, and that only the Lord Jesus can save you. (Romans 3:23)
2. **REPENT:** be willing to turn away from sin and submit to God. (See Luke 13:5)
3. **BELIEVE** that the Lord Jesus Christ died on the cross and shed his blood to pay the price for your sins, and that he arose again. (See Romans 10:9)
4. **ASK** God to save you. (See Romans 10:13)
5. **ASK** Jesus Christ to be the Lord (take control) of your life. (See Romans 12:1-2)

IF YOU REALLY MADE JESUS YOUR LORD (KING), THEN ACT LIKE IT!

1. Read your Bible every day to get to know Christ better.
2. Talk to God in prayer every day.
3. Find a church where the Bible is taught as the complete Word of God and is the final authority.
4. Obey Christ's command and be baptized. (See Matthew 28:19)

WITEZ II
1957 - BY: DANN

Made in the USA
Columbia, SC
12 April 2023

14794129R10076